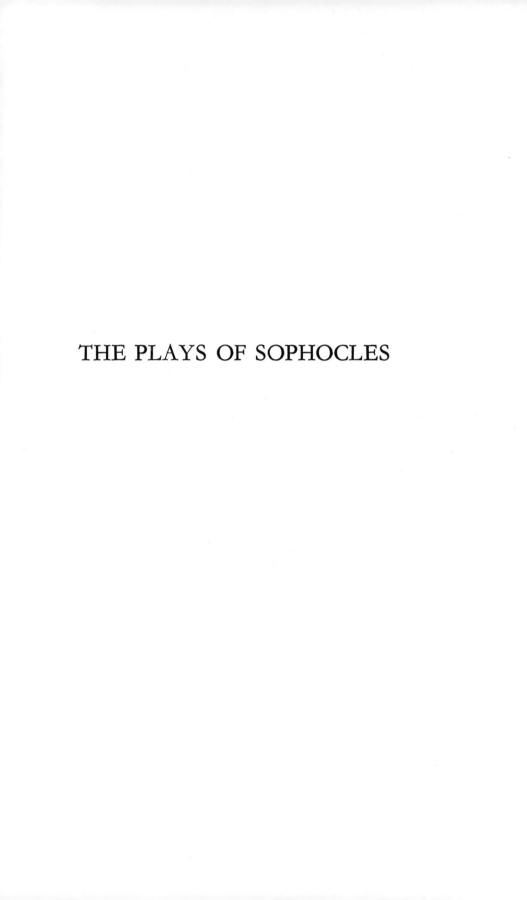

THE PLAYS OF SOPHOCLES

THE PLAYS OF SOPHOCLES

BY

J. C. KAMERBEEK Litt. Dr.

Emeritus Professor of Ancient Greek
in the University of Amsterdam

COMMENTARIES

PART VI

THE PHILOCTETES

LEIDEN
E. J. BRILL
1980

ISBN 90 04 06148 7

Uxori dilectae et diligentissimae

PRAEFATIO

In praeparando hoc sexto commentario in Sophoclis tragoedias, praeter solitas editiones, commentationes, dissertationes, nonnulli libri mihi magno usui fuerunt. Sunt autem hi: *Philoctetes*, edited by T. B. L. Webster (Cambridge 1970), imprimis in rebus ad artem scaenicam pertinentibus, R. D. Dawe, *Studies on the Text of Sophocles*, vol. III (Leiden 1978), Jens-Uwe Schmidt, *Sophokles Philoktet, eine Strukturanalyse* (Heidelberg 1973), *Due Seminari Romani di Eduard Fraenkel, Aiace* e *Filottete* di Sofocle (Roma 1977). Multum mihi profuisse libros illos quos scripserunt K. Reinhardt (*Sophokles*), H. D. F. Kitto (*Form and Meaning in Drama*), B. M. W. Knox (*The heroic Temper*), vix est quod commemorem. Fructum cepi ex observationibus quas M. v.d. Valk v.d. ad me scripsit.

Fortasse non supervacaneum est si hic profiteor me non attigisse quaestiones pertinentes ad ultimas origines quas sumere possis de mytho Philoctetis, quippe quae etiam si contingeret ut firmiter constituerentur vix quicquam ad melius intellegendam artem Sophoclis conferrent.

Restat ut L. van Paassen-van Oosten, discipulae meae, ex animo gratias agam pro opera assidua quam dedit in conquirendis, scrutandis, excerpendis studiis de textu Sophoclis abhinc C annos in lucem editis.

Denique haud facile suo pretio aestimes quaecunque amicus meus David Reid nunc quintum attulit ad emendandum et limandum textum Anglice scriptum.

Santpoort, mense Maio MCMLXXIX *

---

*) Opus absolveram cum Sophoclis pars II (edidit R. D. Dawe) publicata est.

7 πόδα, Webster, alii: πόδα· Campbell, Pearson, alii.

29 στίβου γ' οὐδεὶς κτύπος γ' T κτύπος ΛAGR, edd. complures: τύπος A, edd. complures, Pearson. καὶ codd.: τ' LA δ' GR. Possis, ναί, στίβου τ' vel δ'.

47 ἔλοιτ' ἔμ' Bergk, Cavallin, alii: ἔλοιτό μ' codd. (o *in rasura* L), edd. plerique, Pearson.

53 ὡς codd., edd. plerique: οἷς Musgrave, Pearson.

55 λέγων·: λέγων. edd. plerique, Pearson: λέγων, Webster.

66 τούτῳ γὰρ οὐδέν μ' ἀλγυνεῖς Buttmann, Wunder, Jebb, D.-M., Ed. Fraenkel [1]), alii: τούτων γὰρ οὐδέν μ' ἀλγυνεῖς codd., Campbell (cf. *Paral. Soph.* p. 196): τούτων γὰρ οὐδὲν ἀλγυνεῖ μ' Dindorf, Schn.-N.-Raderm., alii, Pearson.

144 ἐσχατιαῖς LA, edd. plurimi: ἐσχατιᾶς GRQT, Schn.-N.-Raderm., alii, Pearson.

147 δεινὸς ὁδίτης τῶνδ' ἐκ μελάθρων, sic interpunxi (cf. Webster): δεινὸς ὁδίτης, τῶνδ' ἐκ μελάθρων Pearson: δεινὸς ὁδίτης τῶνδ' οὐκ μελάθρων, Linwood, Jebb: δεινὸς ἐδρίτης τῶνδε μελάθρων, Danielsson (Eranos 11-1911-p. 26): δεινὸς ἱδρυτὴς τῶνδε μελάθρων, Dawe (*Studies* III p. 124).

158 ἔναυλον, ἢ θυραῖον; codd., edd. plerique (signum interrogationis post ἕδρα): ἔναυλος, ἢ θυραῖος; Porson (e Thom. Mag. *s.v.* ἔναυλος), Pearson.

166 στυγερὸν στυγερῶς codd., edd. complures: σμυγερὸν σμυγερῶς Brunck, edd. complures, Pearson.

186-88 ἀνήκεστ' ἀμερί-/μνητά τ' ἔχων βάρη · // ἁ δ' Page P.C.Ph.S. 1960, p. 49: ἀνήκεστα μερι-/μνήματ' ἔχων βαρεῖα δ' fere codd., βαρεῖ·//ἁ δ' S (= Vat b), Boeckh, edd. multi: βάρεα·//ἁ δ' Schneidewin: βοᾷ//ἁ δ' Linwood, Pearson.

189-90 πικραῖς / οἰμωγαῖσιν ὑπαχεῖ Emperius: πικρᾶς / οἰμωγᾶς ὑπόκειται codd., Campbell: πικραῖς οἰμωγαῖς (Brunck) ὑπακούει (Auratus) Jebb: πικρὰς / οἰμωγὰς (Pflugk) ὑποχεῖται (post alios Irigoin) D.-M.: πικρὰς / οἰμωγὰς ὑποτάκει J. Jackson: πικρᾶς / οἰμωγᾶς ὕπο χεῖται Erfurdt, Pearson.

---

[1]) *Due Seminari Romani di Eduard Fraenkel*, 1977, p. 66.

196   οὐκ ἔσθ' ὡς οὐ θεῶν του μελέτη Porson, edd. plerique: οὐκ
ἔσθ' ὅπως οὐ θεῶν του μελέτη codd.: οὐκ ἔστιν ὅπως οὐ
θεῶν μελέτη Τ, Pearson.

210   τέκνον,: τέκνον. Pearson.

214   ἀγροβάτας L, D.-M., alii: ἀγροβότας GRA, edd. multi,
Pearson.

228   καλούμενον, vel καλούμενον codd., G. Hermann, Ellendt,
Tournier, Masqueray, D.-M., ego dubitanter: κακούμενον,
Brunck, Campbell, Jebb, Webster, Pearson.

251   οὐδ' οὔνομ' οὐδὲ τῶν ἐμῶν κακῶν κλέος AUᵖᶜZᵒT, D.-M.:
ὄνομ' LΛGR: οὐδ' ὄνομ' ἄρ' οὐδὲ Erfurdt, edd. multi, Ed.
Fraenkel: οὐ τοὔνομ' οὐδὲ Seyffert, Lloyd-Jones Gnomon
33 (1961), p. 545: οὐδ' ὄνομα τοὐμὸν οὐδὲ τῶν κακῶν κλέος
Blaydes, Pearson.

256   μηδαμοῦ codd., edd. complures: μηδαμοῖ Blaydes, Schn.-
N.-Raderm., Pearson.

267   ἀγρίῳ codd., edd. complures, Webster, Ed. Fraenkel:
φοινίῳ Schneidewin (ex Eustath. opusc. 324. 60), Campbell, alii, Pearson.

272   ἀκτῆς, ἐν κατηρεφεῖ πέτρᾳ sic interpunxi: ἀκτῆς ἐν κατηρεφεῖ πέτρᾳ, multi, Pearson.

296   ἐκθλίβων LGR, Seyffert, ego dubitanter: ἐκτρίβων A, edd.
plerique, Pearson.

320   συντυχὼν codd., edd. plerique: σὺν τυχὼν Paley, Pearson.

324   θυμῷ . . . χεῖρα codd., Lloyd-Jones Cl. Rev. 1964, p. 130:
θυμὸν . . . χειρὶ Lambinus, edd., Pearson.

328   ἐγκαλῶν codd., fere edd.: ἐκκαλῶν Pearson: ἐγκοτῶν
Broadhead *Tragica* p. 99 (iam Lawson Cl. Rev. 1929,
pp. 5-7).

333   τόδ' · ἦ τέθνηχ' ὁ Πηλέως γόνος; L, edd. plurimi: εἰ AGR,
Pearson (τόδ, εἰ . . . γόνος.).

342   ὅτῳ σ' ἐνύβρισαν LA, fere edd.: ὅπως ἐνύβρισαν GR (ὅπω
σ' Q): ὅπως σ' ἐφύβρισαν Blaydes *Sp. Tr.* (1902), p. 121:
ὅπως σ' ἐνύβρισαν Pearson.

402   Λαρτίου: Λαρτίου, Pearson.

421, 2   τί δ'; ὃς παλαιὸς κἀγαθὸς φίλος τ' ἐμός, / Νέστωρ ὁ Πύλιος,
ἔστιν; AUY, Campbell, D.-M. [1]): τί δ'; οὐ παλαιὸς . . . /
. . . ἔστιν; Jebb: τί χὠ παλαιὸς . . . / . . . Πύλιος, ἔστιν
Dawe *Studies* III, p. 125: τί δ'; <οὐδ'> ὁ παλαιὸς . . .

_____
[1]) Schn.-N.-Raderm¹¹ (1911) sine commate post Πύλιος.

ἐμός, / Νέστωρ ὁ Πύλιος ἔστιν ('post Wilamowitzium', cf. Schn.-N.-Raderm.[11], p. 152 n. 1) Pearson.

425 ὅσπερ ἦν γόνος codd. (sed e Σ apparet v.l. μόνος extitisse), Campbell, Schn.-N.-Raderm., Wilamowitz, D.-M.: ὃς παρῆν μόνος Toup, Musgrave, alii: ὃς παρῆν (,) γόνος Jebb, alii, Campbell *Paral. Soph.*, p. 205, Pearson.

457 δεινὸς codd., Campbell (sed cf. *Paral. Soph.* p. 207), Kuiper, Webster dubitat: δειλὸς Brunck, edd. plerique, Pearson.

481 ὅπῃ fere codd., edd. plurimi: ὅποι Wakefield, Pearson.

491 δεράδα καὶ τὸν Toup, edd. multi, Ed. Fraenkel: δειράδα καὶ τὸν codd.: δειράδ᾽ ἢ τὸν Pierson, Porson, D.-M., Pearson.

497 ἤ, τά: ἢ τά Pearson.

498 τοὐμὸν ἐν σμικρῷ μέρος LGR Sud. *s.v.* στόλος, edd. multi: τοὐμὸν ἐν σμικρῷ μέρει Sud. *s.v.* διάκονος, Brunck, Schn.-N.-Raderm., Pearson.

502 δεινά, sic interpunxi: δεινὰ Pearson.

509 ὅσσα codd., Campbell, D.-M., alii: οἷα Porson, Schn.- N.- Raderm., Jebb, alii, Pearson.

532 προσφιλῆ;

533, 4 προσκύσαντε τὴν ἔσω / ἄοικον εἰσοίκησιν (vel: εἰς οἴκησιν L) codd. (sed GR habent προσκύσοντες), Campbell, Jebb, D.-M., Wilamowitz(?), Ed. Fraenkel: προσκύσαντε γῆν ἔσω / ἄοικον εἰς οἴκησιν Schneidewin, Pearson.

536 μόνην codd., edd. plerique: μόνον Blaydes, Pearson.

572 ἂν codd., Campbell (etiam *Paral. Soph.*, p. 210), Schn.-N.-Radern.: αὖ Dobree, Jebb, D.-M., alii, Pearson.

608 δόλιος codd., edd. plerique: δόλοις Housman, Tyrrell, Wilamowitz, Pearson.

651 τί γάρ; ἔτ᾽ ἀλλ᾽ ἐρᾷς λαβεῖν; sic interpunxi.

655 ταῦτ᾽, οὐ γὰρ ἀλλ᾽ ἔστ᾽, ἀλλ᾽ ἃ βαστάζω χεροῖν GR, Seyffert, Jebb, Ed. Fraenkel: ἀλλ᾽ ἔσθ᾽ ἃ LΛ: ἄλλα γ᾽ ἔσθ᾽ A, multi edd., Pearson.

666 μ᾽ ἔνερθεν ... ἀνέστησας πέρα LA, edd. plurimi, Ed. Fraenkel: ἔνερθεν ... πέρα GR: ἔνερθεν ... μ᾽ ὕπερ Burges, alii, Pearson.

678 †Ἰξίονα κατ᾽ ἄμπυκα δὴ δρομάδα δέσμιον† fere codd., crucibus notavi: κατὰ δρομάδ᾽ ἄμπυκα δέσμιον (omisso Ἰξίονα) Schneidewin, Jebb, alii, Pearson.

683 ὃς οὔτε τι ῥέξας (Eustath. 763.2) τιν᾽, οὔτε (codd.) νοσφίσας

M. D. Reeve (Cl. Rev. 1971.3, p. 325): ὃς οὔτ' ἔρξας τιν'
codd., edd. plerique, Pearson: οὔτι νοσφίσας Schneidewin,
alii, Pearson: ὃς οὔτι ῥέξας <οὔτιν'>, οὔτι νοσφίσας J.
Jackson (M.S., pp. 111, 2).

685   ὤλλυτ' ἀνάξι' ὧδε Bergk (οὕτως Burges), Wilamowitz
(Gr. Vsk., p. 409 no. 1): ὤλλυθ' ὧδ' ἀναξίως codd., Jebb,
Schn.-N.-Raderm., D.-M., Pearson: ὤλλυθ' ὧδ' ἀτίμως
Erfurdt, Webster: ὤλλυτο τῇδ' ἀναξίως Campbell (1881):
alii aliter.

686   τόδε <δ' αὖ> θαῦμά μ' ἔχει Wunder, J. Jackson (M.S.,
p. 80), D.-M., Webster: τόδε θαῦμ' ἔχει με codd., Campbell
(inserto δή post prius πῶς), Schn.-N.-Raderm.: τόδε
<τοι> (Dindorf) θαῦμά μ' ἔχει (Erfurdt), Jebb. Pearson.

691   πρόσουρος, codd., Campbell, Jebb, Schn.-N.-Raderm.,
D.-M., alii: πρόσουρον Bothe, alii, Wilamowitz (Gr. Vsk.,
p. 409 n. 1), Pearson.

696   ὃς τὰν Hermann, Jebb, alii: οὐδ' ὃς Erfurdt, edd. complures,
Pearson: οὐδ' ὃς τὰν codd.

699   εἴ τις ἐμπέσοι <πόθος> J. Jackson (M.S., p. 113): εἴ τις
ἐμπέσοι, codd., multi edd., Pearson.

700   ἔκ τι γᾶς Page (Proc. Cambr. Phil. Soc., 1960, p. 52),
Webster: ἔκ τε γᾶς codd., Campbell: ἐκ γαίας Dindorf,
Jebb, alii, Jackson, Pearson.
ἑλεῖν codd., Campbell, Jackson, Page, Webster: ἑλών
Turnebus, edd. complures, Pearson.

701   γὰρ codd., Campbell: δ' Hermann, edd. plerique, Pearson.
ἄλλα codd., Schn.-N.-Raderm., Webster, cf. ad 685:
ἀλλαχᾷ Campbell, Jebb, D.-M., Pearson.

711   πτανῶν πτανοῖς ἀνύσειε A, Campbell: πτανῶν ἀνύσειε
πτανοῖς ΛAGR: πτανοῖς ἰοῖς ἀνύσειε Brunck, edd. plerique,
Pearson.

715   δεκέτει χρόνῳ L (δεκατεῖ GR), edd. plurimi: δεκέτη χρόνον
AUY, Pearson.

719   παιδὸς ὑπαντήσας codd., edd. plurimi: παιδὶ συναντήσας
Froehlich, Schn.-N.-Raderm., Pearson.

726, 7 ὄχθαις LA, Campbell, D.-M.: ὄχθας G, Jebb, Schn.-N.-
Raderm., Pearson.

727, 8 ἀνὴρ θεὸς / πλάθει θεοῖς Schneidewin, Schn.-N.-Raderm.:
ἀνὴρ θεοῖς / πλάθει πᾶσι fere codd.: πᾶσι(ν) inter cruces
Campbell, damnat Bergk: ἀνὴρ θεοῖς / πλάθη θεὸς Wila-

mowitz [1]) (*Kl. Schr.* I p. 520 n. 1): ἀνὴρ θεοῖς / πλάθει πᾶσιν nonnulli edd., Pearson.

752 ποιεῖς (ποεῖς) codd., edd. complures: ποιεῖ (ποεῖ, ποῇ) Jebb, Schn.-N.-Raderm., Pearson.

753 ὦ τέκνον. ... ὦ παῖ. edd. plerique: ὦ τέκνον; ... ὦ παῖ; Pearson, Webster.

755 τοὐπίσαγμα edd. plerique: τοὐπείσαγμα LGRQA: τοὐπίσιγμα, Bergk, Pearson.

771 μήτ' ἄκοντα codd., Campbell, Jebb, D.-M., alii: μηδ' ἄκοντα Eustath. 1694.7, Sch.-N.-Raderm., alii, Pearson.

792 ἔχοιτ' codd., edd. plerique: ἵκοιτ' Wakefield, Pearson.

800 ἀνακαλουμένῳ codd., edd. plerique: ἀνακαλούμενον Meineke, Pearson.

834 βάσῃ · cum aliis sic interpunxi: βάσῃ, Pearson.

835 φροντίδος, vel φροντίδος;: φροντίδος. Pearson.
ὁρᾷς ἤδη codd., fere edd.: ὁρᾷς; εὕδει. van Herwerden, Pearson: ὁρᾷς ἤδη; aut ὁρᾷς ἤδη. vel ἤδη · (vide commentarium).

836 μενοῦμεν codd., Jebb, Schn.-N.-Raderm.: μένομεν Erfurdt, Campbell, D.-M., Pearson.

851 ἐξιδοῦ ὅτι πράξεις fere codd., ὅπως L^{sl}Λ^{sl}, ὅτι πως Q, crucibus notavi: ἐξιδοῦ ὅπως πράξεις multi edd., Pearson. Possis ἐξιδοῦ τί πράξεις (vel πῶς πράξεις) vel ἐξιδέ γ' ὅτι (vel ὅπως) πράξεις.

852 ὧν LΛ, Schn.-N.-Raderm.: ὃν L^{sl}Λ^{sl}GRA Campbell, D.-M., alii, Pearson: ἂν Jebb: ὅν γ' Brunck: ὃ γ' Dawe (*Studies* III, p. 131).

853 ταύταν G, Campbell, Jebb, D.-M.: ταὐτὰν vel ταυτὰν LRA alii (nota ΣL et R εἰ τὴν αὐτὴν τῷ 'Οδυσσεῖ γνώμην ἔχεις, hinc, opinor, τὴν αὐτὰν Marc. 616): ταὐτᾷ Dobree, Pearson.

944 θέλει. vel · cum aliis sic interpunxi: θέλει, Pearson, Webster.

957 ὑφ' ὧν codd., edd. plerique: ἀφ' ὧν Wunder, Pearson.

961 ὄλοιο — μήπω Jebb, alii: ὄλοιο μή πω Pearson.

973 οἷς codd., edd. plerique: οἷ' Dindorf, Pearson.

975 εἶ, ... ἐμοί, sic interpunxi: sine interpunctione Pearson.

984 τολμήστατε fere codd., edd. plerique: τόλμης πέρα Pearson.

---

[1]) qui attribuit hanc lectionem G. Hermanno, sed πλάθη coniecit Bergk; θεοῖς / πλάθει θεός est Hermanni δευτέρα φροντίς.

999 οὐδεποτέ γ', οὐδ' ἦν . . . κακόν, sic interpunxi: γ'· . . . κακόν, Pearson.

1022 ζῶ, . . . τάλας, sic interpunxi: ζῶ . . . τάλας, Pearson.

1032, 3 πῶς θεοῖς εὔξεσθ', ὁμοῦ / πλεύσαντος; αἴθειν ἱερὰ πῶς σπένδειν τ' ἔνι; Kuiper *in apparatu*, Radermacher *in apparatu*: εὔξεσθ', ἐμοῦ/πλεύσαντος, αἴθειν ἱερά; πῶς σπένδειν ἔτι; codd. (nisi quod Gʸᵖ habet ὁμοῦ), Campbell: ἔξεστ', ἐμοῦ Pierson, complures, Pearson (probat Ed. Fraenkel, *o.l.* p. 72): ἔξεσθ', ὁμοῦ Jebb.

1054 Textus continuatur sine recessu ('indention').

1071 ἐποικτιρεῖτε: ἐποικτερεῖτε codd., Campbell, Jebb, Pearson (cum Herodian. Gr. 2.559 sed cf. Nauck ad Aesch. fr. 199.6 N²) [1]).

1076 τά τ' ἐκ νεὼς codd. Σ, Campbell, Jebb, alii (Tournier-Desrousseaux³ quoque): τὰ τῆς νεὼς Tournier, Schn.-N.-Raderm. (sine nota critica), Pearson.

1089 τί ποτ' αὖ codd., Campbell, Schn.-N.-Raderm.: τίπτ' αὖ Musgrave, Bothe, Wunder, Jebb, D.-M., Pearson.

1092-94 ἴθ' αἱ πρόσθ' (vel πάρος) ἄνω / πτωκάδες ὀξυτόνου διὰ πνεύματος· / ἄλωσιν οὐκέτ' ἴσχω J. Jackson (*M.S.*, pp. 114-16): εἴθ' αἰθέρος ἄνω / πτωκάδες ὀξυτόνου διὰ πνεύματος / ἔλωσί μ'· οὐ γὰρ ἔτ' ἰσχύω fere codd.: εἶτ' (Schroeder) αἰθέρος ἄνω / πτωκάδες ὀξυτόνου διὰ πνεύματος / ἐλῶσί μ'· (Zn = Paris. gr. 2787) οὐδ' (Wunder) ἔτ' ἰσχύς (Blaydes) Pearson: alii alia.

1095-97 σύ τοι σύ τοι κατηξίωσας, ὦ βαρύποτμ', οὐκ ἄλλοθεν // ἔχη τύχᾳ τᾷδ' ἀπὸ μείζονος· // codd., nisi quod habent βαρύποτμε, Wilamowitz (Übersetzung, p. 113), Schn.-N.-Raderm.: σύ τοι σύ τοι κατηξίωσας, / ὦ βαρύποτμ', οὐκ ἄλλοθεν ἔχει τύχαις ἀπὸ μείζονος, // Campbell: σύ τοι σύ τοι κατηξίωσας, / ὦ βαρύποτμε, κοὐκ / ἄλλοθεν ἔχει τύχᾳ / τᾷδ' ἀπὸ μείζονος· // Jebb: σύ τοι σύ τοι κατηξίω-/σας, ὦ βαρύποτμ'· οὐκ / ἄλλοθεν ἁ τύχα ἅδ' ἀπὸ μείζονος· // Dindorf, alii, D.-M., Pearson.
μείζονος, sic interpunxi: μείζονος· Pearson.

1099 τοῦ λῴονος δαίμονος codd., Campbell, Schn.-N.-Raderm., D.-M.: τοῦ λῴονος †δαίμονος Jebb: λωϊονος δαίμονος Froehlich, Bothe, Blaydes, alii, Dale (Webster): λῴονος ἐκ δαίμονος Pearson.

---

[1]) Schw.-D. I 785 hanc formam accipit in Aesch. et Soph..

1110   κραταιαῖσιν Campbell, Schn.-N.-Raderm.: κρατααῖς codd.,
        Jebb, alii, D.-M., Pearson.

1116-18 πότμος <πότμος> σε δαιμόνων τάδ', οὐδὲ δόλος ἐμᾶς γε
        σὲ // ἔσχεν ὑπὸ χειρός· στυγερὰν ἔχε // Wilamowitz, nisi
        quod inverso ordine σέ γε scripsit (ἔσχεν Bergk): οὐδὲ σέ γε
        δόλος / ἔσχ' ὑπὸ χειρὸς ἐμᾶς. στυγερὰν ἔχε // codd., com-
        plures edd., Pearson, alii alia.

1132, 2 τὸν Ἡράκλειον, / ἄθλιον ὧδέ, LAG[s1], edd. complures,
        Schn.-N.-Raderm., Masqueray, D.-M.: ἆθλον LΣ[γρ]GR:
        τὸν Ἡράκλειον / ἆθλον ἔμ' ὧδέ Campbell (etiam *Paral.*
        Soph., p. 223): τὸν Ἡράκλειον / ἄρθμιον ὧδέ Erfurdt,
        Jebb, alii: τὸν Ἡρακλείῳ ἀεθλίῳ ὧδέ A. Platt, Cl. Qu.
        5-1911-p. 27), Webster: †ἄθλιον† Pearson.

1138   μυρί' ἀπ' αἰσχρῶν codd., Campbell, Schn.-N.-Raderm.,
        D.-M., alii: μυρία τ' (Gernhard) ἀθροῦν (ἀθρῶν Kaibel)
        Pearson.

1144   τοῦδ' codd., Brunck, Campbell, dubitans retinui (κεῖνος
        ad Neoptolemum, τοῦδε ad Ulixem pertinere ratus):
        τοῦτ' Musgrave, Pearson: τῶνδε Thudichum, Gernhard,
        edd. multi.

1192   προύφαινες GRQ, Campbell, Jebb, Schn.-N.-Raderm.,
        D.-M.: προύφανες LA: προφαίνεις Pearson.

1207   κρᾶτ' ἀπὸ πάντα καὶ ἄρθρα τέμω codd., Campbell, Schn.-
        N.-Raderm. (nisi quod τεμῶ scripserunt), D.-M.: κρᾶτα
        καὶ ἄρθρ' ἀπὸ πάντα τέμω Bergk, Pearson.

1212-14 οὐ γὰρ ἔστ ἐν φάει γ' ἔτ'. ὦ πόλις // ὦ πόλις πατρία, πῶς ...
        ἀνήρ, codd., sic divisit Radermacher: οὐ γὰρ ἐν φάει γ'
        ἔτι. // ὦ πολις ὦ πόλις πατρία, // πῶς ... ἀνήρ, G. Hermann,
        vulg., Pearson.

1265, 6 μέγα codd. / ... κακόν AGRQL[s1], Campbell, D.-M., alii:
        νέα (Bergk) / ... κακά L, Jebb, Schn.-N.-Raderm.,
        Pearson.

1284   ἔχθιστος codd., Campbell, Jebb, D.-M., alii: αἴσχιστος
        Pierson, Porson, Wunder, Schn.-N.-Raderm., Pearson.

1289   ἁγνοῦ ... ὕψιστον codd., Campbell, Jebb, D.-M.: ἁγνὸν ...
        ὑψίστον Wakefield, Wunder, Schn.-N.-Raderm., alii, Ed.
        Fraenkel (*o.l.* p. 74), Pearson.

1313   δὲ codd., edd. complures: τε Turnebus, Schn.-N.-Raderm.,
        Pearson.

1314   πατέρα τε τὸν ἐμὸν τε add. AUY, Campbell, Schn.-N.-

Raderm., alii: πατέρα τὸν ἐμὸν fere codd.: πατέρα τὸν ἀμὸν T, Jebb, D.-M., alii, Pearson.

1329 ἐντυχεῖν codd.: ἂν τυχεῖν Porson, multi, Pearson.

1337 ἔστιν Jebb, alii: ἐστιν Pearson.

1361 τἄλλα . . . κακά codd., Campbell, D.-M.: τἄλλα . . . κακούς Dobree, Doederlein, Wunder, Bergk, Jebb, alii: πάντα (Reiske) . . . κακούς Pearson.

1364sqq. οἵ τε σοῦ καθύβρισαν / πατρὸς γέρας συλῶντες ὕστερόν τε σὲ / Ὀδυσσέως ἔκριναν —, εἶτα τοῖσδε σὺ tentavi (cf. Pearson in apparatu; οἵ τε σοῦ codd., οἵ γέ σου Heath, multi, Pearson).

1366 τόδε LGRQ (τὸ δὲ Λ), Jebb, Schn.-N.-Raderm., D.-M.: τάδε AGʸᵖ Campbell, Pearson.

1367 ἀλλ' ἅ μοι ξυνώμοσας codd., edd. plerique, Ed. Fraenkel (o.l., p. 75): ἀλλά μ' ὃ ξυνήνεσας Blaydes (ξυνήνεσας van Herwerden), Pearson.

1392 οὐδέποθ', sic interpunxit Jebb: οὐδέποθ alii, Pearson.

1394 πείσειν codd., edd. plerique: πείθειν Schaefer, Pearson.

1406 Ἡρακλέοις Wackernagel: Ἡρακλείοις codd.: Ἡρακλέους Brunck, edd., Pearson.

1407, 8 Νε. πῶς λέγεις; Φι. εἴρξω πελάζειν σῆς πάτρας. Νε. ἀλλ' εἰ <θέλεις> / δρᾶν <σὺ> ταῦθ' ὅπωσπερ αὐδᾷς, στεῖχε προσκύσας χθόνα Housman (Cl. Rev. 1925, p. 78): πῶς . . . σῆς πάτρας / δρᾷς ταῦθ' ὥσπερ αὐδᾷς . . . χθόνα fere codd.: Νε. πῶς λέγεις; Φι. εἴρξω πελάζειν. Νε. στεῖχε προσκύσας χθόνα Dindorf, Jebb, D.-M., alii: Νε. πῶς λέγεις; Φι. εἴρξω πελάζειν σῆς πάτρας. Νε. ἀλλ' εἰ <δοκεῖ / σοὶ τὸ> δρᾶν τάδ' ὥσπερ αὐδᾷς, στεῖχε προσκύσας χθόνα Pearson.

1433 ταῦτ' codd., edd. plerique: ταῦτ' Heath, Pearson.

1448 ταύτῃ fere codd.: ταὐτῇ Dobree, Pearson.

1451 ὅδ' ·: ὅδ' Pearson.

INTRODUCTION

I. Sources and Predecessors

1. The Philoctetes saga belongs to the Trojan cycle and has an important connection with the Heracles story. In Hom. *Il.* II 716-725 we read:

οἳ δ' ἄρα Μηθώνην καὶ Θαυμακίην ἐνέμοντο,
καὶ Μελίβοιαν ἔχον καὶ Ὀλιζῶνα τρηχεῖαν,
τῶν δὲ Φιλοκτήτης ἦρχεν, τόξων εὖ εἰδώς,
ἑπτὰ νεῶν· ἐρέται δ' ἐν ἑκάστῃ πεντήκοντα
ἐμβέβασαν, τόξων εὖ εἰδότες ἶφι μάχεσθαι.
ἀλλ' ὃ μὲν ἐν νήσῳ κεῖτο κρατέρ' ἄλγεα πάσχων,
Λήμνῳ ἐν ἠγαθέῃ, ὅθι μιν λίπον υἷες Ἀχαιῶν
ἕλκεϊ μοχθίζοντα κακῷ ὀλοόφρονος ὕδρου·
ἔνθ' ὅ γε κεῖτ' ἀχέων, τάχα δὲ μνήσεσθαι ἔμελλον
Ἀργεῖοι παρὰ νηυσὶ Φιλοκτήταο ἄνακτος.

The poet knows of Philoctetes' bowmanship, of his misfortune, his sad detention on Lemnos where the Achaeans left him behind, but he also alludes—unmistakably—to the reversal of his fortunes and the rôle he is destined to play in the capture of Troy. His bowmanship is mentioned by Odysseus when among the Phaeacians *Od.* VIII 219 sq.: οἷος δή με Φιλοκτήτης ἀπεκαίνυτο τόξῳ / δήμῳ ἔνι Τρώων, ὅτε τοξαζοίμεθ' Ἀχαιοί·. At *Od.* III 190—Nestor speaking to Telemachus—he is numbered among the chieftains who had a safe return home after the Trojan war (εὖ δὲ Φιλοκτήτην, Ποιάντιον ἀγλαὸν υἱόν).

It is to be noted that the localities mentioned at *Il.* II 716, 7 belong to the peninsula of Magnesia, whereas his 'classic' homeland is situated at Malis near mount Oeta, and is traversed by the river Spercheus. Possibly this shift is to be attributed to his rôle in the Heracles saga [1]).

In the *Cypria*, Agamemnon's fleet, after the second departure for Troy (from Aulis), was said to have made for the isle of Tenedos, where Philoctetes was bitten by a water-snake, after which διὰ τὴν δυσοσμίαν ἐν Λήμνῳ κατελείφθη (Proclus 144-146, Severijns). In

---

[1]) Cf. Schn.-N.-Radermacher, Einl.[11] p. 3 n.

Proclus' brief account of the Ἰλιὰς μικρὰ we read that after the ὅπλων κρίσις and Aiax's death Ὀδυσσεὺς λοχήσας Ἕλενον λαμβάνει, καὶ χρήσαντος περὶ τῆς ἀλώσεως τούτου Διομήδης ἐκ Λήμνου Φιλοκτήτην ἀνάγει. ἰαθεὶς δὲ οὗτος ὑπὸ Μαχάονος καὶ μονομαχήσας Ἀλεξάνδρῳ κτείνει· (Proclus 211-214), and: καὶ Νεοπτόλεμον Ὀδυσσεὺς ἐκ Σκύρου ἀγαγὼν τὰ ὅπλα δίδωσι τὰ τοῦ πατρός· (ib. 217, 8; cf. Od. XI 508, 9).

We should, of course, bear in mind that Proclus' extracts are extremely succinct, many details, possibly borrowed by tragic (and other) poets from the cyclic epics, are left out or mentioned so briefly that it remains impossible for us to establish the measure of originality of the latter in handling the epic material. Helenus' oracle, for instance, is a case in point. From Proclus' text we can infer that Philoctetes and his bow (and possibly also Neoptolemus) are necessary for the capture of Troy; we learn that the bowman Philoctetes kills the archer Paris, but nothing more is said about his rôle in the war, nor about the conditions and circumstances of his return, except that he is healed by Machaon. There is no special mention of the bow.

In Hesiod no mention is made of Philoctetes, nor do we find much about him in the remnants of the lyric poets (as far as we are aware, there was no poem of Stesichorus dealing with his fortunes). In Pind. *Pyth.* I 50 sqq. the ailing Hiero leading his army is compared to Philoctetes taking part in the capture of Troy. In the schol. it is noted: τῇ ἱστορίᾳ καὶ Βακχυλίδης συμφωνεῖ ἐν τοῖς διθυράμβοις, ὅτι οἱ Ἕλληνες ἐκ Λήμνου μετεστείλαντο τὸν Φιλοκτήτην Ἑλένου μαντευσαμένου· εἵμαρτο γὰρ ἄνευ τῶν Ἡρακλείων τόξων μὴ πορθηθῆναι τὴν Ἴλιον (= Bacch. *fr.* 7).

2. Both Aeschylus and Euripides wrote a tragedy on Philoctetes and his bow being fetched from Lemnos to Troy. From both plays a number of fragments survive; we have, on papyrus, remnants of their hypotheses, and more important, we have Dio Chrysostomus' comparative essay on Aeschylus', Euripides' and Sophocles' *Philoctetes* (*Or.* LII); the same wrote a sort of paraphrase of the Prologue of Euripides' play (*Or.* LIX).

The date of Aeschylus' tragedy is unknown (but since it seems to have needed only two actors and to have had a simple dramatic structure I should guess it to be comparatively early [1])), nor do we

---

[1]) This remains very uncertain, however. See O. Taplin's pertinent remarks, *The Stagecraft of Aeschylus*, 1977, p. 430.

know whether it belonged to a closely connected trilogy; Euripides' *Philoctetes* is the second play of the tetralogy of which *Medea* is the first (431 B.C.).

The fragment of the hypothesis of Aeschylus' *Philoctetes* (Pap. Ox. 2256 fr. 5) is very scrappy. In Mette's *Fragmente der Trag. des Aisch.* 392 it runs as follows:

```
                ] · ἀδύνα-
τον δ' ἦν τὴν Τροία]ν λημφθῆ(ναι),
εἰ μὴ οἱ Ἕλληνες μετεπέ]μπον-
το ἐκ τῆς Λήμνου τὸν Φ]ιλο[κ]τ[ή(την).
κεῖται δ' ὁ μῦθος καὶ π]αρ' Εὐριπί-
δηι. παρὰ Σοφοκλεῖ δὲ Νεο]πτόλεμο(ς)
                ] Φιλοκτή(τ . . )
                'Οδυσ]σεύς
                ]
                ]
                ]ω οὗ
```

This partial reconstruction of the text has the merit of not introducing Neoptolemus as a *dramatis persona* into Aeschylus' play [1] (there is no mention of Neoptolemus in Dio's remarks on Aeschylus' play, whereas Diomedes in Euripides and Neoptolemus in Sophocles are referred to by him). We do not learn anything new from the fragment.

From Dio's comments we learn that Odysseus, undisguised but not recognized by Philoctetes, gained the latter's trust by the false story that Agamemnon was dead and Odysseus 'destroyed' on a most shameful charge. Further that the Chorus consisted of Lemnians, who were apparently approaching him for the first time (without any excuse for their neglect) and to whom he related his story. Whether or not there was a prologue-parodos we cannot tell (see Taplin *o.l.* p. 430) [2]. From the frr. 398, 399 Mette it appears that an attack of his νόσος occurred in the course of the play. We may surmise that this provided Odysseus with an occasion to take the bow; after that he must have persuaded Philoctetes, or forced him, to follow him to Troy.

---

[1] Cf. Taplin, *o.l.* p. 430 n. 1, and Mette's note *a.l.*.
[2] W. Calder, Gr. Rom. Byz. St. 11 (1970) pp. 173 sq., argues in favour of it. Webster, *Philoctetes*, (1970) p. 3 assumes a prologue spoken by Odysseus.

Three important features in Aeschylus' handling of the story stand out: it was Odysseus who came to fetch Philoctetes (Diomedes in the *Little Iliad*); he attempted to win the other's confidence by a false story speculating on his enmity against the Achaean chieftains and himself; an attack of Philoctetes' disease was made to occur.

The fragmentary hypothesis of Euripides' play, Pap. Oxy. 2455, fr. 17 (edited by Turner in Pap. Oxy. XXVII 1962; the text also in C. Austin, *Nova Fragmenta Euripidea*, 1968, p. 100) does not shed much new light on what was known from Dio LII and LIX:

. ξ[
.. ρα[...]. ας Φιλοκτ[η]τ[......] οι
λευς.[..]ες ἐν τοῖς τόποις [ἐν οἷς ἐδ]ή-
χθη· περιαλγῆ δ' α[ὐτὸν γενόμ]ενον
ἐπὶ τὴν παρακειμένην Λ[ῆ]μνον δια-
κομ[ίσ]αντες εἴασαν· ὁ δ[ὲ] τὸν δεκαετῆ
χρό[ν]ον διέζησεν ἀτυχῶν, ὡς ἂν βίον
ἔχ[ων] τὸν ἔλεον τῶν ἐντυγχανόντων·
..]ε[.]τα ¹) καὶ Ἕλενος εἶπεν τ[ο]ῖς Τρωσ[ὶ] τοῖ[ς
Ἡρακλέο[υς] τόξοις ἀσφαλίσασθα[ι] τὴν πόλιν καὶ λ[η]φθεὶς δ' αἰχμάλωτος τὴν αὐτὴν ποιεῖσθ]αι συμμαχ[ί]α[ν] ἔ[πε]ισεν
        ] τὸν Φιλοκτ[ήτην
        ] Ὀδυσσεὺς εχ[
    ἐνε]τείλατο μὲν ἐμφ[
        ] Ἀθηνᾶς βου[λ
    ]η[.....]υτο[
    ]ε[......]φι[
        desunt lineae fere 17
                ]ισκα[..]ει
                ]ην ἀσφάλει-
αν ἀναγκάζει[πρὸς τὴν ν]αῦν συνακ[ο]λουθεῖν. —

ληφθεὶς αἰχμάλωτος confirms, perhaps, the exactness of Dio's paraphrase of the Prologue (LIX 2); ὡς ἂν βίον ... ἐντυγχανόντων is in agreement with Dio LII 8 (Actor), Ἀθηνᾶς βου[λ ... with Dio LIX 3.

---

¹) ἔπ]ε[ι]τα Turner, 'vix recte' Austin; but it is difficult to imagine another possibility.

From Dio we learn that Odysseus, in the Prologue, expounded the circumstances under which he has come to Lemnos in order to fetch Philoctetes and his bow: ὁ μὲν δὴ μαντικώτατος Φρυγῶν Ἕλενος ὁ Πριάμου κατεμήνυσεν, ὡς ἔτυχεν αἰχμαλωτὸς ληφθείς, ἄνευ τούτων (Philoctetes and his bow) μήποτ' ἂν ἁλῶναι τὴν πόλιν. Conscious of Philoctetes' hatred—because it was at his instigation that Philoctetes had been left behind at Lemnos—, Odysseus would not have dared to fetch the sick man but for the exhortation of Athena and her promise that she would disguise him out of all recognition. Moreover he knew that a Trojan embassy was on its way with the intention of winning over Philoctetes and his bow to the Trojan side. So it was a case of *periculum in mora*. We have to imagine Odysseus in disguise arriving before Philoctetes' abode; after Odysseus' fairly long monologue Philoctetes is seen approaching and a dialogue between the two ensues. Odysseus overcomes Philoctetes' suspicion by making himself out to be a fugitive friend of Palamedes'. He is, then, invited by Philoctetes to share with him for the time being his miserable life [1]).

After this—see Webster, *The Tragedies of Euripides*, p. 59—the parodos of the Chorus of Lemnians—as in Aeschylus, but they excuse themselves for their neglect of the unhappy hero—must have taken place. Dio makes mention of the Lemnian Actor introduced as dramatis persona by Euripides, ὡς γνώριμον τῷ Φιλοκτήτῃ προσιόντα καὶ πολλάκις συμβεβληκότα [2]). Webster (*The Tragedies of Euripides*, p. 59 [3])) makes the shrewd observation, that Actor may have supplied Philoctetes not only with food, but also with news. 'The news which is needed and which Odysseus cannot give is the arrival of a Trojan ship'. We may surmise that after the parodos there came a scene in which Philoctetes, Odysseus and Actor were on stage. Then, after a stasimon, the arrival of the Trojan embassy occurred. Paris, probably,—cf. 797 N².—offered Philoctetes gold and royal power; Odysseus, still in his rôle of

---

[1]) In the dialogue between Odysseus and Philoctetes the *fr. ad.* 389 N.² = Eur. *fr.* 790 a, (*Supplementum* Snell, 1964, p. 12) will have occurred: οὐκ ἔστ' ἐν ἄντροις λευκός, ὦ ξέν', ἄργυρος.

[2]) It is not clear whether this Actor is of Euripides' invention. In Hyginus 102 (*Philoctetes*) the same rôle is attributed to a 'pastor regis Actoris, nomine Iphimachus Dolopionis filius'. This may have been borrowed from Euphorion's *Philoctetes*; for the remnants of this poem cf. van Groningen, *Euphorion* (1977), *frr.* 48 and 49, pp. 113-116.

[3]) I regard Webster's reconstruction of the play on the whole as plausible.

fugitive victim, prevailed on Philoctetes, by appealing to his
'patriotic' feelings, to drive away the Trojans (Webster's interpretation of *Urne Etrusche* I 80 pl. 69-72 is very convincing). We
can imagine, that, just as after the Emporos scene in Sophocles,
the poet has thought fit to place after the exciting ἀγών, in which
two parties seek to win over the sick man, a violent attack of
Philoctetes' disease, as a result of which he falls into a coma (*fr.*
801 N² ἀπέπνευσεν αἰῶνα). We know from Dio that Diomedes made
his appearance in the play; he can be thought to have entered
during Philoctetes' sleep, and to have taken the bow away. At the
end of the fragmentary hypothesis we read the words ἀναγκάζει
[πρὸς τὴν ν]αῦν συνακολουθεῖν. (This is, at least, not contradictory to
Dio's τὸ δέ τι καὶ πειθοῖ ἀναγκαίᾳ, ἐπειδὴ τῶν ὅπλων ἐστέρητο LII 2).

3. We can now, up to a point, gauge the measure of Sophocles'
originality in handling the dramatization of the saga. From Aeschylus and Euripides he took over the assigning to Odysseus of the
task of bringing back Philoctetes and Heracles' bow to the Achaean
army. He discarded Diomedes (*Little Iliad* and as second man in
Euripides); he made Odysseus choose Neoptolemus, the youthful
son of Achilles, as his companion and collaborator (note that in the
Little Iliad Odysseus fetched Neoptolemus from Scyros, but only
after Diomedes had secured the arrival of Philoctetes, if we can
trust Proclus; according to Neoptolemus' story to Philoctetes
Odysseus had taken him from Scyros—*Phil.* 344 sqq.—).

He made Philoctetes' loneliness and isolation absolute, and
equally absolute his rancour and refusal to comply with the wish of
the Achaeans even after Neoptolemus has restored the bow, and
despite the promise of healing and glory. So Heracles' appearance is
needed to bring the ending of the drama into line with the main
data of the saga (there is no indication of a deus ex machina in
Euripides' *Philoctetes*) [1]. He made the Chorus consist of Neoptolemus' sailors who have to follow their chieftain's lead. But his
chief originality lies in the rôle assigned to Neoptolemus.

2. Prior Assumptions of the Play

Philoctetes, son of Poeas, king of Malis, had been endowed by
Heracles with the latter's bow and its inescapable arrows because

---

[1] It is noteworthy that Sophocles made use of Heracles as deus ex
machina in another play: *Athamas*; cf. ΣVM Ar. *Nub.* 257; see further
S. L. Radt, *T.G.F.* iv (1977) Sophocles, pp. 99, 100.

he alone among mortals had dared to kindle Heracles' pyre on Mount Oeta. By means of this bow Heracles had at one time conquered Troy. In the tenth year of Agamemnon's expedition against the town, after Achilles' and Aiax' death, the Trojan seer Helenus, who had been captured by Odysseus, acquainted the Achaean chieftains with the oracle that Troy's fall depended on Philoctetes' voluntary assistance by means of the Heraclean bow.

Furthermore the Achaeans had to call to their aid Neoptolemus, Achilles' son, fetch him from Scyros, and restore to him Achilles' armour. For the collaboration between Achilles' son (with his father's armour) and Philoctetes (with Heracles' bow) was necessary for their ultimate success. (From Sophocles' text it is not clear whether the fetching of Neoptolemus is thought to belong to the Helenus oracle. At any rate, at the start of the play Neoptolemus had been fetched from Scyros [1]), and he had been given the assurance that his arrival was necessary to the victory of the Greeks).

As to Philoctetes: before reaching Troy the Greek fleet had to sail to the little isle of Chryse (to the East of Lemnos), for there they had to offer to the deity Chryse. In the precinct of Chryse Philoctetes had been bitten in his foot by her sacred snake [2]). The wound festered and its fetid odour and the hero's cries of pain caused the chieftains to expose Philoctetes, with his bow, on the uninhabited isle of Lemnos (or at least in a part of it without any inhabitants).

3. Course of the Action of the Play

Prologue (1-134). Odysseus and Neoptolemus, with an attendant, enter, supposedly having come from their ships in the little harbour nearby, moving in the direction of the centre of the skene, where the entrance of Philoctetes' cave is visible, some steps above ground-level. The panels of the skene suggest a wall of rock.

In his introductory speech Odysseus makes Neoptolemus and the audience acquainted with the place of the action; he mentions his rôle in the exposure of Philoctetes and the causes which led to

---

[1]) Probably the argument of Sophocles' *Scyrioi*; cf. Radt, *T.G.F.* iv Sophocles, pp. 418, 9.

[2]) Sophocles appears to be the first to mention Chryse (isle and nymph); that is not to say that this detail must be of his invention. See Pearson on Soph. *fr*. 384 (*Lemniae*). 'Chryse' also in *fr*. 40, (*Aichmalotides*) but there a town in the Troad is meant.

it. He wants Neoptolemus to make sure that this is the very spot where they abandoned the sufferer, and to spy whether he is absent or in the cave. So the hearer is orientated, in more than one sense, as to the presuppositions of the action. By means of Neoptolemus' report of what he sees in the cave he gets an impression of Philoctetes' condition. From Odysseus' keeping aloof from the cave and from some utterances of his the hearer will infer that, after Philoctetes' absence has been ascertained, he will hear more about things to come (presumably in a dialogue between Odysseus and Neoptolemus): the very fact that Neoptolemus, Achilles' son, is Odysseus' companion (in contrast with the traditional story; not for nothing is the young man solemnly addressed in ll. 4, 5) will have stretched the hearer's curiosity as to the rôle he will have to play. The attendant is sent to look out for Philoctetes—note the close relation between 46, 7 and 13, 14, and between 24, 5 and 49—, and Odysseus is ready to expound his σόφισμα (announced in 14). After four preparatory lines (50-54), in which the singular task that will be asked of Achilles' son is alluded to, and his subordinate position is emphatically mentioned, Odysseus gives Neoptolemus his instructions, complete with explanatory comments: he has to win Philoctetes' trust by deceit, by pretending that he, Achilles' son, is sailing home, because when he had been fetched to Troy under the pretence that by his aid alone Troy could be captured, the Achaean chieftains refused to render him his father's armour which they had awarded to Odysseus. He, unlike Odysseus, can converse with Philoctetes, and thus he will be able to steal the bow. By nature, it is true, Neoptolemus would not be disposed to commit fraud, but in this case the end justifies the means and the glory will be his.

Neoptolemus objects that although he is ready to take Philoctetes by force, he is averse to deceit, and on Odysseus' arguing that words are more effective than acts, he asks why, then, attempt deceit rather than persuasion. But neither force nor persuasion will avail (thus Odysseus). 'And what gain is it to me—asks Neoptolemus—that he should come to Troy' (112, Jebb's translation). That bow alone will capture Troy. So it will not be Neoptolemus who will destroy the town, as had been claimed (thus the young man's disappointed words). But Odysseus' next line οὔτ' ἂν σὺ κείνων χωρὶς οὔτ' ἐκεῖνα σοῦ (115) tips the balance in his mind, between honesty and ambition, in favour of the latter.

Odysseus leaves, taking with him the attendant whom he will send back in the disguise of a merchant sailor when matters appear to progress too slowly.

It is not clear whether Odysseus means Neoptolemus to steal the bow only or whether he intends him to take Philoctetes as well to the harbour. We get the impression that Odysseus is thinking of the bow as the all-important element of success and that all will be well once they have it in their possession. Nothing is said explicitly about the Helenus oracle in the prologue, and in particular nothing about the condition that Philoctetes will have to come of his own free will. The typically Sophoclean method is followed throughout in this play, in that only at the end will the hearer be in possession of all the elements which determine the course of the action. We may wonder at Neoptolemus' apparent ignorance of some of them, but this ignorance, I think, is apparent rather than real, and caused by the necessity of sketching within the brief compass of the exposition the mental situation of the young man. If we had to do with a novel, not with a non-naturalistic drama, we might say that Neoptolemus' questions 103, 106, 112, 114 ought to belong to a previous chapter. As it is, they belong to the prologue where the audience is provided with the information necessary to follow the unfolding of the action.

After hearing the prologue the hearer knows a good deal about the interrelation between the very different characters of Odysseus and Neoptolemus. He will be enmeshed in the problem of how the young man will acquit himself of the difficult, inappropriate task; he will eagerly await the arrival of Philoctetes, soon to be expected.

Parodos (135-218) in the form of an amoibaion between Neoptolemus and the Chorus of sailors (antistrophic pairs sung by the Chorus, anapaests recited by Neoptolemus).

The Chorus begin by asking what is expected from them. Neoptolemus invites them to take a view of Philoctetes' abode and asks them τὸ παρὸν θεραπεύειν on the latter's arrival. He informs them of Philoctetes' absence, and of his way of providing for his livelihood. The Chorus sing an antistrophic dirge in which they imagine the miserable and solitary life of the sufferer. This is answered by Neoptolemus with a theological explanation of Philoctetes' fate (191-200). Then the Chorus warn that they hear his approach accompanied by cries of pain.

It is remarkable that there is no mention made of *seeing* his

approach from afar, as for instance on the approach of Creon in
O.T., or of Heracles' litter in *Trach.*. At 219 it is as if Philoctetes
suddenly makes his appearance before them. I think that this is
immediately understandable, if we assume (with A. M. Dale,
Wiener Studien 69 (1956) p. 104 (= *Collected Papers* p. 127) and
Webster Introduction, p. 8) 'that the cave was conceived as a
kind of tunnel, so that it also has an entrance behind'. Philoctetes
is supposed to enter his cave, through the back entrance, and so
unseen; then he makes his appearance at the entrance which
overlooks the stage.

First Epeisodion, first scene 219-540; three parts marked off by
two responding choral interludes. Philoctetes, Neoptolemus,
Chorus.

The appearance of the haggard sufferer at the entrance of the
cave (we may imagine that he climbs down between 219-230 and
henceforth occupies the centre of the stage at ground level) is well-
calculated to make a deep impression on the others, and on the
audience. The silence to be assumed after 229 is more eloquent than
cries of horror or distress would be.

Neoptolemus' first awkward and stiff reply (232, 3) significantly
contrasts with the urgency and the pathos of Philoctetes' opening
words. This remains so in the ensuing dialogue 234-253, in which
Neoptolemus' identity is made known to Philoctetes, and the
deceit is started by the young man's feigned ignorance of his interlocutor's person and fate, to the latter's distressed amazement.
Then Philoctetes embarks on the story of his misfortunes, his
Crusoësque life and desolation, his frustrating experiences with the
rare visitors to his hermitage—and all this due to the guilt of the
Atreidae and Odysseus, whom the gods may punish (254-284, 285-
299, 300-316).

After two lines expressing pity spoken by the Coryphaeus,
Neoptolemus introduces his false story by chiming in with Philoctetes' last words: he, too, has been injured by the Achaean
chieftains and Odysseus. This, of course, impresses Philoctetes very
much, and he wants to be informed. Neoptolemus complies, but is
interrupted when he begins by mentioning Achilles' death: Philoctetes first wants to hear more about this. The supposed friendship between Philoctetes and Achilles is an important element in
the development of their interrelation. He is very much distressed
by the news. Neoptolemus brings him back to the matter in hand

and goes on telling his story (343-390). He was fetched from Scyros by Odysseus and Phoenix, because, according to them, after Achilles' death none other than his son was destined to capture Troy. But on his arrival the chieftains, and Odysseus in particular, refused to render him his father's armour. So he decided to turn his back on the Achaean army [1]).

The false story is confirmed by a curious interlude of the Chorus: they are supposed to θεραπεύειν τὸ παρόν (391-402).

Philoctetes recognizes, from Neoptolemus' ill-treatment by the Atreidae and Odysseus, the affinity between their fates; he expresses his surprise that Aiax should suffer Neoptolemus' ill-treatment to happen. But Aiax is dead, and thus is introduced the dialogue in which Philoctetes is informed of the evil fortune of some good friends of his, in contrast to the survival of others regarded by him as wicked (Diomedes, Odysseus, Thersites, whereas (Achilles), Aiax, Antilochus, Patroclus are dead) (414-445). This leads up to Philoctetes' despairing outcry: ποῦ χρὴ τίθεσθαι ταῦτα, ποῦ δ' αἰνεῖν, ὅταν / τὰ θεῖ' ἐπαινῶν τοὺς θεοὺς εὕρω κακούς; (451, 2). This meets with the approval of Neoptolemus, who declares that henceforth he will beware of Ilium and the Atreidae, content to live on rocky Scyros (453-460), to which he immediately adds that now he is about to leave, ὡς ὁπηνίκ' ἂν θεὸς / πλοῦν ἡμὶν εἴκη, τηνικαῦθ' ὁρμώμεθα (464, 5).

To this, Philoctetes' natural reaction is a passionate entreaty to take him aboard his ship; from Scyros or from Euboea he can then easily reach his home. He beseeches the young man by his father and mother, by Zeus ἱκέσιος for any place on board, even the humblest. He points to the glory of performing this loathsome task, he appeals to the human condition and human solidarity, which requires pity for fellow-beings in distress (468-506).

The Chorus, just as they confirmed Neoptolemus' false story at 391-402, now eagerly support Philoctetes' entreaty (507-517).

Neoptolemus' warning against making light of the matter is countered by the Coryphaeus, and Neoptolemus declares himself ready to sail with Philoctetes (519-29; his last words are as ambiguous as any). Neoptolemus and Philoctetes are about to take leave of the latter's abode and then to make for the ship, when they are stopped by the Coryphaeus who announces the arrival of

---

[1]) Knox (*The Heroic Temper*, p. 123) rightly observes: 'the lies Neoptolemos proceeds to tell present him as a sort of spurious Achilles'.

two men, one of Neoptolemus' sailors and a stranger. The latter,
of course, is the attendant from the Prologue, disguised as a merchant skipper.

Apparently we are to suppose that Odysseus has grown im-
patient, deeming the delay too long, and wants to hurry things up.
We may ask ourselves, whether Odysseus is supposed to follow the
confrontation between Philoctetes and Neoptolemus from a hidden
post of observation, or to be waiting on his ship and taking action
at the moment he thinks fit. Since the text does not mention such
a hiding-place (see notes ad 974, 5 and 1013-51), it seems better not
to speculate about such a device. (Such speculations are dangerous,
for in the end they may lead to Verrallian fantasies).

First Epeisodion, second scene 541-627. 'Emporos' (with 'guide',
persona muta), Neoptolemus, Philoctetes, (Chorus, silent).

The expected 'ἔμπορος' arrives; he poses as a wine-trafficker
between Peparethus and the army before Troy. He pretends to
notify Neoptolemus, in the latter's interest, that Phoenix and
Theseus' sons have sailed in pursuit of him, and on Neoptolemus'
asking 'why not Odysseus?' he declares that Odysseus and Diomedes were about to fetch another man; after much hesitation he is
persuaded to disclose that this other man is Philoctetes (all this.
of course, belongs to the deceit). On Neoptolemus' question why
this need of Philoctetes was felt, the 'ἔμπορος' tells the story of the
Helenus oracle and Odysseus' boasting that he will take back
Philoctetes either willingly, or by force.

What is the result of the ἔμπορος scene? It enhances Philoctetes'
trust in Neoptolemus and adds an urgent reason to his eagerness
for departure. On the whole ,the scene lends a feeling of urgency to
the course of the action. But it does not solve Neoptolemus' problem as to the bow and arrows. Perhaps we may assume that Odysseus' apparent impatience lies at the bottom of Neoptolemus'
mentioning of the bow in the next scene: it becomes, then, clear,
from Philoctetes' reaction, that the latter's trust in the young man
leaves nothing to be desired.

On the other hand it may be correct to assume that for all
Odysseus' cleverness the sending of the 'emporos' is an erroneous
move on his part and intended as such by the dramatist [1]). Let

---

[1]) I do not believe that the poet wants us to understand that it was
Odysseus' set purpose to carry the bow away, leaving Philoctetes on the
island, as is suggested by Knox, *The Heroic Temper*, p. 128 and cp. p. 134.

us not forget that, after all, the whole of Odysseus' σόφισμα boils down to a chain of errors and miscalculations.

First Epeisodion, third scene 628-675. Philoctetes, Neoptolemus, (Chorus, silent).

Things are much as they were before the arrival of the ἔμπορος, but for Philoctetes' excitement and feeling of being hunted, and Neoptolemus' feeling of being hurried by Odysseus. Further, for the hearer as well as for Neoptolemus, the reaction of Philoctetes to the report of the Helenus oracle delivered by the 'emporos' is very important. One thing is certain: Neoptolemus cannot go to the ship with Philoctetes without having the bow in his possession. Hence his objections against Philoctetes' urgent prayer for immediate departure (635-644), his returning to Philoctetes' proposal first to visit the cave (533 sqq. ∼ 645 sqq.) and his mentioning of the bow (654). So the scene ends with their entering the cave together, after their dialogue called forth by Neoptolemus' question 654, in which Philoctetes' complete trust in the young man has been poignantly shown. Still more than in the preceding scenes the hearer will be aware how false Neoptolemus' position is. It is difficult to believe that the poet did not mean us to understand that this awareness is also growing in the mind of the young man.

From the standpoint of composition technique it is to be noted that Philoctetes' words about the bow (658, 9, 667-69) prepare us for its handing over to Neoptolemus at 762 sqq. There is, moreover, a discreet preparation for the attack of Philoctetes' illness in the next act to be heard in his last words of this scene: τὸ γὰρ / νοσοῦν ποθεῖ σε ξυμπαραστάτην λαβεῖν.

Stasimon 676-729. Two antistrophic pairs.

For this song, the only stasimon proper of the play, see my introductory note in the Commentary.

Second Epeisodion 730-826. Neoptolemus, Philoctetes, (Chorus silent).

It seems best to assume that Neoptolemus and Philoctetes have descended from the cave and are on the stage proper at the beginning of the scene. Philoctetes suddenly comes to a standstill. Despite his repeated heroic efforts to hide the attack of his illness he is at last overcome by it; he asks Neoptolemus to cut off his foot, not to spare his life. He tries to explain to Neoptolemus the nature of the ailment, its periodicity; above all he beseeches him not to leave him alone. He does not want to be touched, but what he wants is that Neoptolemus should take charge of the bow lest it be taken away during the sleep that will follow the attack. Neoptolemus shall not give up the bow to the Achaeans, for that will involve his own and Philoctetes' death (730-741, 742-752, 753-768, 769-773).

The bow, thus Neoptolemus, will not be given to another, only to him and to Philoctetes. Philoctetes gives the bow and Neoptolemus utters a prayer of ambiguous meaning (779-781). Although these lines still belong to the deceit (they are to be compared with 528, 9), their wording is such that we cannot believe any more in Neoptolemus' firm decision to carry out the fraud under all circumstances. (Here I am not quite of the same opinion as J. U. Schmidt, *Sophokles-Philoktet*—1973—p. 143: 'N. gibt unzweideutig das unveränderte Ziel seines Strebens zu erkennen').

A second attack of the illness breaks out; again its unspeakable horror is directly impressed on Neoptolemus and the audience. Again, and still more forcibly, the sufferer prays for death. He wants Neoptolemus to help to burn him, as he did Heracles. He asks him again not to leave him, he requires him solemnly to promise that. Then he falls down and sinks into a coma. Again some of Neoptolemus' answers, although still remaining within the framework of the deceit, are such that his real pity with the sufferer cannot be doubted (806 ἀλγῶ πάλαι δὴ τἀπὶ σοὶ στένων κακά, 812 ὡς οὐ θέμις γ' ἐμοῦστι σοῦ μολεῖν ἄτερ, where θέμις shows the same ambiguity as ὅποι ποτὲ θεὸς δικαιοῖ 780, 1).

Lyrical interlude 827-864. Chorus, Neoptolemus, (Philoctetes sleeping). Strophe, four hexameters recited by Neoptolemus, antistrophe, epode.

The Chorus seem to start a lullaby [1]), but, actually, after invoking Hypnos to maintain his power over Philoctetes' eyes, exhort Neoptolemus in veiled terms to make away stealthily with the bow. Neoptolemus, appealing to the import of the Helenus oracle, rejects their suggestion. The Chorus urgently but still in veiled terms pray him to remember the situation and warn him not to let slip the opportunity for action offered by Philoctetes' sleep.

Third Epeisodion, first scene 865-974. Neoptolemus, Philoctetes, Chorus.

---

[1]) Cf. K. Reinhardt, *Sophokles*[1], p. 192: 'vielmehr ein Lied der leisen, aber umso stärkeren Verführung zum Verrat'.

Philoctetes, still lying on the ground, recovers his consciousness; first of all he gives vent to his overwhelming gratitude for Neoptolemus' having stood by his promise: never would the Atreidae have brought themselves to do such a thing, but he, generous offspring of a noble breed, took as a light burden the cries of pain and the ill smell. He now asks of Neoptolemus to raise him, so that they can make for the ship as soon as possible (867-881).

The apparent aloofness of Neoptolemus' reply is surely meant as suggestive of his discomfort, of his mental ἀπορία and shame, that will break forth at 895. His offer of having Philoctetes carried by the sailors is refused, and so he helps him to rise, and then, just at the moment the other is standing by his side, clinging closely to him, the cry of desperate embarrassment comes from his lips: παπαῖ· τί δῆτ' ἂν δρῷμ' ἐγὼ τοὐνθένδε γε (895: for further comment see the Commentary a.l.). Philoctetes is quite at sea as to Neoptolemus' ἀπορία, even when his questions have called forth Neoptolemus' ἅπαντα δυσχέρεια, τὴν αὑτοῦ φύσιν / ὅταν λιπών τις δρᾷ τὰ μὴ προσεικότα. (902, 3, those verses fundamental for a correct understanding of the play). At last, after more questions, more replies, truth will out: 915, 6. When this deadly disclosure has been more fully explained, it causes Philoctetes' despair, and retentless rage since Neoptolemus refuses to give back the bow (904-926). His furious outburst (927 sqq.) is followed by a pathetic apostrophe to the surrounding landscape, witness of the evil that Achilles' son has done to him. His repeated request that his bow be returned is not answered, and at last, moving to the cave, he addresses his wonted haunt; he will fall a prey to the beasts he used to hunt for. A conditional curse on Neoptolemus concludes his passionate rhesis (927-962).

There is no reply from Neoptolemus; instead the Coryphaeus points out to his master that it rests with him either to sail (to Troy with the bow; whether with or without Philoctetes is not made explicit), or to give in to Philoctetes' wish. Neoptolemus speaks of the οἶκτος δεινός that has now long overtaken him (965, 6). He remains in his terrible quandary (τί δράσω; 969, τί δρῶμεν, ἄνδρες; 974) without directly answering Philoctetes' repeated urgent entreaties to act accordingly and render him the bow (967, 8, 971-73). Then, immediately after Neoptolemus' τί δρῶμεν, ἄνδρες; Odysseus breaks in, shouting ὦ κάκιστ' ἀνδρῶν, τί δρᾷς; (974) and orders him to move back, after having delivered the bow to him.

Third Epeisodion, second scene 974-1069. Odysseus, Philoctetes, Neoptolemus (silent), Chorus, attendants of Odysseus (personae mutae). From this moment on all attention is centred on the confrontation between the two antagonists. Neoptolemus, not complying with Odysseus' command as to the bow—nor does he leave the stage—remains a silent witness of the scene; his silence is suggestive of his utter ἀπορία.

Odysseus has no difficulty in admitting that he is the real manager of the deceit; Neoptolemus shall not return the bow to Philoctetes, Philoctetes has to go to the ship; if not willingly then by force. Together with the best of the Greeks he will conquer and destroy Troy. An attempt at suicide on his part is prevented by Odysseus' attendants (976-1003). Held fast by the latter he utters a long lament and complaint about his treatment now and formerly. He scathingly comments upon Odysseus' wiles, contrasting the latter's unwillingness to take part in Agamemnon's expedition with his own loyalty, Odysseus' good fortune with his misery, and calling on the gods to wreak vengeance upon the Greek leaders; a vengeance to be expected: for it was a θεῖον κέντρον that drove them to send for him, a wretched outcast (1004-1044).

After the correct diagnosis of Philoctetes' stubborn attitude made by the Coryphaeus (1045, 6), Odysseus performs what seems a *volte-face*: he bids the attendants to release Philoctetes. He will no longer insist: since they have the bow, which can be handled just as well by Teucer or Odysseus himself, Philoctetes' assistance is not needed, he may remain on Lemnos, if such is his pleasure. He brushes away Philoctetes' protest, and when the latter appeals to Neoptolemus, commands the young man to follow him.

Third Epeisodion, third scene 1070-1080. Philoctetes, Neoptolemus, Chorus. Philoctetes beseeches the Chorus to have pity on his loneliness. The Coryphaeus leaves the matter to Neoptolemus, and Neoptolemus, evidently lagging behind Odysseus (and always holding the bow), gives the Chorus leave to remain until the ship is ready to sail, in the hope that Philoctetes will change his mind (1074-1080).

Kommos 1081-1217. Philoctetes, Chorus. Two antistrophic pairs (1081-1100 = 1101-1122, 1123-1145 = 1146-1168) and a long epode. In the strophic part each strophe and antistrophe is regularly divided between Philoctetes and Chorus; the choral sections, being much shorter than the actor's, have the character of ephymnia. In this part the Chorus react to the preceding words of Philoctetes, but Philoctetes never reacts to the words addressed to him. But the epode starts with Philoctetes' reply to the Chorus' last ephymnium, and the epode throughout is a passionate exchange of interrelated utterances and replies on both sides, in various metres and of varying length; a number of cola or verses is divided between actor and Chorus.

In str. α Philoctetes addresses his abode, which is to be the witness of his death, and laments his powerlessness. The Chorus point out his own choice in the matter. In antistr. α Philoctetes continues his lament, complains against the deceit and prays for vengeance on the deceiver. The Chorus bid him to direct his imprecation against others, and not to rebuke their friendly intentions. In str. β Philoctetes imagines the derisive laughter of Odysseus, now in possession of the bow. He addresses the bow and pities its fate because it is to be handled by one unworthy of it. The Chorus point out that what has happened has been done by a man who acted under orders on behalf of his friends. In antistr. β Philoctetes addresses the beasts and birds of prey who now will easily make him their quarry. Now the Chorus observe, assuring him of their good intentions, that it is in his power to be healed of his deadly sickness (implying, of course, that by giving in, he will be healed). Philoctetes understands the implication and his reaction is vehement. Let them leave him alone. The Chorus answer, what amounts to: 'we ask no better than that', and start to go. But he stops them, lamenting over his foot. The Chorus make a last attempt. But he refuses: away with Ilium and all those who have plunged him into misery. He asks for a sword to rend himself into pieces. He only longs for death.

Philoctetes retires into the cave. The Chorus is supposed to show signs of departure.

Fourth epeisodion, first scene 1218-1262. Coryphaeus, Odysseus, Neoptolemus. It seems to me better to regard 1218-1408 as a fourth 'act' of the play than as forming, together with 1409-1471, the Exodos. Its last part, it is true, has the character of a 'false' Exodos, but the term is hardly applicable to the rest.

The Coryphaeus, more or less addressing the invisible Philoctetes, announces Neoptolemus' and Odysseus' arrival. Neoptolemus, bow in hand, is seen hastily making for Philoctetes' abode, closely followed by Odysseus. They are involved in a vehement discussion, and the upshot of the long stichomythia 1224-1256 (with two 'irregularities', 1247-49, 1254-56, which prevent the passage from growing monotonous) is that Neoptolemus upholds his firm resolve to restore justice by returning the bow to Philoctetes in the face of Odysseus' dismay, indignation and threats. At the end Odysseus retires: he will tell the army and Neoptolemus will get his punishment (1257, 8).

Fourth Epeisodion, second scene 1263 (or 1261)-1307 (or 1302). Neoptolemus, Philoctetes, Odysseus (from 1293 to 1302), (Chorus silent).

Neoptolemus calls Philoctetes to come out. The latter complies, though somewhat fearfully and showing much mistrust. Neoptolemus asks whether he insists on sticking to his refusal. The other makes clear that all attempts at persuasion will be in vain, and curses the Atreidae and Odysseus, being interrupted by Neoptolemus when he is in the act of including the latter in the curse: he bids him to receive the bow back from his hands. Philoctetes can not believe him, upon which the young man invokes Zeus. Philoctetes' mistrust is all but overcome, and Neoptolemus passes him the bow. At that crucial moment Odysseus tries to intervene, but Philoctetes proceeds to direct the bow against his enemy. Neoptolemus prevents the shot, while Odysseus disgracefully quits the scene—and the play [1]). The moment is one of the highest dramatic skill and meaningful action.

Fourth Epeisodion, third scene (or: pseudo-Exodos) 1308-1408. Philoctetes is reconciled with Neoptolemus, once more recognizing in him Achilles' son. In the new situation Neoptolemus earnestly tries to prevail upon Philoctetes to give in: (1) his refusal would mean that he persists in self-willed misery; (2) his sickness, caused by divine dispensation, can only be terminated if he goes to Troy, is healed by the Asclepiadae, and takes part, by means of his bow and together with Neoptolemus, in the destruction of Ilium; (3) all this is fated to happen as shown by Helenus' incontrovertible prophecy, to happen in the summer that is at hand; (4) it is a glorious prospect to be reckoned the best of men, to be healed and to be the conqueror of Troy (1310-1347). For one moment it seems that Philoctetes considers surrendering (οἴμοι, τί δράσω; πῶς ἀπιστήσω λόγοις / τοῖς τοῦδ', ὃς εὔνους ὢν ἐμοὶ παρῄνεσεν (1450, 1)).

---

[1]) M. Pohlenz, *Die Griechische Tragödie* I², p. 335: 'Und was ist in dieser Tragödie der Erfolg der vielgepriesenen Weltklugheit? Ein völliges Fiasko'.

But feelings of shame, wrath and fear when he thinks of the eventual confrontation with the Atreidae and Odysseus immediately get the upperhand. Neoptolemus himself ought to part company with the people who bereft him of his father's armour (the delusion of the fraud as to that persists in Philoctetes' mind); he bids him to make good his promise by taking Philoctetes home, and to remain himself on Scyros, away from the war (1352-1372). Neoptolemus does not yet give up his attempt at persuasion.

A heated stichomythia ensues. Neoptolemus' arguments, based on the will of the gods, his friendship, his well-wishing, the benefit to be gained, are all frustrated by the other's stubbornness. In the end he is inclined to give up and leave Philoctetes to his fate. Philoctetes reminds him of his solemn promise. Neoptolemus gives in, and they are about to leave in order to sail home. The final tetrameters are suggestive of their departure. At this juncture the audience must be supposed to have followed the acting with bated breath. What is about to happen, nay, what actually seems to happen, must strike them as an innovation bolder than anything even Euripides ever dared confront them with.

Exodos proper (1409-1471). Heracles, Philoctetes, Neoptolemus, Chorus: 1409-1417 anapaests (Heracles), 1418-1444 trimeters (Heracles), 1445-1472 anapaests (Philoctetes, Neoptolemus, Heracles, Philoctetes, Chorus).

But now Heracles, probably immediately recognizable from his attributes, makes his appearance (on the roof of the skene). What no mortal, not even Neoptolemus after giving back the bow, was qualified to perform, the persuasion of Philoctetes to comply with his destiny, proves for him an easy task. The old bond of friendship with the heir of his bow and his divine status preclude any remnant of mistrust or protest on the part of Philoctetes. Furthermore he addresses Philoctetes as all but his equal, comparing his own life of toil crowned with divine glory with the other's destiny in store for him. He will be healed by Asclepius himself, he will kill Paris and, in collaboration with Neoptolemus, destroy Troy, destined to fall for the second time by means of Heracles' bow. Thankful, though not without a vestige of bitterness (χρόνιός τε φανείς 1446), Philoctetes vows his obedience. So does Neoptolemus. Heracles urges them to make haste.

Then the poet assigns to the central character of the play a moving farewell-speech to his abode and its surroundings. Its tone is one of resignation to his fate rather than of any feeling either of bitterness or of triumph. The Chorus, addressing the Nymphs of the sea, recite a final prayer for safe return.

A stage-manager would do well to place Heracles' exit immediately after 1451.

4. MEANING OF THE PLAY

What could have moved Sophocles to compose a *Philoctetes* on the lines sketched above? One thing is certain: if he wanted to dramatize the sufferer's destiny, the conclusion had to be his return to the Achaean army. This was what happened according to the most venerable tradition. It is perhaps not too speculative an assumption to imagine that the poet when pondering on the treatment of the story by his predecessors felt two difficulties: (1) How, after the fraud and the stealing of the bow, was it possible for Philoctetes, in the end, to be persuaded by Odysseus, or, if not persuaded, how then could he convincingly be represented as yielding to force? Persuasion (and force), it is true, could be based on an appeal to divine ordinance, but how little power of conviction would such an appeal, spoken by an Odysseus, have had for an injured and deceived hero [1]). And if, after all, force had to prevail, how very unsatisfactory such an ending would be [2]). (2) How unsatisfactory also if the fraud and the deceit were not to be shown up as shameful in the course of the action, and only to be excused, after the event, by means of an appeal to the gods. Would it not have seemed to him that in such a way the gods were represented as approving of the fraud, and that one directed not against an enemy but towards an injured and innocent friend?

Two courses, it seems, could be envisaged: he might have created an Odysseus after the fashion of his own Odysseus in *Aiax*, a paragon of humaneness whose sincere confession of guilt as to the events of the past might have favourably impressed Philoctetes; this would have necessitated quite another Philoctetes than the one we know from the play (imagine a confrontation between Aiax

---

[1]) How could a Sophoclean hero yield to force? It is difficult to imagine such a thing.

[2]) Euripides, it is true, by means of the Trojan embassy, introduced the 'patriotic' motif. This, perhaps, made his treatment more convincing than it seems. (Cf. *Erechtheus* and *I.A.*). Persuasion may have been, at the end of Euripides' play, more important than force.

alive and the Odysseus of the tragedy), a forgiving and forgetting man, not a Sophoclean hero at all. The result would hardly have been a tragic drama, at best a serious comedy of manners. And how, within such a design, could the first confrontation between Philoctetes and Odysseus have been brought about without the evidently unsatisfactory means used by Aeschylus and Euripides?

The other course was the course chosen by the poet. In order, first, to avoid the improbability of Odysseus not being recognized through the lapse of time or through his being metamorphosed by Athena, and, second, to demonstrate the immorality of fraud and deceit—and, in the end, its unavailingness—, he decided to introduce the young Neoptolemus. By this choice he could plausibly create the character of a very young man, ambitious and upright by hereditary nature [1]. (Let us not forget that αἰὲν ἀριστεύειν καὶ ὑπείροχον ἔμμεναι ἄλλων was Peleus' instruction to Achilles—Il. XI 784—and that ἐχθρὸς γάρ μοι κεῖνος ὁμῶς 'Αΐδαο πύλῃσιν, / ὅς χ' ἕτερον μὲν κεύθῃ ἐνὶ φρεσίν, ἄλλο δὲ εἴπῃ. are Achilles' words spoken to Odysseus—Il IX 312, 3—). Neoptolemus, recently fetched from Scyros, with the prospect that he is to be the capturer of Troy, and standing under Odysseus' command, is persuaded by the latter to capture Philoctetes' bow by deceit in order to render Philoctetes' return possible. The problem of achieving seemingly glorious ends by devious means is clearly mirrored in the dialogue of the Prologue. Odysseus overcomes the scruples of the young man's inner nature by playing on his ambition and his military sense of duty. Persuaded by Odysseus' overbearing sophistry—implying an apparently full understanding of the young man's reluctance—Neoptolemus undertakes a task at variance with his nature. Odysseus is represented as entirely unscrupulous where success and gain are at stake (ὅταν τι δρᾷς ἐς κέρδος, οὐκ ὀκνεῖν πρέπει); he knows the 'ways of the world', he is not aware of the force of moral values [2]. He is not allowed by the poet to utter a single word of pity on behalf of Philoctetes. He does not foresee how Neoptolemus will be impressed when confronted with the sufferer.

Now the hearer is indubitably meant to understand that Philoctetes' appearance does make a shattering impression on Neoptolemus (and the Chorus); cf. 225 sqq., 230 sq.. Moreover the hearer

---

[1] Cf. B. M. W. Knox, The Heroic Temper (1964), p. 121.
[2] Cf. Knox, The Heroic Temper, pp. 124, 5, who calls Odysseus' οὗ γὰρ τοιούτων δεῖ, τοιοῦτός εἰμ' ἐγώ (1049) 'the quintessence of moral relativism'.

has been led to ponder on Philoctetes' condition by the choral song 169-190. The sense of Neoptolemus' false position is enhanced by Philoctetes' words 242, 3 disclosing the friendship between him and Achilles. The long rhesis of Philoctetes in which he tells the story of his misfortunes, confronts the young man with the reality of the injury and misery suffered by an innocent man and the pitiless cruelty of those who were responsible for it. But the effect, at this stage of the action, is that it renders the fraud easier to perform. Neoptolemus' false story perfectly agrees with Philoctetes' experience, and Philoctetes has no inkling that Achilles' son could be mistrusted. So it is only natural that Philoctetes beseeches Neoptolemus to take him home.

Matters, however, are complicated by the intervention of the pseudo-emporos. Its only effect seems to be the enhanced feeling of urgency on the part of Philoctetes and of Neoptolemus: Philoctetes wants to hasten the departure, Neoptolemus to find means of capturing the bow (hence 654 sqq.). But the words of the emporos have also another effect [1]), on the hearer and also on Neoptolemus: for at 610 sqq. the audience perceives for the first time that Philoctetes has to go of his own free will, while the fact that these words have also their effect on Neoptolemus implicitly appears from 839 sqq.. For, although there nothing is said about Philoctetes' free will, what, if not the notion that Philoctetes had to be persuaded to be brought to Troy, prevents Neoptolemus, at that point, instead of following the suggestion of the Chorus to depart with the bow and without Philoctetes, from having Philoctetes, unconscious, carried to the ship, while retaining the bow himself?

The attack of the illness, occurring at the moment of the proposed departure is calculated to have an overwhelming influence on Neoptolemus' mind. Here, at last, the horrible reality of Philoctetes' condition is revealed *ad oculos*. Thereafter it is impossible for the young man to continue the fraud. Although retaining the bow, he cannot but disclose the truth. Philoctetes' vehement reaction brings him near to giving back the bow, when Odysseus' sudden arrival prevents him from doing so (but he does not hand over the bow to Odysseus).

Odysseus' remonstrances addressed to Philoctetes are in vain, and Philoctetes is left alone with the Chorus. In the ensuing Kommos it is demonstrated how Philoctetes, perfectly aware of the

---

[2]) See further my comments ad 603-621.

terrible fate that is in store for him if he is left behind on Lemnos
without the bow, and certainly not without fear of such a fate,
nevertheless refuses to yield. And again, when Neoptolemus has
given back the bow and made a last attempt at persuasion, he
persists in his refusal. Now Neoptolemus, accepting the full consequences of his conversion and sticking to his promise once given,
undertakes the bringing home of Philoctetes.

Thus they are about to depart, their fourth false start (though
now without any ambiguity), when Heracles appears and restores
legend its rights.

This takes place after Philoctetes' righteous inexorability and
heroic stand, Neoptolemus' noble and honest inner nature and
Odysseus' vain trickery and wily sophistry have each received their
ample due. (It is to be noted that Odysseus, who boasted at the
end of the Prologue of 'Αθάνα Πολιάς, ἣ σῴζει μ' ἀεί 134, has to fly
for his life at 1299; I cannot understand why the idea that Odysseus
is the villain of the piece has met with such resistance, e.g. from
Reinhardt [1])).

Sophocles' introduction of Heracles is almost as much a stroke of
genius as that of Neoptolemus. There was one person capable of
reconciling Philoctetes with his fate (and his fate is to partake in
the capture of Troy) because of their ancient friendship, because of
Philoctetes' heirship to Heracles' bow and because of the exemplary
nature of Heracles' destiny. And this he does with sober words and
great authority.

To my mind the end of the play does not leave us under the
impression that the poet wants us to understand that Philoctetes
ought not to have withstood Neoptolemus' last attempt at persuasion in the preceding scene. All that has been said of his destiny
in the course of the play, even Neoptolemus' urgent and honest
plea, could not break through the barriers of his bitterness and
mistrust because it seemed to derive from a troubled source (Helenus could easily be regarded as Odysseus' instrument). The poet
has done his utmost to justify Philoctetes' resistance and to suggest
its grandeur, by insisting on his misery and the awful way in which

---

[1]) See his comment on 1035 sqq., *Sophokles*[1], p. 197. Cf. also Lesky's
remark in *G.G.L.*[3], p. 333. In this I side with W. B. Stanford, *The Ulysses
Theme*[1], 1954, pp. 108 sqq.. Bowra's opinion: 'Odysseus does not consciously
or deliberately disobey the oracle' (*Sophoclean Tragedy*[1], p. 268, see also
pp. 284, 5) is to be rejected.

he has been treated in the past and is deceived in the course of the action ('the victim of a barely credible inhumanity' [1])).

Because it is Heracles who now reveals to him the truth, he gives in, but there is nothing in Heracles' words coming near to a reproach, nor anything in Philoctetes' approximating to a confession of guilt: he bows to what is to be, and will sail, ἔνθ' ἡ μεγάλη Μοῖρα κομίζει / γνώμη τε φίλων χὠ πανδαμάτωρ / δαίμων, ὃς ταῦτ' ἐπέκρανεν. His ultimate surrender might strike one as an anticlimax, but on the other hand it is the only condition for his being healed, and so the fulfilment of the legend and of the hearer's desire for Philoctetes' healing are shrewdly combined [2]). That is not to say, that I entirely agree with Knox when he posits that in the *Philoctetes* the hearer hopes for the success of the compromises offered to the hero. I cannot but feel rather that the sentiments of the hearer will be ambivalent.

5. CHRONOLOGY

Ἐδιδάχθη ἐπὶ Γλαυκίππου (Hypothesis II), i.e. *Ol.* 92.3 = 409 B.C. It is not clear how Webster (edition of the play, p. 5) could state: 'Sophocles' play was produced in 408 B.C.', unless by an oversight. This date, combined with a number of similarities in dramaturgic design, lyric metre and character drawing between this play and *Electra*, are in favour of a late dating of the latter.

---

[1] H. D. F. Kitto, *Form and Meaning in Drama*[1] (1956), p. 105, and cf. B. M. W. Knox, *The heroic Temper* (1964), p. 117.

[2] Cf. Knox, *o.l.*, p. 118. I am out of sympathy with Bowra's verdict (*o.l.*, p. 292): 'His excuse of distrust is wrong and can only be deplored'.

PHILOCTETES

Prologue 1-134

On the vexed problems of the suggested scenery see the Introduction pp. 9, 10 and comm. ad 16-19. Enter Odysseus and Neoptolemus, the latter followed by one of his mariners. Design and function of this Prologue have some things in common with the Prologue of *Electra*, but the differences are more important. The spectator is made acquainted with the circumstances of the chief character of the play in the dialogue [1]; in the *Electra* this happens—after the ominous cry 77—in quite another way, viz. by Electra's own solo-anapaests. In the *Electra* the μηχάνημα is expounded by Orestes' long rhesis; it offers, so to say, no dilemma. Here the young Neoptolemus has to be persuaded to take his essential part in Odysseus' σόφισμα. By and large this Prologue is highly dramatic and dynamic; the first 76 trimeters of the *Electra* on the other hand strike us as rather static.

1-11. Ἀκτὴ ... / ... στενάζων: opening sentence of extraordinary length (cf. *Ai.* 7 ll., *El.* 3, *O.T.* 3, *Ant.* 3, *Trach.* 8, *O.C.* 2) and packed with a great amount of information of the utmost importance as to the interrelation between the three main dramatis personae.

1-3. Ἀκτὴ ... ἥδε τῆς ... / Λήμνου ... / ἔνθ': 'This is the ἀκτὴ ('headland', 'promontory', 'region of rugged coast') belonging to Lemnos where ...' [2]. The antecedent of ἔνθ' is ἀκτή, not Λήμνου. It is this region that is said to be uninhabited [3], not the whole of Lemnos (in Homer this is not the case), but for practical purposes this makes little difference: Philoctetes is supposed not to have had any intercourse with whatever inhabitants the isle may have had: his loneliness is absolute (this in contradistinction to the situations in Aeschylus' and Euripides' plays).

1. μέν: 'inceptive' μέν 'scarcely answered by 11 ἀλλὰ ταῦτα μὲν τί δεῖ λέγειν' (Denniston *G.P.*² p. 383).

---

[1]) Cp. Kitto, *Form and Meaning*¹ (1956), p. 107: 'In fact, the stinking rags and the rough-hewn cup are part of a consistent building-up of Philoctetes' part, and are essential to the structure and the idea of the whole play'.

[2]) Not: 'This coast belongs to Lemnos' (Campbell).

[3]) Cf. Σ 2 ἐν ἐρήμῳ γὰρ μέρει τῆς Λήμνου ἐξετέθη; but cf. 221.

1, 2. τῆς περιρρύτου χθονὸς / Λήμνου: τῆς περιρρύτου χθονὸς amounts to 'isle' (but περιρρύτου is suggestive of the 'isolation') and Λήμνου is probably an apposition, not a genitive dependent on χθονὸς.

ἄστιπτος: probably the correct form (ἄστειπτος A and older editions). Στίβος is almost a key word of the first part of the play.

3, 4 ὦ ... / ... Νεοπτόλεμε: cf. *El.* 1, 2 (but Orestes' name in 6). The very full wording of this vocative is entirely functional. Not only does the audience hear the identity of the young man but it is also reminded of his father's fame; and on the other hand it is only natural for Odysseus to address his companion in so flattering a way: he wants to secure his support in a tricky case.

πατρὸς ... τραφείς: genit. of origin, cf. Aesch. *Sept.* 792. As Jebb rightly remarks, 'more forcible than γεγώς, as suggesting, not birth merely, but the inborn qualities'.

Νεοπτόλεμε: the name, awkward to handle in iambics, only here and in vs. 241, where it is indispensable, in both cases with synizesis of the first two syllables, here filling with παῖ the second metre (– – ⏑⏑⏑), there with the first syllable of οἶσθα (–⏑⏑ ⏑ –). In Eur. *Andr.* 14 it fills the second metre with the last syllable of νησιώτη (– – ⏑⏑–), similarly *Troad.* 1126 with the last syllable of ἀνῆκται (– – ⏑⏑–); in *Or.* 1655 the name, without synizesis, occupies the first metre (⏑– ⏑⏑–): in all three cases its last three syllables form an anapaest in the second foot of the metre. See Stevens ad *Andr.* 14. Neoptolemus' later second name, Pyrrhus, is unknown to epic poetry and Tragedy [1]. (But note the *varia lectio antiqua Il.* XIX 327 Πυρῆς ἐμὸς ὃν κατέλειπον and v. Wilamowitz' comment in the Introduction of his translation of *Phil.* p. 15 n. 1 (*Griechische Tragoedien* XII, *Philoktet*[2]. 1929)).

4, 5. τὸν Μηλιᾶ / Ποίαντος υἱόν: the audience, or at least many among them, will have understood who is meant. For the name of Philoctetes' father, though not a very illustrious hero—he was one of the Argonauts—must have occurred frequently in the lost epic poetry dealing with Troy's capture—we have only *Od.* III 190 εὖ δὲ Φιλοκτήτην, Ποιάντιον ἀγλαὸν υἱόν, evidently a traditional formula—and moreover in Aeschylus' and Euripides' plays, not to mention Sophocles' own Φιλοκτήτης ὁ ἐν Τροίᾳ of unknown date. Pind. *Pyth.* I 53 has Ποίαντος υἱὸν τοξόταν (but Philoctetes' own

---

[1]) From Paus. X 26. 4 (*Cypria* test. XIV Allen) it does not follow clearly that the name Pyrrhus was known to the author of the *Cypria*.

name has been mentioned *ib.* 50). Philoctetes' own name occurs six times in the text of the play, twice combined with 'Poeas' son', 'Poeas' son' without 'Philoctetes' six times.

ἐξέθηκ': 'expose'; only here in Sophocles; frequently used of foundlings (Hdt., Eur., Men.), so ἔκθεσις 'exposure', but also of the putting out of Odysseus on the shore of Ithaca Arist. *Poet.* 1460 a 3 b.

6. ταχθεὶς . . . ὕπο: by these words Odysseus emphatically casts back upon the Atreidae the responsibility for the deed [1]). Implicitly his obedience to orders may serve as an example for Neoptolemus.

7. νόσῳ . . . πόδα: καταστάζοντα—lit. 'running down'—goes with Ποίαντος υἱὸν, πόδα is accus. of respect. In νόσῳ διαβόρῳ κατά- σταζοντα the cause (the 'gnawing sore'—Jebb—) and its effect (the dripping pus) are briefly compressed in one pregnant phrase. On διαβόρῳ Σ comments: τῇ τὸν πόδα ἐσθιούσῃ, σηπτικῇ, τῇ δια- βιβρωσκούσῃ, τῇ καλουμένῃ φαγεδαίνη· πάθος δὲ τοῦτό ἐστιν οὕτω λεγόμενον παρὰ τοῖς ἰατροῖς. This is true, and the word was used by Aesch. in his *Phil.* (fr. 253 N.[2]) and by Eur. in his (*fr.* 792 N.[2]). For the underlying image of the νόσος as a θήρ (cf. ἐνθήρου 698) see my *Sophoclea* II, Mnemos. 1948, pp. 198-204.

Webster rightly rejects the colon at the end of the line (Campbell, Pearson) because it obscures the construction of the sentence: 'This is Lemnos . . . where (ἔνθα) . . . I exposed Philoctetes once (ποτε) . . . when (ὅτε) . . .' Some causal element may be felt in ὅτε, but it is never used, unlike ἐπεί, to introduce what amounts to an additional main sentence expressing the cause of what precedes (Dutch: 'immers').

9. ἐκήλοις: 'undisturbed'. It is well-known that εὐφημία, amount- ing to 'piously observed silence', is an essential requisite for sac- rifices.

9-11. ἀλλ' . . . / . . . / . . . στενάζων: logically these words contain the cause of οὔτε . . . παρῆν . . . προσθιγεῖν. We cannot be sure whether syntactically κατεῖχ' (subject Philoctetes) is on a par with παρῆν or whether the words have to be regarded as a main sentence; Greek usage seems rather in favour of the latter.

ἀγρίαις: cf. 173, 265, 267.

κατεῖχ': 'non *morabatur* sed *implebat*' (so correctly E.). Cf. *Ai.* 142 μεγάλοι θόρυβοι κατέχουσ' ἡμᾶς ἐπὶ δυσκλείᾳ; *Il.* XVI 79 οἳ δ' ἀλαλητῷ / πᾶν πεδίον κατέχουσι, Eur. *Troad.* 556 φοινία βοὰ κατεῖχε Περγάμων

---

[1]) Cf. on this detail Kitto, *Form and Meaning*, p. 109. To Philoctetes' mind there is no difference, cf. 263-265.

ἕδρας (both quoted by Schn.-N.-Raderm.). From these words it is far from clear that 'the sacrifice which the cries of Philoctetes interrupted must be that which an oracle had commanded the Greeks to offer at Chrysè's altar' (Jebb, referring to 270); a hearer would, rather, be inclined to think of the camp before Troy and of sacrifices in general. (From the dialogue between Neoptolemus and Philoctetes we do not get the impression that Philoctetes was never there before his exposure, on the contrary; but see note ad 268-270).

βοῶν, στενάζων: cf. *Trach.* 786, 7 (Heracles) ἐσπᾶτο γὰρ πέδονδε καὶ μετάρσιος, / βοῶν, ἰύζων and the note there. For instances of this type of asyndeton, see Bruhn, *Anhang* § 158. Instead of στενάζων R has ἰύζον, G ἠύζον, *i.e.* ἰύζων. Dawe, *Studies on the Text of Sophocles* I (1973), p. 84, may be right in preferring ἰύζων here also.

δυσφημίαις: cf. the oxymoron ἀνευφήμησεν οἰμωγῇ *Trach.* 783.

11-14. ἀλλά: breaking off. ἀλλά ... ἀκμὴ γὰρ ... λόγων is, so to say, an explicit way of expressing what could have been expressed by ἀλλ' ἀκμὴ γὰρ οὐ μακρῶν ἡμῖν λόγων.

μέν: emphatic, but possibly there is some measure of correlation with ἀλλ' ἔργον 15 ('μέν opposes ταῦτα, κ.τ.λ. to ἀλλ' ἔργον, κ.τ.λ. in l. 15', Campbell).

12. ἀκμή: cf. *El.* 22 ἵν' οὐκέτ' ὀκνεῖν καιρός, ἀλλ' ἔργων ἀκμή.

13. μὴ καὶ μάθῃ: for καὶ 'even', 'actually' in negative final clauses see *G.P.*[2] p. 298; cf. *infra* 46.

ἐκχέω: 'spill', 'spoil', *irritum facio*. ἀπὸ μεταφορᾶς τῶν ἀμελγόντων Σ.

14. αἱρήσειν: the meaning is ambiguous, wavering between 'to take hold of' and 'to take in'. Whether Odysseus wants to make clear from the start, that Philoctetes himself has to go to Troy or whether he refers to the capture of the bow by art and contrivance, remains uncertain. In either case what he says seems contrary to the Helenus oracle according to which Philoctetes will have to go willingly to Troy [1]).

15. ἀλλ' ... ὑπηρετεῖν: Mazon's translation well catches the military flavour of the words: 'Pour le reste, à toi, et sans retard, de faire ton service'.

---

[1]) For opinions on these words cf. Kitto, *Form and Meaning*, pp. 96, 108, C. M. Bowra, *Sophoclean Tragedy*[1] (1943), p. 268, I. M. Linforth, *Philoctetes, The Play and the Man* (Univ. of Calif. Publ. in Class. Philol. 15, 3, 1956), p. 102, A. E. Hinds, *The Prophesy of Helenus in Sophocles' Philoctetes*, Cl. Qu. 61. 1967, p. 171.

τὰ λοίφ': either accus. of respect (which I prefer) or internal accus. with ὑπηρετεῖν (Jebb, Webster and others).

ἔργον . . . σὸν: whether as familiar a phrase as Jebb will have it, is a moot question. It often occurs in Ar., it is true, but also in Aesch. *Prom.* 635, *Eum.* 734.

16-19. Authorities disagree about the problem whether any attempt was made to use scenic devices to suggest the landscape where the play is supposed to occur. P. Arnott [1]) is inclined to deny this altogether, Webster [2]) remarks: 'The long back wall (of the σκηνή) took painted panels: here the set representing rocks, which was designed for satyr-plays, would probably be employed'. Another problem is this: were both or was only one opening into the cave visible to the audience? The latter view was defended by W. J. Woodhouse [3]) and by A. M. Dale [4]) (followed by Webster), but strongly opposed by Linforth, *o.l.*, p. 97 n. 2. Linforth's arguments *contra*, however, ('Since in 16 Odysseus tells Neoptolemos to search for a cave with two openings, and N. in 159 says to the chorus, "You see yonder living place with two entrances", both openings must be visible; if N. should speak 38-39 from inside the cave, his words would be inaudible etc.') are not convincing. As Webster comments (n. ad 16): 'On stage one mouth is the central door of the *skene* so that we know that we must imagine a corresponding rear door, through which Philoctetes may return'. I am inclined to accept this view without feeling absolutely sure about it. See note ad 146-9.

16. ὅπου . . . ἐνταῦθ': ἐνταῦθ' refers in general to the place where they have arrived. Commentators compare Ar. *Ran.* 431, 2 ἔχοιτ' ἂν οὖν φράσαι νῷν / Πλούτων' ὅπου 'νθάδ' οἰκεῖ;

δίστομος πέτρα: 'cave in the rock with a double entrance' (L.-Sc.).

17, 8. τοιάδ', ἵν': 'such that in it'. Sophocles and Euripides frequently use ἵνα as local adverb (respectively 30 and 53 instances [5])).

ἡλίου διπλῆ / . . . ἐνθάκησις: = a θάκησις ἐν ἡλίῳ on both sides (see Campbell's note).

---

[1]) *Greek Scenic Conventions* (1962), pp. 93 sq., p. 99.
[2]) *Philoctetes, Introduction* (1970), p. 8.
[3]) *The Scenic Arrangements of the Philoctetes of Sophocles*, J.H.S. 32 (1912), pp. 239 sqq.
[4]) Wiener Studien 69 (1956), p. 104 = *Collected Papers*, p. 127.
[5]) Cf. P. Monteil, *La phrase relative en grec ancien* (1963), p. 377.

19. δι' ἀμφιτρῆτος αὐλίου: αὐλίον is used four times with reference to Philoctetes' abode, the cave (see 954, 1087, 1134). It is used of rural abode, stable, fold and the like. ἀμφιτρής: = ἀμφίτρητος 'pierced through on both sides'. Cf. Eur. *Cycl.* 707. For the formation see Schwyzer I 451.

20, 1. ποτὸν κρηναῖον: 'drinking water from a κρήνη' (in the rock).

22, 3. ἅ μοι ... / ... κυρεῖ: There are three interrelated problems in these two lines: (1) it is not clear at first sight whether ἅ or Philoctetes is the subject of ἔχει and κυρεῖ; (2) how, in either case, can we understand the accusative with πρός; (3) should we read (with GRA) τόνδε γ' εἴτ' or τόνδ' ἔτ' εἴτ' (with Elmsley; L has τόνδ' ἤτ'). If we take ἅ, referring to cave and spring (or 'fountain'), as going with προσελθὼν and σήμαιν' as object, and as the subject of ἔχει and κυρεῖ, or, (better) as solely the subject of ἔχει and κυρεῖ, the words have to mean: 'whether these things—cave and spring— are near this very place here' (thus Webster) 'or whether they are elsewhere'. It is, then, better to follow GRA. But it is very difficult to think of an excuse for the use of the accusative with πρός. If we take ἅ with προσελθὼν and regard Philoctetes as the subject of ἔχει and κυρεῖ, the difficulty of the accusative may seem diminished by assuming that Philoctetes' life is implied to be directed to this place, that it is the centre of his life [1]). (v. Wilamowitz remarks: 'πρός lokal mit dem Akk. sieht so aus, als nähme es späten Gebrauch voraus, vgl. aber Aisch. *Prom.* 348'; we might also quote Eur. *El.* 315, 16 πρὸς δ' ἕδρας 'Ασιήτιδες / δμωαὶ στατίζουσ', but see Denniston's strong objection against this mss reading); τόνδ' ἔτ' and τόνδε γε are both possible. Blaydes' τὸν αὐτὸν, accepted by Jebb, makes things much easier, to such a degree that one feels uneasy about it [2]). (The old conjecture ἐκεῖ instead of ἔχει is not helpful; Mazon, as appears from his translation, takes ἔχειν πρός in the sense of 'apply to', 'be valid'—'si ces indications valent encore -ou non- pour l'endroit où nous sommes'—: I cannot find any convincing parallel).

μοι: ethic dative. σῖγα: has to be connected with προσελθὼν

---

[1]) Cf. Campbell, *Paralip. Sophoclea* (1907), p. 196: 'But may not ἔχειν πρὸς χῶρον τόνδε have the sense of "clinging" or "adhering to this place"?' Similarly Lloyd-Jones, Gnomon 1961, p. 545 and Ed. Fraenkel, *Due Seminari Romani* (Sussidi Eruditi 28), Roma 1977, p. 43.

[2]) Despite Jens-Uwe Schmidt's note (*Sophokles. Philoktet*—1973—p. 20 n. 7); he subscribes to Blaydes' conjecture and repeats the argument drawn from προσ- in the preceding line.

('Geh leis hinauf' v. Wilamowitz [1])), not with σήμαιν' for that would mean that Neoptolemus is asked to make gestures without speaking (hardly: 'fais-moi savoir, mais sans élever la voix,' Mazon), and he will do nothing of the kind.

σήμαιν': Rather than alter σήμαιν' into μάνθαν' (Dawe, *Studies on the Text of Sophocles* III, 1978, pp. 121, 2) I would accept the breach of the regula Porsoniana. Eur. *Heracl.* 529 καὶ στεμματοῦτε καὶ κατάρχεσθ', εἰ δοκεῖ is retained (with misgivings) by Murray and by Pearson (1907). And I do not see the difference between our case and *Ai.* 1101 ἔξεστ' ἀνάσσειν ὧν ὅδ' ἡγεῖτ' οἴκοθεν (quoted by Koster, *Traité*[3], p. 105, and retained by Pearson; here, it is true, Dawe reads ἥγετ' with Elmsley). It would seem better to speak of *regula* than of *lex Porsoniana* and to regard the elision of the last vowel of the word preceding final ‿‿ as constituting a legitimate exception to the rule. For a useful survey of violations of the *regula* in Euripides cf. Platnauer ad *I.T.* 580

24, 5. τἀπίλοιπα τῶν λόγων: amounts to: the rest of my informations and instructions. If we assume that Odysseus has foremost in mind his plan of action, the idea 'course of action' may be regarded as the implied subject of ἴῃ and κοινά as predicative adjunct: 'and that our endeavour may proceed by joint action' (or the like). Jebb prefers to take κοινά as subject.

Neoptolemus is seen to mount the stage and to arrive before the visible entrance of the cave.

26, 7. οὐ μακράν: 'not far-away'. A very condensed way of expressing: 'I had not far to go in order to discharge my task'. Adverbs of place can be used as predicates. Jebb aptly quotes *Trach.* 962, 3 ἀγχοῦ δ' ἄρα κοὐ μακράν (sc. ὄν [2])) προὔκλαιον. Mazon's 'la tâche sera vite remplie' is not satisfactory.

28. ἄνωθεν, ἢ κάτωθεν: 'above (you) or beneath'. We have to assume that Neoptolemus has mounted the stage but is not on a level with the cave entrance. I suppose that this has been put up at a height roughly half of that of the stage building entrance and that some steps lead up to it from the stage [3]). It is probably correct to assume that Odysseus is not standing in the orchestra

---

[1]) Similarly Ellendt, Campbell, Jebb. But in L.-Sc. we find Mazon's interpretation.

[2]) So Jebb; but <οὖσα> seems better; see my note *a.l.*

[3]) I do not believe, as Webster does, that we have to assume the use of an eccyclema.

directly before the stage building but near to the parodos at the
right of the audience. He must have an easy exit, should Philoctetes
be in his cave. Moreover it is hard to understand how otherwise his
οὐ γὰρ ἐννοῶ would have any credibility.

οὐ ... ἐννοῶ: 'I perceive it not' (Jebb). In ἐννοῶ the old meaning of
νοεῖν, sc. 'see', is clearly present. Perhaps: 'I have no clear conception of it'.

29. τόδ' ἐξύπερθε: ἄντρον εἰσορῶ. For τόδ' amounting to 'here':
cf. K.-G. I 642.

καὶ ... κτύπος: if καὶ is correct τ' LA is impossible and δ' GR
nearly so. γ' Tricl. seems the only way out (G.P.² p. 157). If we
alter into, ναί, (cp. Reiske's emendation of El. 1445), τ' is excellent
and δ' possible.

στίβου ... κτύπος: sound of foot-fall. This is perfectly in harmony with Odysseus' next question and with Webster's assumption
as to the other entrance of the cave. στίβος can mean 'footstep' as
well as 'track'; τύπος (A, preferred by Pearson) is an inferior
reading; its origin is either mechanical (ICK) or to be ascribed to a
misapprehension of στίβος. Neoptolemus, moreover, cannot as yet
see into the cave (as appears from τόδ' ἐξύπερθε).

30. ὅρα ... μὴ ... κυρῇ: the subjunctive, because ὅρα combines
the notions 'see' and 'cave'.

καταυλισθείς: LAGR clearly better than κατακλιθείς A; καταυλισθείς amounts to 'lodged'; the words are well rendered by Campbell:
'See whether he be not within and asleep'.

31. ὁρῶ: now Neoptolemus is on a level with the entrance of the
cave.

32. τροφή: abstract noun, denoting 'provision' and including
both food and utensils, means of sustenance (= διατροφή). τρυφή
(Welcker) is preferred by Schn.-N.-R. and by Ed. Fraenkel. o.l.
p. 44.

οἰκοποιός: 'constituting a house'. Utensilia quibus locus aliquis in
modum domus instruitur (G. Hermann).

33. γε: 'Yes',. Cf. 35.

στιπτή ... φυλλάς: 'a bed of pressed leaves'; cf. L.-Sc. s.v. στιβάς
I and s.v. φυλλάς II 1.

ὡς ἐναυλίζοντί τῳ: 'as for somebody lodging here', ὡς with the
participle expressing that this is the unmistakable impression one
gets. The dative may depend on στιπτή as a dativus auctoris (this is
preferred by Campbell and Webster).

35, 6. αὐτόξυλον: 'of mere wood' (without polish or ornament). Determinative compound, comparable with αὐτόπαις, αὐθόμαιμος, αὐτάδελφος, and cf. Musgrave's conjecture αὐτοπέτρου O.C. 192, the note ad *fr.* 130 P. and the controversial interpretation of αὐτοσίδαρον Eur. *Hel.* 356, see comments by Pearson and by Kannicht. For αὐτο- compounds in Soph. see J. C. F. Nuchelmans, *Die Nomina des sophokleischen Wortschatzes* (1949) pp. 105 sq..

πυρεῖα: firesticks and perhaps stones (cf. 296), or perhaps, some embers left covered up (Campbell).

37. θησαύρισμα: 'store'; the irony has a tinge of cruelty.

κείνου: predicative and by its placing very emphatic: 'His are these possessions which you announce' (Webster).

38, 9. ἰοὺ ἰού: perhaps the best paraphrase of the exclamation as used in Tragedy is Campbell's: 'an exclamation of discovery mixed with dislike' (we may add sorrow, horror, disgust).

ταῦτα γ᾽ ἄλλα: and there <I see> other things: ῥάκη <which> θάλπεται. There is no need to assume Neoptolemus to have entered the cave in order to be able to see the rags 'drying in the sun' [1]) at its second entrance. So Linforth's objection against Woodhouse's (and Webster's) reconstruction of the scenery is not valid. As it is, this important detail reinforces this reconstruction. Without urging the difference, it is at least noteworthy that the rags are referred to by ταῦτα, the πυρεῖα by τάδε, just as the cave itself by τόδε 29. ἄλλα, amounting to 'besides', is a clear instance of the idiom discussed by K.-G. I 275 Anm. 1; O.T. 290 is probably not comparable, O.T. 7 up to a point.

νοσηλείας: derives from νοσηλός; the context requires us to interpret βαρείας του νοσηλείας πλέα together as meaning: 'infected through ministration to some grievous sore' (Campbell). In itself νοσηλεία cannot mean 'matter discharged from a sore'; its (later attested) meaning is 'care of the sick', or 'sickness which needs tending'. See *fr.* 264 P. ἀνοσήλευτον with the note.

41, 2. κηρί: combines the notions 'disease' and 'disgrace'.

προσβαίη μακράν: προσ- is to be excused by the idea of direction in the accus. μακράν (Radermacher, v. Wilamowitz *o.l.* p. 112, ad v. 23).

43, 4. (ἐ)πὶ φορβῆς νόστον: we should not think of νόστον as internal accus. with ἐξελήλυθεν (if we do, φορβῆς has to be altered into φορβὴν). It is a well-known fact that νόστος (νέομαι, νοστέω)

---

[1]) Cf. *Trach.* 697, Eur. *Hel.* 181.

does not always mean 'return' but also 'come' or 'go' (See in the last instance W. J. Verdenius, Mnemos. 1969, p. 195 and Chantraine, *Dict. Ét. s.v.* νέομαι). So νόστον can be taken as 'ὁδός', 'journey', 'expedition' and the genitive as denoting the object of the journey (Jebb, quoting *I.T.* 1066 γῆς πατρῴας νόστος). Broadhead's objection to this (the associated genitive should signify the *terminus ad quem, Tragica* - 1968 - p. 97), is not valid, for the φορβή, when found, will be the *terminus* of Philoctetes' journey. So φορβῆς νόστον amounts to 'foraging expedition' (Campbell; his other interpretation: 'for the purpose of a return with food', though attractive, lays too heavy a strain on the use of the genitive; it is accepted by Ed. Fraenkel, *o.l.* p. 44). φύλλον ... που: sc. ἐκεῖσε ἐξελήλυθεν. νώδυνον causative 'allaying pain' = ἀνώδυνον Hippocr. *Aph.* 5.22; *Ai.* 554 b, meaning 'causing no pain'.

45-47. τὸν ... παρόντα: Neoptolemus' attendant.

μὴ καὶ λάθῃ: cf. 13.

ἕλοιτό μ᾽: there is much to be said for reading ἕλοιτ᾽ ἔμ᾽ (Bergk, Cavallin); in L o is in *rasura*, the original letter was ε.

Odysseus, as appears from his first rhesis, has the following preoccupations: he wants to ascertain whether the place where they have arrived is really Philoctetes' abode; he wants to remain unseen by the latter; so he wants to be sure that Philoctetes, for the moment, is absent. He wants to give his instructions to Neoptolemus regarding his μηχάνημα. Now that he is satisfied as to the place of Philoctetes' abode and as to his absence for the time being, and after taking precautionary measures in view of the latter's expected arrival, he is ready for his instructions to Neoptolemus. Ἀχιλλέως παῖ (50, cf. 4) marks the beginning of the second part of the Prologue.

48. ἔρχεται: Neoptolemus' attendant.

στίβος: either Philoctetes' approach (his 'footfall', 'walking', cf. 29)—and in that case, if Webster's assumption (see ad 16-19) is correct, the man has to be sent near the entrance of the cave— or 'path', 'track', in which case the watch has to go in the direction of one of the parodoi but not the one Neoptolemus and Odysseus have used, Webster's improbable idea. Vs. 125 does not compel us to this line of thought. After 125 Odysseus can be supposed to signal to the watch to leave his post at the entrance of the cave (for instance), or near the other parodos. There is time enough for the man's return during Odysseus' words before his exit.

49. σὺ δ' . . . λόγῳ: referring to 24, 5. δευτέρῳ λόγῳ: in a second or further discourse. Actually Odysseus' instructions are expounded in his second rhesis.

50, 1. 'Ἀχιλλέως παῖ: this has to be seen in close connection with γενναῖον, for γενναῖος properly means 'true to one's birth or descent'. The difficulty for Odysseus is of course this, that lies and trickery are just what are contrary to the φύσις of Achilles' true son.

ἐφ' οἷς: ἐπὶ τούτοις ἐφ' οἷς.

μὴ μόνον τῷ σώματι: see 90, where Neoptolemus declares himself ready to πρὸς βίαν τὸν ἄνδρ' ἄγειν / καὶ μὴ δόλοισιν.

52, 3. ἤν: κἤν would be what we expect.

ὧν: τούτων ἅ. Up till now Neoptolemus has been left in the dark about Odysseus' σόφισμα.

ὑπουργεῖν: on a par with γενναῖον εἶναι, where for instance τῇ γνώμῃ προθύμως ὑπουργοῦντα would have expressed more explicitly Odysseus' meaning. The somewhat cryptic, implicit wording enhances the suspense as to the unfolding of his instructions.

ὡς ὑπηρέτης πάρει: reminding Neoptolemus of his subordinate position: 'tu es en service' (Mazon). Musgrave's οἷς (Pearson) is quite unnecessary.

54, 5. τί δῆτ' ἄνωγας: 'Eh bien! quels sont tes ordres?' (Mazon).

τὴν Φιλοκτήτου σε δεῖ / ψυχὴν . . . λέγων·: The construction δεῖ σε ὅπως fut. ind. occurs also at *Ai.* 556. We may regard δεῖ σε ὅπως ἐκκλέψεις as a combination or contamination of δεῖ σε ἐκκλέψαι and the elliptical ὅπως ἐκκλέψεις (cf. K.-G. II 377). We have, then, to put a point or, better, a semi-colon after λέγων. Then follows asyndetically the next sentence with λέγειν inf. pro imperat. Webster, putting a comma after λέγων, prefers to construe ὅπως τὴν Φιλοκτήτου ψυχὴν λόγοισιν ἐκκλέψεις λέγων, and makes the sentence run right on to 65. This is possible, but it would seem to me that the character of general announcement of Neoptolemus' line of conduct which 54, 5 convey when taken as one introductory sentence is more apposite.

λόγοισιν ἐκκλέψεις: λόγοισιν is instrumental dative and the pleonastic λέγων 'helps to emphasize the unwelcome lesson that words and not deeds are required of Neoptolemus' (Campbell). ἐκκλέψεις amounts to ἐξαπατήσεις. On κλέπτειν and compounds cf. Denniston ad Eur. *El.* 364.

56, 7. 'Ἀχιλλέως παῖς: either ''Ἀχιλλέως παῖς' (sc. εἰμι or πάρειμι) or 'Ἀχιλλέως παῖς (sc. εἶναι or παρεῖναι).

κλεπτέον: amounts to 'deceitfully conceal'.

58, 9. πλεῖς δ' ὡς πρὸς οἶκον: δ' adversative. πλεῖς interrupts the construction and is much more lively than πλεῖν would be; Campbell notes: sc. ὡς φήσεις λέγων. ὡς marks the purpose of the sailing. (Another possibility would be that ὡς = ὅτι introduces an object clause dependent on λέγειν; hyperbaton is a very common phenomenon in Sophocles; then there would be not interruption, but variation of the construction).

ἔχθος ἐχθήρας: the same figura etymologica *El.* 1034.

60, 1. ἐν λιταῖς: by means of prayers. ἐν, as often, with the instrumental dative.

στείλαντες: for στέλλω 'summon' see L.-Sc. *s.v.* III.

τήνδ': *i.e.* your arrival. μόνην δ' LRG would not be impossible.

62, 3. οὐκ ἠξίωσαν . . . ὅπλων / ἐλθόντι: contamination of σε οὐκ ἠξίωσαν τῶν Ἀχιλλείων ὅπλων and οὐκ ἠξίωσάν σοι δοῦναι τὰ Ἀχίλλεια ὅπλα. δοῦναι has the character of an epexegetic infinitive, with the dative added.

κυρίως: as was your right, by right.

ἐλθόντι: <to you> when you had arrived.

64, 5. παρέδοσαν: they had handed them over.

λέγων: thus the construction returns to the inf. pro imper. λέγειν 57. (If we take ὡς 58 = ὅτι, there is no irregularity at all but the liveliness of the discourse is diminished).

ἔσχατ' ἐσχάτων: cf. K.-G. I 339. Intensification of ἔσχατα κακά, or ἔσχατα κακῶν, cf. H. Thesleff, *Studies on Intensification in Early and Classical Greek*, 1954, § 342. Perhaps Alc. 117 b 33 L.-P. κάκων ἐσχατ[is comparable.

66, 7. τούτῳ γὰρ οὐδέν μ' ἀλγυνεῖς: codd. τούτων, corr. Buttmann (L has οὐδέ μ', corr. L¹); this seems better than Dindorf's τούτων γὰρ οὐδὲν ἀλγυνεῖ μ', as is well argued by Jebb. The mss reading (with τούτων οὐδέν as internal accusative: 'with none of these things will you hurt me' Webster: it is retained by Campbell) is possible at a pinch. For the sentiment expressed, *El.* 59, 60 is, up to a point, comparable (as is the situation).

εἰ δ' ἐργάσῃ / μὴ ταῦτα: typical Sophoclean hyperbaton coinciding with syntactic enjambment. The words, of course, refer to Neoptolemus' performing of the fraud, not only to the taunts against Odysseus.

βαλεῖς: = προσβαλεῖς 'inflict' (thus, correctly, Campbell and Jebb).

68, 9. εἰ γὰρ ... / ... πέδον: these words can leave us with the impression that the taking of the bow will suffice. But the next lines (prepared by 13 and 46, 7) make clear that Odysseus cannot have dealings with Philoctetes so long as the latter is in control of his bow. So, evidently, Odysseus wants Neoptolemus to insinuate himself into Philoctetes' trust by guile and to take advantage of every opportunity to obtain the bow. We must assume that Odysseus' calculations are based on the idea that Philoctetes once bereaved of his bow, can be persuaded to follow them to Troy.

70, 1. ὁμιλία / ... πιστὴ καὶ βέβαιος: 'intercourse based on trust, and safe'.

72-74. πέπλευκας: denoting the voyage to Troy.

οὔτ' ἔνορκος οὐδενί: ὤμοσαν γὰρ τῷ Τυνδάρεῳ πάντες Ἕλληνες συνελθεῖν ἐὰν ἁρπασθῇ ἡ Ἑλένη. So Neoptolemus' lie as to his returning home would be plausible.

οὔτ' ἐξ ἀνάγκης: cf. 1025. Referring to Odysseus' feigning madness and its detection by Palamedes.

οὔτε τοῦ πρώτου στόλου: nor <a member> of the first expedition. What is meant, is more clearly expressed in Philoctetes' words 246, 7 οὐ γὰρ δὴ σύ γ' ἦσθα ναυβάτης / ἡμῖν κατ' ἀρχὴν τοῦ πρὸς Ἴλιον στόλου.

Von Wilamowitz (*Einleitung* translation p. 17 n. 1) pertinently remarks: 'Dass Philoktet ihn persönlich hassen muss, weil er ihn ausgesetzt hat, lässt er hier im Dunkeln',—although a thoughtful spectator will remember ll. 5-7.

τούτων: the three items 72, 3.

75, 6. ὄλωλα: see K.-G. I 150, Schw.-Debr. II 287.

77, 8. σοφισθῆναι: passive form and passive meaning [1]).

κλοπεύς / ὅπως γενήσῃ: again hyperbaton and syntactic enjambment coincide.—'Lorsque Sophocle emploie κλοπεύς, le choix du dérivé en -εύς répond plus à une recherche de style qu'a une nuance de sens' (Chantraine, *Formation des Noms*, p. 130). Cf. *Ant.* 493. Jebb's translation is exact: 'No; the thing that must be plotted is just this,—how thou mayest win the resistless arms by stealth'.

I imagine that after these words a gesture of anger and aversion must be made by Neoptolemus, followed by a moment of painful silence. Odysseus is made to forestall an outburst of indignation on his partner's part (this is marked by the asyndeton) by declaring

---

[1]) But Σ has: σοφισθῆναι: σοφίσασθαι. This would be without parallels but not without analogies.

that he is perfectly aware that the σόφισμα is against the grain of Neoptolemus' φύσις.

79, 80. ἔξοιδα: cf. Philoctetes on Odysseus' wily ways 407. The φύσις, *indoles ingenita*, of Neoptolemus recurs 874, 902, 1310 in meaningful contexts.

παῖ: Erfurdt's conjecture instead of καί mss, adopted by many editors, but not by Campbell and Dain-Mazon. But Jebb's discussion (*Appendix*) in favour of παῖ seems to me convincing (Campbell, *Paralip. Soph.* p. 197, conceded that his parallels for καί were insufficient). See *G.P.*², p. 325. If καί were to be retained, it should be connected, not with ἔξοιδα, but with φύσει . . . πεφυκότα ('actually'). The mss reading has been defended by F. de Ruyt, R.B.Ph. 1933, pp. 113-118.

81, 2. ἀλλ' . . . γάρ: 'complex' use of the idiom, ἀλλά going with the main sentence, γάρ with the dependent clause (*G.P*²., p. 98); but that is not to say that the interrelation between the two particles is not close.

ἡδύ . . . νίκης: a condensed way of saying <τὸ > τῆς νίκης <κτῆμα > ἡδύ τι κτῆμά <ἐστιν > and λαβεῖν is epexegetic infinitive. The idiom is common with χρῆμα, e.g. Eur. *Andr.* 181 ἐπίφθονόν τι χρῆμα θηλειῶν ἔφυ, *ib.* 957. τι LGR is surely better than τοι A (accepted by Masqueray 1924).

τόλμα: as often, the meaning of τολμᾶν is *a se impetrare, in animum inducere*. Sc. τοιαῦτα φωνεῖν καὶ τεχνᾶσθαι κακά.

δίκαιοι: 'honest', 'redlich'.

αὖθις: 'another day'.

ἐκφανούμεθα: the first person plural is suggestive of their close fellowship.

83-85. εἰς ἀναιδές: for a 'shameless' <deed>, or (perhaps better) 'for shamelessness', to be connected with δός μοι σεαυτόν. I cannot understand why the article should be obligatory with ἀναιδές used as a noun (so Jebb, who implausibly takes it as attribute with μέρος), the less so if we take it as a substitute for ἀναίδεια: abstract nouns often go without the article, not only in poetry. The concept ἀναίδεια is illustrated by πᾶσαν αἰσχύνην ἀφείς [1]).

ἡμέρας μέρος βραχύ: accus. of duration. For the idea cf. Eur. *Or.* 656 μίαν πονήσας ἡμέραν.

---

[1]) Cf. von Erffa, Αἰδώς *und verwandte Begriffe in ihrer Entwicklung von Homer bis Demokrit* (Philol. Suppl. 30: 2, 1937), p. 117.

κέκλησο: on this expressive use of the imperative of κεκλῆσθαι cf. C. J. Ruijgh, *L'emploi onomastique de* κεκλῆσθαι, *Miscellanea Tragica*, 1976, pp. 377 sq..

εὐσεβέστατος: 'scrupulous' rather than 'religious', 'pious', cf. 1051 [1]).

86, 7. μέν: *solitarium*, emphasizing ἐγώ.

οὓς ἄν ... / ... στυγῶ: 'When counsels pain my ear, son of Laertes, then I abhor to aid them with my hand', thus Jebb, better than 'Wie ich nicht liebe durch Lügen getäuscht zu werden, so ist es mir verhasst Lügen zu erfinden' (Radermacher). τῶν λόγων is partitive genitive. τούσδε refers back to the preceding relative.

88, 9. ἔφυν· ... / ... οὐκφύσας: cf. 79 and 3, 4. For practical purposes the difference between ἔφυν and πέφυκα is often negligible; metrical convenience often seems the decisive factor in the choice.

ἐκ: 'by means of'.

ὥς φασιν: Neoptolemus had not known his father.

90-92. καὶ μὴ δόλοισιν: on a par with πρὸς βίαν. Jebb calls μὴ 'generic' (noting that the phrase means: 'and by such means as are not frauds'). Campbell (*Paral. Soph.* p. 197 sq.), questioning this, speaks of μὴ as 'deprecatory', to be construed with ἄγειν, implying μὴ ἄγω (subj.). Related to this is Webster's comment: 'Possibly "and never by guile" like the use of μή with a future indicative after an oath (Goodwin, *G.M.T.*, § 686)'. There are, at any rate, cases of the use of μή instead of the expected οὐ, where the firm intention of the subject or the speaker is involved. Perhaps a case like Hdt. III 127.2 τίς ἄν μοι τοῦτο ἐπιτελέσειε σοφίῃ καὶ μὴ ('aber ja nicht' K.-G. II 187) βίῃ τε καὶ ὁμίλῳ; is comparable. The emendation οὐ μὴν (Schn.-N.-Radermacher) seems unnecessary.

ἐξ ἑνὸς ποδός: 'with only one foot to rely on' (Campbell) and similarly Jebb, Mazon. Webster ('we should say "single-handed" ...') follows Schn.-N.-Radermacher (and probably v. Wilamowitz) in denying that the phrase has anything to do with Philoctetes' lameness, implausibly in my opinion. How can the spectator, on hearing the phrase ἐξ ἑνὸς ποδός, be expected not to think of the hero's lameness?

93-95. γε μέντοι: adversative (*G.P.*[2] p. 412). It is adversative in so far as the words express that he shrinks from taking the consequences of his preceding statement (we might assume that it

---

[1]) See J. C. Bolkestein, Ὅσιος *en* Εὐσεβής, thesis Utrecht, 1936, p. 32 n. 6.

answers μὲν 86, though the distance is somewhat long); the tenor of this sentence in its turn is limited by the adversative βούλομαι δ' κτλ.

καλῶς: goes with δρῶν; 'honourably', its moral sense taken up by its antithesis κακῶς.

ἐξαμαρτεῖν: 'fail', (in the sense of: 'be unsuccessful'—'regarded as an event at some one moment' (Jebb)).

νικᾶν κακῶς: 'be victorious in a dishonourable way'. Σ paraphrases: θέλω εἰπὼν τὸ ἀληθὲς ἀποτυχεῖν μᾶλλον ἢ ἐξαπατᾶν τὸν ἄνδρα καὶ ἐπιτυχεῖν and comments: εἰσάγει δὲ αὐτὸν ὁ Σοφοκλῆς τὸν τοῦ πατρὸς λόγον λέγοντα 'ἐχθρὸς γάρ μοι κεῖνος κτλ'. (Il. IX 312 sq.).

96, 7. ἐσθλοῦ πατρὸς παῖ: again Odysseus tries to insinuate himself into his partner's favour by referring to his noble father, thus introducing the argument drawn from his own experience: words are more powerful than deeds. Odysseus is made to play the part of the older man grown wise by experience, showing sympathy with youthful naïvety by mentioning the ways of his own youth, feigning regretful disillusionment.

98, 9. εἰς ἔλεγχον: εἰς πεῖραν <τῶν> πραγμάτων Σ.

πάνθ' ἡγουμένην: 'lead the way in all things.' βροτοῖς: 'where mortals are concerned' (Campbell), the use of ἡγουμένην being absolute; but close dependence upon ἡγουμένην is at least possible.

100. τί οὖν μ' ἄνωγας: In addition to the instances of hiatus in Tragedy after τί listed by Jebb (who, however, here prefers Wakefield's τί μ' οὖν) we now have a very good parallel in Eur. Teleph. fr. 10.2 τί οὖν σ' ἀπείργει (see Handley-Rea, The Telephus of Euripides, Bull. Inst. Cl. Stud. Suppl. 5 - 1957 - a.l.). It should, moreover, be stated that this hiatus, very common in Comedy, cannot create surprise in a late tragedy of Sophocles. See also Campbell Paralip. Soph., p. 198 and Ed. Fraenkel, Zu den Phoenissen des Euripides, Sitzungsber. München 1965, I, p. 40 n. 3.

Most commentators seem to understand the verse as meaning: 'Que m'enjoins-tu donc là, si ce n'est pas mentir?' (Mazon). But surely there is something to be said for Campbell's slightly different interpretation: 'I see you want me to tell a lie: have you any further commands?' (Cp. v. Wilamowitz: 'Verlangst du mehr, als dass ich lügen soll?'). ὃ θέλεις κέλευε πλὴν τοῦ ψεύδεσθαι Σ is probably to be rejected (if Σ means: order me whatever you will but not the telling of lies); there seems to be a confusion between πλήν preposition and πλήν conjunction.

101. λέγω σ' . . . λαβεῖν: λέγω with the acc. c. inf. amounts to *iubeo*, as often (K.-G. II 26 Anm. 2).

Neither the wording of 55 nor that of this line is such that we can unhesitatingly subscribe to v. Wilamowitz' verdict 'dass es auf seine Person auch ankommt, wird unzweideutig gesagt (55.101)' (*Einl.* translation p. 18), for δόλῳ λαβεῖν can be taken as a paraphrase of δολῶσαι. That is not how Neoptolemus takes the phrase (ἄγειν 102 !), but it appears from Odysseus' further instructions that Neoptolemus' task is to make himself master of the bow by guile, but how he is then to deal with Philoctetes is left in the dark. It would seem that Odysseus in using the phrase δόλῳ λαβεῖν is supposed to mean 'overmaster him by guile' *i.e.* 'by getting hold of his bow by lie and deceit'. But perhaps this is oversubtle, for δόλῳ λαβόντα γ' 107 (evidently with Philoctetes as object) does not mean more than δολώσαντά γ'. So Odysseus' intention seems rather to be: 'take him by lie and deceit (in order to have the occasion of getting hold of his bow)'.

102. ἐν δόλῳ: 'instrumental' ἐν is fairly common in the language of Tragedy and elsewhere. ἐν δόλῳ is on a par with πείσαντ'. Cf. 60.

103. Πειθώ and βία will not avail; there remains δόλος.

104. οὕτως . . . τι δεινὸν ἰσχύος θράσος: lit. 'such a dread boldness consisting in strength', *i.e.* 'such a terrible emboldening strength'. Cf. Eur. *Phoen.* 267, 8 ὡπλισμένος δὲ χεῖρα τῷδε φασγάνῳ / τὰ πίστ' ἐμαυτῷ τοῦ θράσους παρέξομαι.

105. προπέμποντας: 'sending forth'. Dobree wanted to insert γ' after ἰούς.

106. ἐκείνῳ . . . θρασύ: 'one cannot even dare to have intercourse with him'. θρασύ of the thing to be dared, to be ventured. Commentators refer to Pind. *Nem.* VII 50 θρασύ μοι τόδ' εἰπεῖν.

108. δῆτα τὰ ψευδῆ: reading of RGA, rightly preferred by Jebb, Campbell, Pearson, Webster to δῆτα τὸ (Vauvilliers, D.-M.) and to the improbable δὴ τάδε of LΛ. Jebb refers to *fr.* 352 P. καλὸν μὲν οὖν οὐκ ἔστι τὰ ψευδῆ λέγειν ('those things which are false').

109. οὐκ . . . γε: 'No, at least not if . . .'.

110. πῶς . . . βλέπων: 'de quel front' (D.-M.), 'with what *face*' (L.-Sc.). Cf. *O.T.* 1371.

οὖν: implies 'if so'.

λακεῖν: only in Lᵃᶜ (the other mss have λαλεῖν); λακεῖν is used of loud utterances, here it is evidently expressive of effrontery. Perhaps *Ant.* 1094 μή πώ ποτ' αὐτὸν ψεῦδος ἐσ πόλιν λακεῖν (quoted by Jebb) implies the same suggestion.

113. This wording and again 115 are suggestive of the idea that the bow alone will suffice. This does not signify that Odysseus is supposed to be unaware that it will not; only that he wants Neoptolemus to be under the impression that for the moment the stealing of the bow is essential.

114. This refers back to the means of persuasion by which Odysseus and Phoenix had prevailed upon Neoptolemus to come to Troy. An element of chagrin is to be perceived in Neoptolemus' words. Cf. note ad 603.

115. οὔτ' ἂν σύ: sc. πέρσειας.

116. θηρατέ' οὖν: Triclinius' reading (mss have θηρατέα) seems better than G. Hermann's and Elmsley's θηρατέ' ἄν; Mazon conjectured θηρατέ' ἄρα ¹): the mistake of the mss is then to be attributed to haplography.

γίγνοιτ' ἄν: 'they would then *become* (by logical inference) desirable prizes' (Jebb).

117. ὡς: <know>, <be sure> that (see L.-Sc. s.v. ὡς F2).

τοῦτο: the seizing of the bow.

118. τὸ δρᾶν: for the article see K.-G. II 43-45. Cf. for instance *El.* 467, *Ant.* 27, 78, 266, 1106, *infra* 1241, 1252 (πείθομαι τὸ δρᾶν).

119. σοφός: in the sense applicable to Odysseus himself, 'clever', 'adroit'. This consideration may leave some doubt as to the inevitability of Vauvilliers' correction αὐτός (for αὑτός), adopted by all editors and very plausible in itself.

120. ἴτω: *fiat*; its force is best illustrated by Eur. *Med.* 819 ἴτω· περισσοὶ πάντες οὖν μέσῳ λόγοι. See also *ib.* 798.

αἰσχύνην: sense of shame (= αἰδώς, cf. 83), scruple.

121, 2. ἢ μνημονεύεις: implying his acting accordingly.

παρήνεσα / . . . συνήνεσα: the rhyming marks the end of the stichomythia, as is well remarked by Webster (I do not know exact parallels in Sophocles), and, above all, summarizes the two men's different rôles in these preliminaries and Neoptolemus' final yielding.

125. τὸν σκοπόν: cf. 45.

πρὸς ναῦν: Neoptolemus' ship (see Jebb's sensible remarks *Introduction* p. XX n. 1) ²). On the question of the whereabouts of the σκοπός see note ad 48.

---

¹) Tournier (R. Ph. VI (1882) 113-148) θηρατέ' ἄν γίγνοιτ'ἄρ'.

²) It seems desirable to assume that Odysseus and Neoptolemus have sailed each in a ship of his own, although nowhere this is stated explicitly.

126, 7. τοῦ χρόνου δοκῆτέ τι / κατασχολάζειν: Radermacher's explication: 'müssig sein zum Schaden der Zeit' (τι adverbial or internal accus.), approved by Groeneboom ad Herod. 1.17 seems preferable to taking χρόνου as a partitive genitive with the object τι. I cannot understand ἔτι (codd.) approved by Webster.

128, 9. ναυκλήρου τρόποις / μορφὴν δολώσας: *i.e.* he will be disguised after the fashion of[1]) a merchant skipper. (On ναύκληρος and ἔμπορος[2]) see H. Knorringa, *Emporos*, thesis Utrecht pp. 96, 97: 'also a trader with a ship of his own was usually called ἔμπορος; if such a trader was called ναύκληρος, he was more looked upon as the owner of a ship than as a trader'). For his costume cf. Plaut. *Miles* 1172 sqq..

ὡς ἂν ἀγνοία προσῇ: 'that he may not be recognized', viz. as the man he really is, a sailor of Neoptolemus' ship just as are the members of the Chorus. For ἀγνοία cf. *Trach.* 350.

130, 1. οὗ ... αὐδωμένου: either genitive absolute or genitive dependent on δέχου or on λόγων. αὐδωμένου is middle, cf. *infra* 852, *Ai.* 772 (K.-G. I 102) [3]).

ποικίλως: 'craftily', cf. Alc. fr. 69.6, 7 ὁ δ' ὡς ἀλώπα / ποικιλόφρων, L.-Sc. *s.v.* ποικίλος III 3 a, b, c, ποικίλλω 'speak equivocally' Pl. *Symp.* 218 c.

δέχου: 'pick up' (Webster's rendering).

τὰ συμφέροντα τῶν ἀεὶ λόγων: 'whatever in his speech from time to time is profitable' (Campbell). The Emporos' last words are σφῷν δ' ὅπως ἄριστα συμφέροι θεός (627).

132. παρείς: for παρίημι 'leave to' (Dutch 'overlaten aan') cf. *fr. ad.* 353 N.[2]: Ζεὺς γὰρ τὰ μὲν μέγιστα φροντίζει βροτῶν, / τὰ μικρὰ δ' ἄλλοις δαίμοσιν παρεὶς ἐᾷ.

133, 4. Ἑρμῆς δ' ὁ πέμπων Δόλιος: Ἑρμῆς Δόλιος ὁ πέμπων; ὁ πέμπων not <ἡμᾶς> but men generally who pursue something by cunning. For Hermes 'Patron der Intrigue' see W. Schmid, *G.L.G.* I 2 p. 398 n. 2; cf. *El.* 1396, Aesch. *Choëph.* 727 sqq..

Νίκη τ' Ἀθάνα Πολιάς: the identification of Athena, always Odysseus' patroness in Homer, with Νίκη and Ἀθάνα Πολιάς is only natural in the mouth of a Vth century Odysseus figure. Ed. Fraenkel (*o.l.* p. 47) wants to athetize the line; I do not agree. For Athena Νίκη cf. Eur. *Ion* 454 ~ 457, 1529.

---

[1]) For the idiom cf. Groeneboom ad Aesch. *Ag.* 918.

[2]) See, however, my note ad 542.

[3]) One could think of conjecturing αὐδωμένων (with Nauck, but without altering οὗ into σύ). Then οὗ would be dependent on λόγων and ποικίλως αὐδωμένων would be predicative adjunct to λόγων.

Parodos 135-218

Three antistrophic pairs; anapaestic recitatives between str. and antistr. α, between antistr. α and str. β and between antistr. β and str. γ. The recitatives are spoken by Neoptolemus (with the exception of one question by the Coryphaeus 161). The first line of str. and antistr. γ is divided between Chorus and Neoptolemus. The songs are in aeolochoriambics with iambic and dactylic (142 = 157) elements.

The Chorus, consisting of sailors in the service of Neoptolemus, is supposed to arrive from the latter's ship and enters the orchestra from the same side whence Odysseus has made his exit. They are supposed to know something about Philoctetes and the aim of the expedition and its difficulties.

135, 6. με δέσποτ᾽: Triclinius' reading instead of δέσποτά μ᾽, which would yield a choriamb, where the antistr. has an iambic metre [1]).

ἐν ξένᾳ ξένον: cf. *O.C.* 184 τόλμα ξεῖνος ἐπὶ ξένας and the many instances of this schema listed by Bruhn, *Anhang* § 223.

στέγειν: 'keep hidden', a usage of the verb recurring several times in Soph. and Eur.; but the rhyming play with the antithesis στέγειν / λέγειν only here, as far as I am aware. Cf. *Trach.* 596, Eur. *El.* 273.

ὑπόπταν: only here in Tragedy, but both Soph. and Eur. use ὑποπτεύω.

138-40. τέχνα ... / ... γνώμα: *i.e.* τέχνα καὶ γνώμα <ἐκείνου> παρ᾽ ὅτῳ κτλ., τέχνας <καὶ γνώμας> ἑτέρας προύχει. This τέχνα τέχνας ἑτέρας προύχουσα is the 'royal art', cf. *O.T.* 380, 1 ὦ ... τέχνη τέχνης / ὑπερφέρουσα.

παρ᾽ ὅτῳ: 'in whose hands' (L.-Sc. s.v. παρά B II. 2).

ἀνάσσεται: the passive of the verb is exceptional but it occurs in Hom. *Od.* IV 177 ἀνάσσονται δ᾽ ἐμοὶ αὐτῷ, and ἀνάσσω τινός (of things) is common: its passive form ἀνάσσεταί τι is according to Greek usage; moreover, since the royal sceptre is the symbol of royalty the phrase can be regarded as the passive form of an active ἀνάσσω with internal accusative or of ἀνάσσω ἔχων, νέμων, κραίνων (cf. σκῆπτρα κραίνειν *O.C.* 449).

---

[1]) Cf. v. Wilamowitz, *Gr. Vsk.* p. 531 n. 1: '135 ist der überlieferte Choriamb ... an sich willkommen, aber man muss wohl mit Triklinios με δέσποτ᾽ ἐν annehmen, weil die Gegenstrophe einen normalen Trimeter hat oder gehabt hat'. I am, nevertheless, not so sure about the necessity of the alteration.

τὸ θεῖον Διὸς σκῆπτρον: Διὸς amounts to ἐκ Διὸς; cf. *Il.* II 101-108.

141, 2. σε . . . ἐλήλυθεν: 'on you has descended'. The acc. pers. is rare with ἔρχομαι; *Il.* XVIII 180 αἴ κέν τι νέκυς (acc. pl.) ᾐσχυμμένος ἔλθῃ is not a striking parallel. Better the instances with βαίνω Eur. *Hipp.* 1371, Ar. *Nub.* 30 quoted by Jebb; it is, of course, common with ἱκάνω, ἱκνέομαι.

ὦ τέκνον: the sailors were presumably Achilles' companions.

τόδ' . . . πᾶν κράτος: 'this (implied in σκῆπτρον) complete power'.

ὠγύγιον: predicative adjunct: 'from earliest ages'. The word, of unknown origin, means 'primeval', 'uralt'. Ogyges was said to be a king of Attica or of Boeotia. But see Broadhead ad Aesch. *Pers.* 37. With ᾿Αθάνας *Pers.* 975. First occurrence Hes. *Theog.* 806 with Στυγὸς ὕδωρ. In Soph. it recurs in *O.C.* 1770 (Θήβας).

142, 3. τό: 'therefore' (as ταῦτα in prose); Denniston *G.P.*² p. 565. Cf. ὃ Eur. *Hec.* 13.

144-46. ἐσχατιαῖς: locative, 'in the extreme parts'. There is nothing against the plural.

κεῖται: amounts to 'resides'.

δέρκου θαρσῶν: 'regarde, n'aie pas peur' (Mazon).

146-49. δεινὸς ὁδίτης: impressively suggestive of Philoctetes' fear- and pity-inspiring gait; another memorable occurrence of this epic word in Theocr. 16.93.

τῶνδ' ἐκ μελάθρων: these words contain the strongest argument in favour of Webster's assumptions about the cave ¹) (see ad 16-19). For if we connect them with the previous words—by far the most natural way of taking them—it follows that Neoptolemus is supposed to think that the now absent Philoctetes will enter his cave by way of the off-stage entrance, and will appear to them coming out from its visible entrance. To connect the phrase with the main sentence, does not yield a satisfactory sense (τῶν μελάθρων ἀποστὰς Σ); Campbell's interpretation 'who inhabits here'—to be connected with the temporal clause—is impossible without the altering of ἐκ into οὐκ, conjectured by Linwood and Jebb and put into the latter's text. If we follow Webster there is no difficulty and no need for emendation. The comma has to be put after μελάθρων.

πρὸς ἐμὴν ἀεὶ χεῖρα προχωρῶν: Jebb rejects a figurative sense and translates: 'come forward at my beck from time to time'. It would seem more natural to interpret with Mazon and others: 'réglant tes

---

¹) Dawe's scornful objections against this idea (*Studies on the Text of Sophocles* III, pp. 123, 4) and against ὁδίτης are not justified in my opinion.

démarches sur chacune des miennes', 'proceeding according to my beck'.

τὸ παρὸν θεραπεύειν: to serve each momentary situation, 'to meet each occasion duly' (Campbell). See my note ad *El.* 1251 (ὅταν παρουσία φράζῃ) and cf. *El.* 1305, 6 οὐ γὰρ ἂν καλῶς / ὑπηρετοίην τῷ παρόντι δαίμονι. For θεραπεύειν cf. Thuc. III 56.3 τὸ δὲ ξυμφέρον μᾶλλον θεραπεύοντες.

150, 1. In 150 codd. have one foot too many: μέλον πάλαι μέλημά μοι λέγεις ἄναξ τὸ σόν; Triclinius leaves out τὸ σόν, followed by most editors: τὸ σόν, then, has to be regarded as an intrusive gloss referring to ὄμμ' (or ἄναξ τὸ σόν as a conflation of two ancient readings) and ὄμμ' refers to the Chorus' eye, either as the subject of φρουρεῖν (Jebb) or as a sort of internal accusative with φρουρεῖν (Campbell—also in *Paral. Soph.* p. 199,—Webster). But v. Wilamowitz (*Gr. Vsk.*, p. 531, n. 1) and Radermacher (*Kritischer Apparat*, p. 151) prefer to omit ἄναξ; the Chorus, then, say that to watch Neoptolemus' eye, *i.e.* his winking as to their course of conduct, is since long their chief concern.

ἐπὶ σῷ μάλιστα καιρῷ: precisely with a view to 'your opportunity', 'to what is most opportune for you' (Campbell).

152-54. αὐλὰς ποίας ἔνεδρος ναίει καὶ χῶρον τίν' ἔχει: the first member of the clause asks after Philoctetes' dwelling-place [1]), the second after his whereabouts now. The plural αὐλὰς does not bear a specific significance.

154-58. τὸ: pronoun, and subject of the sentence, μαθεῖν epexegetic infinitive.

ἀποκαίριον: = ἄκαιρον. But the interrelation of the sentences or clauses from τὸ γάρ to the end of the antistrophe is not quite certain. If we put a comma after ποθέν (Campbell and Pearson) τὸ looks forward to the clauses τίς τόπος, ἢ τίς ἕδρα, τίν' ἔχει στίβον, ἔναυλον ἢ θυραῖον, questions dependent on μαθεῖν. But if we put a semi-colon after ποθέν and preferably also before τὸ γάρ (instead of a full stop), τὸ refers to the preceding words and τίς τόπος κτλ. are independent questions. This course, I think, is to be preferred.

156. μὴ προσπεσών με λάθῃ ποθέν: the rearrangement of the transmitted text (μή με λάθῃ προσπεσών) by G. Hermann is probable for reasons of response.

157, 8. τίς τόπος, ἢ τίς ἕδρα: the first phrase asks the same

---

[1]) αὐλή is often used of 'uncivilized habitations' (Denniston ad Eur. *El.* 304).

question as the second one 154 (χῶρον τίν' ἔχει), and the second the
same as the first in 154. The order is again reversed in τίν' ἔχει
στίβον, ἔναυλον ἢ θυραῖον, which means: 'does he walk in his dwelling-
place or abroad?' It is quite unnecessary to alter ἔναυλον ἢ θυραῖον
into ἔναυλος ἢ θυραῖος (Porson followed by Pearson). For στίβος cf.
supra 29.

159, 60. οἶκον μὲν ὁρᾷς τόνδ' ἀμφίθυρον: Neoptolemus answers
the Chorus' first question (153, 4). μὲν suggests that the answer to
the second question is to follow. τόνδ': deictic. 'Here you see . . .',
pointing to the visible entrance. He adds ἀμφίθυρον as a further information. We have not to assume that the Chorus or one of its
members has ascended near to the entrance [1]).

πετρίνης κοίτης: defining genitive, lit. 'consisting of a rocky
couch', *i.e.* 'where he has his couch on the rocky ground' (with
οἶκον, not with ἀμφίθυρον).

161. ποῦ γὰρ: on this use of 'progressive' γὰρ see Denniston
*G.P.*² p. 81 ('a speaker . . . having been satisfied on one subject,
wishes to learn something further') and the instances p. 82 (2 II);
further pp. 84, 5. If we insist on 'translating' γὰρ, perhaps 'well,
then' will do, but Denniston is probably right in arguing that γὰρ
in such questions is used 'as a purely transitional particle'.

ἄπεστιν: there is a peculiar anticipatory element in ἄπεστιν. We
might divide the line into two questions: ποῦ γὰρ ὁ τλήμων αὐτός;
ἄπεστιν;, but in view of 146 we had perhaps better not.

162, 3. φορβῆς χρείᾳ: Neoptolemus takes up Odysseus' supposition (43).

στίβον ὀγμεύει: ὄγμος denotes *inter alia* a 'furrow in ploughing'
and so ὀγμεύω 'move as ploughmen do'. 'He ploughs his way along'
is Webster's correct translation.

τῇδε πέλας που: cf. 41. τῇδε is Blaydes' conjecture, τόνδε LA,
τήνδε GR, impossible reading but corroborating the conjecture
(accepted by Jebb, Radermacher, Pearson, Webster); τόνδε is
accepted by Campbell ('this way, somewhere not far off. With
τόνδε N. points to the way Ph. must have taken') and by Dain-
Mazon. In *Paral. Soph.* p. 199 Campbell shows some sympathy with
τῇδε in view of the *v.l.*. I do not regard the matter as settled.

164-66. ταύτην: sc. by such laborious expeditions, but also
pointing forwards to θηροβολοῦντα.

βιοτῆς: h.l. meaning 'sustenance'.

---

[1]) See v. Wilamowitz' correct remarks *Gr. Vsk.* p. 533.

φύσιν: *genus, modus*. Cf. D. Holwerda Φύσις, thesis Groningen 1955, p. 67.

λόγος ἐστί: Neoptolemus is supposed to know more about Philoctetes than appears from the *Prologue*.

θηροβολοῦντα: neither θηροβολέω nor θηροβόλος occur elsewhere. But compounds in -βόλος are numerous; cf. in Tragedy ἐλαφαβόλος *Trach*. 213, ἰχθυβόλος Aesch. *Sept*. 132.

στυγερὸν στυγερῶς: 'as a wretch wretchedly'. The schema is very common with κακός . . . κακῶς (or vice versa): *Ai*. 839, 1177, 1391, *O.T*. 248, *infra* 1369. (Bruhn, *Anhang* § 223 II). There is no need to alter into σμυγερὸν σμυγερῶς (Brunck, followed by many editors): στυγερός can very well mean 'wretched' (*Trach*. 1016). See Jebb's and Webster's comments.

πτηνοῖς ἰοῖς: cf. *infra* 711.

167, 8. οὐδέ ... / ... ἐπινωμᾶν: with αὐτῷ (LAΣ) ἐπινωμᾶν is trans. meaning 'bring to'; whether or not παιῶνα κακῶν, then, is literal, 'a healer of ills', or metaphorical, 'a cure' [1]) (no instances of such a use of παιών are known) is a moot point. With αὐτῷ (GRQ) ἐπινωμᾶν has to be taken intransitively (no instances, but προσενώμα *infra* 717 is so taken by many commentators—not by Campbell in his edition nor in *Paralip. Soph*. p. 109—). Broadhead, *Tragica* (1968) pp. 97, 8 regards ἐπινωμᾶν as corrupt and suggests ἐπαμύνειν. (Another way, with αὐτῷ, is to take τίν' as the subject and παιῶνα κακῶν as the object of ἐπινωμᾶν, as proposed by Linwood; παιῶνα κακῶν should then preferably be taken metaphorically).

169-190. The Chorus' expression of sympathy with Philoctetes, in no way conflicting with the rôle they have to play as Neoptolemus' supporters in the fraud, prepares the hearers for the formidable impact of Philoctetes' own appearance in the next scene. Sympathetic entering into another's fate by means of imagination is followed by 'reality' itself.

169-72. μή του κηδομένου βροτῶν: this is not in favour of the metaphorical interpretation of παιῶνα κακῶν (with αὐτῷ); it is perhaps relevant to remember that such a person existed in Euripides' *Philoctetes*.

μηδὲ ξύντροφον ὄμμ' ἔχων: on a par with the preceding genitive absolute, cf. Eur. *Heracl*. 520, 1.

---

[1]) Webster inclines to this interpretation if we read αὐτῷ, but prefers intransitive ἐπινωμᾶν with αὐτῷ.

ξύντροφον ὄμμ᾽: *vitae consortem* (E.) but ὄμμα is suggestive of somebody who would take care of him.

μόνος: the solitariness and isolation of Philoctetes is emphasized throughout the play. What this really means will appear from Philoctetes' own words.

173. νόσον ἀγρίαν: the concept ἄγριος belongs to the motifs connected with Philoctetes: cf. 226, 265, 267, 1321.

174-76. ἀλύει: 'is at a loss', 'perplexed', 'distracted'. In Sophocles the word always has an unfavourable meaning, cf. *infra* 1194, *O.T.* 695, *El.* 135.

ἐπὶ παντί τῳ χρείας ἱσταμένῳ: much more forceful than ἐπὶ πάσῃ χρείᾳ ἱσταμένῃ, stressing each individual case of need as it arises.

ἀντέχει: absolute 'hold out'. This meaning is well-known from Vth and IVth century Attic.

πῶς ποτε πῶς: cf. *infra* 687.

177-79. ὦ παλάμαι θνητῶν: Σ explains by ὦ τέχναι καὶ γνῶμαι: τοῦτο θαυμάζων τὸν Φιλοκτήτην φησὶ πῶς μόνος ὢν ἐξευρίσκει τὰ πρὸς τὴν ζωὴν ἑαυτῷ. παλάμαι 'devices' as in Theogn. I 624 βιότου παλάμαι. (It will not do to see in the words an allusion to the 'tricks' of his enemies by which he has been brought into this situation). Instead of θνητῶν Dindorf adopted Lachmann's θεῶν (mainly for metrical reasons, but –◡◡–◡– 188 can very well respond to –◡◡–––); he was followed by many subsequent edd., but not by von Wilamowitz (*Gr. Vsk.* p. 532), who also accepts Σ's interpretation, or by Pearson or by D.-M.. Though θεῶν yields an easy contrast with the next lines, I prefer to retain the mss reading (I cannot regard θνητῶν as an intrusive gloss on βροτῶν—see Webster—nor see in βροτῶν of the next line an objection against θνητῶν here), but not without misgivings.

οἷς μὴ μέτριος αἰών: οἷς ὁ βίος οὐκ ἔχει τῶν κακῶν μέτρον (Σ). In this context this seems better than 'whose destiny exceeds due measure' (Jebb and others); μέτριος is rightly rendered by 'tolerable' in L.-Sc. s.v. III 2 and we can compare *El.* 140 ἀλλ᾽ ἀπὸ τῶν μετρίων ἐπ᾽ ἀμήχανον ἄλγος or 236 καὶ τί μέτρον κακότατος ἔφυ, Eur. *Alc.* 884 μέτριον ἄχθος, *Troad.* 722 οὐ γὰρ μέτρια πάσχομεν κακά. But the wider explication is possible [1]).

180, 1. πρωτογόνων ... / οἴκων: dependent on οὐδένος· 'no man belonging to', πρωτογόνων being somewhat catachrestically used for εὐγενῶν.

---

[1]) Cf. Eur. *Med.* 125 τῶν γὰρ μετρίων τοὔνομα νικᾷ.

ἴσως: 'I imagine'. No need of any alteration (v. Wilamowitz' conjecture ἴσος in particular is a bad one).

οὐδενὸς ὕστερος: *nulli secundus*.

182-85. ἐν βίῳ: to be connected neither with κεῖται (Campbell, Radermacher), nor with πάντων, but with ἄμμορος (Jebb).

κεῖται: reminiscent of *Il.* II 721 ἐν νήσῳ κεῖτο (Philoctetes) and cp. the instances of 'lie sick, wounded, in misery' listed in L.-Sc. s.v. I 3.

μοῦνος ἀπ' ἄλλων: 'alone, apart from others'. The phrase occurs in *Hymn. Merc.* 193. ἀπό does not differ from epic νόσφι, ἄνευθε.

μέτα: thus correctly v. Wilamowitz (*Gr. Vsk.* p. 532) and Webster because there is period-end after μέτα, as appears from the *brevis in longo*.

185-87. At the end of 187 the reading βαρεῖα is impossible, for there must be period-end after ἔχων ◡– and moreover the first syllable of 188 must be long. The simplest remedy is to read, with Boeckh [1]) and many editors and with the ms S (Turyn = Vat b Campbell, Pearson) βαρεῖ· / ἁ δ'. But there is some awkwardness in connecting βαρεῖ with λιμῷ. If we consider the words from ἔν τ' to the end, we see that this connection is hardly possible: ἔν τ' ὀδύναις ὁμοῦ λιμῷ τ' / οἰκτρὸς / ἀνήκεστα μεριμνήματ' ἔχων / βαρεῖ. We do not expect a special attribute belonging to λιμῷ after all the intervening words. So I think Page's proposal (approved by Webster) [2]) most attractive (Proc. Cambr. Philol. Soc. 6 - 1960 - p. 49): ἀνήκεστ' ἀμερίμνητά τ' ἔχων βάρη; ἀμερίμνητος, it is true, does not occur elsewhere, but we have ἀμέριμνος 'uncared for' at *Ai.* 1207.

188-90. ἁ δ' ἀθυρόστομος / ... / ... †ὑπόκειται†: if ὑπόκειται is retained it will not do to connect πικρᾶς οἰμωγᾶς with τηλεφανὴς (Dübner's and Tournier's idea, repeated by von Wilamowitz in Radermacher's commentary, see J. Jackson, *Marginalia Scaenica*, pp. 206-208: there are no adjectives in -φανής with an active, causal sense), nor with ὑπόκειται. It has to be connected with ἀχὼ and τηλεφανὴς simply means 'coming from afar' (lit. 'appearing far away'). ὑπόκειται, then, has to be taken = ὑπάρχει 'is there'. In the long list of proposed corrections, collected in Jebb's *Appendix*,

---

[1]) *De metris Pindaricis*, p. 323.
[2]) Forestalled by G. Hermann but without the alteration of μεριμνήματ'; Schneidewin proposed βάρεα· ἁ δ'.

Emperius' conjecture πικραῖς / οἰμωγαῖσιν ὑπᾶχεῖ is in my opinion the best, better than πικραῖς οἰμωγαῖς (Brunck, Blaydes) ὑπακούει (Auratus), adopted by Jebb, or πικρᾶς οἰμωγᾶς ὗπο χεῖται (Erfurdt, adopted by Pearson), or πικρὰς οἰμωγὰς ὑποχεῖται (Irigoin, adopted by Dain-Mazon). Better also than Jackson's oversubtle πικρὰς οἰμωγὰς ὑποτάκει.

ἀθυρόστομος: from ἄθυρος 'without a door', hence 'ever-babbling'. Simonides 541. 2 Page has ἄθυρον στόμα, Eur. Or. 903 ἀθυρόγλωσσος. (No connection with ἀθύρω save that in the case of ἀθυρόνομος popular etymology may have played a part, see Chantraine Dict. Étym. s.v. θύρα).

191-200. Again Neoptolemus is supposed to know more about Philoctetes than appears from the Prologue. For nothing has been said there about Χρύση. Further it has to be noted that, without entering into the pity worded by the Chorus, he is endowed with a theological speculation as to the divine intentions bearing on Philoctetes' fate in connection with the fall of Troy, and that he appears to be convinced that not only the bow but Philoctetes and his bow will have to be conveyed to Troy.

It is interesting to read the words spoken by Agamemnon Q.S. IX 491 sqq. on Philoctetes' return to Troy. See F. Vian in his edition III p. 172 sqq., his notes ad Q.S. VII and his Recherches sur les Posthomerica pp. 45, 48.

192. θεῖα: predicative adjunct = θεόθεν πεμφθέντα.

κἀγώ: (not only others but) 'I also' (or: 'even I', notwith-standing my youth). Cf. Ant. 719 (Haemon) γνώμη γὰρ εἴ τις κἀπ' ἐμοῦ νεωτέρου πρόσεστι.

193. καὶ: correlative with καὶ 195.

194. τῆς ὠμόφρονος Χρύσης: 'deriving from the savage-minded Chryse', to be connected with τὰ παθήματα κεῖνα, rather than with ἐπέβη (pace Jebb).

ἐπέβη: 'attack', here with πρός, Ai. 138 cum acc. pers. On Chryse and the snake see Introduction, p. 7 and n. 2.

195. κηδεμόνων: κηδεμών 'one who cares for', cf. Theogn. 360, Ant. 549.

196. οὐκ . . . μελέτη: sc. πονεῖ. Mss have οὐκ ἔσθ' ὅπως οὐ θεῶν του μελέτη and we have to choose between Triclinius' οὐκ ἔστιν ὅπως οὐ θεῶν μελέτη and Porson's οὐκ ἔσθ' ὡς οὐ θεῶν του μελέτη; the latter seems somewhat preferable: the rare οὐκ ἔσθ' ὡς may easily have been ousted by the common οὐκ ἔσθ' ὅπως.

197, 8. τοῦ μὴ ... τόνδ' ... / τεῖναι: on this final use of the genitive of an inf. with the article, rare in poetry, common in Thuc. and other prose-writers, see K.-G. II 40 c.

τεῖναι ... βέλη: cf. P. Oxy. 2805 .6, 7 ο[ὑ] τενεῖς ταχὺν / ἰὸ]ν (Barrett in Carden, *The Papyrus Fragments of Sophocles* (1974), p. 179); *tendere sagittas arcu.*

199. ὅδ': on ὅδ' in the antecedent of a relative clause see K.-G. I 647; a remarkable instance is Eur. *Or.* 896, 7 ὅδε ... / ὅς ἂν ...; it is more emphatic than οὗτος and it points to the time that has come now.

ἐξήκοι: Jebb ably defends the optative with the words 'since a secondary tense is implied in the phrase θεῶν του μελέτη'; this is also Ellendt's vindication against Schaefer's ἐξήκη. For ἐξήκειν used to express the 'running out of time' implying a supposed or predicted fulfilment cf. *Ant.* 896 πρίν μοι μοῖραν ἐξήκειν βίου.

201-03. εὔστομ' ἔχε: the same as εὐστόμως ἔχε, εὐστόμει, εὐφήμει. For εὐστομέω = εὐφημέω cf. Aesch. *Cho.* 997 (but there it does not amount to 'be silent'), Ar. *Nub.* 833 (quite another meaning at *O.C.* 18). Adverbial εὔστομα Hdt. II 171.1 περὶ μέν νυν τούτων εἰδότι μοι ἐπὶ πλέον ὡς ἕκαστα αὐτῶν ἔχει, εὔστομα κείσθω and the same *ib.* 171.2.

παῖ: see 141 with note.

προυφάνη: of sound, cf. 189 τηλεφανής.

κτύπος: cf. 29. In my opinion the word can hardly refer to Philoctetes' cries of pain; primarily it must express the noise of his difficult gait; secondarily the sounds that the act of walking forces him to produce may be implied, whereas these are explicitly stated in φθογγάς ... ἕρποντος and still more clearly in βαρεῖα ... αὐδὰ τρυσάνωρ. So far as I can ascertain κτύπος is never used of the human voice.

φωτός ...<του>: ὡς σύντροφος φωτός <του> τειρομένου. σύντροφος may be regarded as a noun ('companion') or as an adjective construed with the genitive on the analogy of the (possessive) genitive with ἴδιος, οἰκεῖος, κοινός and the like (K.-G. I 432 Anm. 2, 376.4).

<του>: Porson's conjecture is convincing.

205-07. ἐτύμα: 'true' (implying 'typical', Dutch 'echt').

φθογγά: φθογγή, it is true, seems to be exclusively used of the human voice and of birds and animals, but since φθόγγος is also used of other sounds, I should not find it strange if, although the human voice (groaning and moaning included) is primarily meant here, there is also reference to the noises of his stumbling along.

τοu ... / ... ἕρποντος: I do not think τοῦ would be better (Webster, if Porson's <τοu> 202 is accepted).

στίβου (LA) or στίβον (GR): στίβου is defended by Campbell (comm. and *Paralip. Soph.* p. 201), and by Webster as second choice: 'in the constraint of walking'. I think it the more exquisite reading.

207-09. βαρεῖα: 'douloureux' (Mazon).

αὐδὰ τρυσάνωρ: 'the crying of a man in distress', 'qui exprime la misère de l'homme' (Chantraine, *Dict. Ét. s.v.* τρύω). Cf. *fr.* 174 P. δραπέτιν στέγην 'a run-away home'. The idea expressed by τειρομένου is repeated; τρύω and τείρω are cognates.

διάσημα θροεῖ γάρ: Triclinius' reading instead of δ. γὰρ θροεῖ. In this way the text of the antistrophe προβοᾶ γάρ τι δεινόν can be left unaltered. Postponement of γάρ is fairly common in Soph. and γάρ at the end of the sentence does not seem to me an obstacle, if we compare Eur. *I.T.* 1036.

διάσημα: 'clear', 'distinct'; in this meaning without parallels.

210. ἀλλ' ἔχε, τέκνον,: surely the comma, not a full stop after τέκνον is correct, and φροντίδας νέας is the object of ἔχε. Nevertheless it has to be borne in mind that ἀλλ' ἔχε could have been a complete sentence: 'Come, listen'. Then, after Neoptolemus' interruption, follows what he has to give his attention to: 'new thoughts', *i.e.* thoughts pertaining to a new event.

210-14. ὡς: has to be rendered by 'for' (Dutch 'immers').

οὐκ ἔξεδρος, ἀλλ' ἔντοπος: 'not far from home but in the place'. The words express the same as θυραῖος and ἔναυλος; they tally very well with Webster's idea about the locality and the way Philoctetes is supposed to have entered the cave.

οὐ ... ἔχων: cf. γόους ... ἔχειν *Ai.* 319, 20. The contrast with 'bucolic' sweetness is used in order to emphasize the desolateness of Philoctetes' cries.

ἀγροβάτας: L's reading, as *lectio rarior* perhaps to be preferred to ἀγροβότας. Cf. Eur. *Cycl.* 54 and Chantraine, *Études sur le Vocabulaire grec* (1956), p. 39 with n. 1.: 'berger qui vit aux champs' (lit. 'qui foule les champs').

215-18. Instead of continuing with a participle on a par with ἔχων, the sentence is carried on by the finite verb βοᾶ with two dependent participles.

πταίων ὑπ' ἀνάγ/κας: ἀνάγκας sc. στίβου, cf. *supra* στίβου κατ' ἀνάγκαν.

τηλωπὸν: 'heard from afar'; same metaphor as in τηλεφανής. Closer to the literal meaning in *Ai.* 564 κεῖ τὰ νῦν τηλωπὸς οἰχνεῖ (*procul e conspectu*).

ἰω-/ἀν: it is surely correct to relate this to Philoctetes' exclamation when appearing 219: ἰὼ ξένοι. ἰωά (ἰωή), fairly common in epic, is too rare a word elsewhere (ἅπαξ in Tragedy) to have been chosen without a special purpose. This is all the more cogent if, as seems plausible, we interpret ναὸς ἄξενον αὐγάζων ὅρμον as meaning 'seeing the (*i.e.* our) ship at its inhospitable anchorage' (Campbell, Webster, cf. also 302) rather than 'gazing on the haven that hath no ship for guest' (Jebb [1]) and others), that is if we connect ναὸς with ὅρμον and not with ἄξενον [2]).

αὐγάζων: 'discern', rare in Tragedy; αὐγασθεῖσα is transmitted *fr.* 659.6 P. (and see my conjecture in *Skyrioi* P. Oxy. 2077 fr. 2.21, Mnem. 1975, p. 116). Not in Aesch., three or four instances in Eur..

γάρ: <such or such must be the reason for his crying > 'for'.

προβοᾷ: only here and at. *Il.* XII 277. I do not regard the meaning of προ- as absolutely certain; 'he shouts forth' or, perhaps, 'he goes on shouting'? Mark that with either interpretation of ναὸς ... ὅρμον his 'dread' cries are understandable: he may be supposed to lament the inhospitality of the island-coast as well as the presence of a ship that will again frustrate his hope.

First Epeisodion 219-675

First scene, 219-540
  first part 219-390, Philoctetes, Neoptolemus, Chorus.
  choral interlude 391-402
  second part 403-506, Philoctetes, Neoptolemus, (Chorus).
  choral interlude 507-518
  third part 519-541, Philoctetes, Neoptolemus, Chorus.
Second scene 542-627, Emporos, Philoctetes, Neoptolemus (Chorus).
Third scene 628-675, Philoctetes, Neoptolemus (Chorus).

---

[1]) I fail to see how it follows from 467 that the ship was not visible from the cave.

[2]) Thus also Ellendt: 'dicitur navis statio inhospitalis, quod constituta est in loco alias solitario'. See also D. B. Robinson, Cl. Qu. 1969, p. 40.

219. ἰὼ ξένοι: if we follow Webster, Philoctetes shows himself in the entrance of his cave; we have then to assume that between 219 and 230 he descends from the higher level to the level of the stage where Neoptolemus is standing. We may imagine that this happens between 221, 2, 224, 5, 229, 30. If, as seems plausible, we hear a relation between ἰὼ and ἰωάν 216, the import of ἰὼ may be thought to lie between surprise and agonizing invocation. Brief iambic *membra* (or their syncopated forms ◡– –, – ◡ –) are found in Sophocles, introducing or concluding or interrupting passages in trimeters, always with emotional effect. Cf. 730 sqq..

220, 1. ναυτίλῳ πλάτῃ ZoZpAUY [1]), according to Turyn a Byzantine interpolation, the ancient reading being represented by κἀκ ποίας πάτρας LΛGᵞᵖQZgZnTTo (κἀκ ποίας πέτρας GR). But would a Byzantine scholar dare such an interpolation simply because of ποίας πάτρας 222? *Pace* Jebb, who in contradistinction to many others prefers L's reading, I can hardly believe it, and I prefer to admit the wandering eye of a scribe, who anticipated the first words of 222, supplying them with κἀκ (or καὶ). (cf. Dawe, *The Collation ... of Mss of Aesch.*, p. 66 note: 'However that reading—ναυτίλῳ πλάτῃ—arose, it was never the result of capricious Byzantine emendation'). Even if we alter πάτρας 222 into πόλεως (Jebb), the tautology of the two phrases is not to be endured.

ναυτίλῳ πλάτῃ: perhaps amounts to 'by ship', but it seems better to connect the phrase still closer with κατέσχετε: 'have you put in with the oars of your ship'. For the phrase cf. also *fr.* 430 P. ναύκληρον πλάτην.

οὔτ' εὔορμον: see ad 217.

οὔτ' οἰκουμένην: see ad 1-3.

222, 3. ποίας ... ποτε: LGR have the metrically impossible πάτρας ἂν ὑμᾶς ἢ γένους [2]), A and collaterals the not very elegant πάτρας ὑμᾶς ἂν ἢ γένους. So it is perhaps best to accept Triclinius' ποίας πάτρας ἂν ἢ γένους ὑμᾶς ποτε.

ποίας πάτρας ... γένους: genitives of origin to be connected with ὑμᾶς ... εἰπών.

τύχοιμ' ἂν: with its forceful meaning of 'hitting the mark' ('Shall

---

[1]) Turyn, *Manuscript Tradition*, p. 179; the reading 'is an obvious interpolation from Aristophanes' (*Ran.* 1207 = Eur. *fr.* 846.2 N.²). Ed. Fraenkel (*o.l.* p. 48) is of the same opinion.

[2]) Unless we accept the form ὕμας, defended by Wackernagel, *Sprachl. Unters. zu Homer* (1916) p. 6 n. 1. (he compares *Od.* XVI 372).

I be right by naming you . . .', Campbell). Cf. Aesch. *Ag.* 622 (with Fraenkel's note), 1233, *Choeph.* 14 sq., 315 sqq., 418; *O.C.* 1580.

223, 4. σχῆμα . . . Ἑλλάδος / στολῆς: 'the (visible) type of Greek dress'. For the combination with φωνή (here forming, up to a point, a contrast), cf. [Xen.] *Resp. Ath.* II 8 καὶ οἱ μὲν Ἕλληνες ἰδίᾳ μᾶλλον καὶ φωνῇ καὶ διαίτῃ καὶ σχήματι χρῶνται.

προσφιλεστάτης: a strong word expressive of the castaway's feeling of nearness to things Greek despite the bitterness of his experience.

225, 6. καὶ μή . . . / . . . ἀπηγριωμένον: these words make clear the stunning impression made by Philoctetes' appearance on Neoptolemus and the Chorus. In addition to their being struck dumb this must be apparent from their gestures.

μ': the accusative is to be construed with ἐκπλαγῆτ' in the first instance and also with δείσαντες (cf. *El.* 1045, Thuc. III 82.5); ὄκνῳ belongs to the whole sentence.

ἀπηγριωμένον: 'transformé en sauvage' (Mazon).

227-29. If καλούμενον is retained, it either amounts to ὄντα (thus for instance Radermacher) or it has to be regarded as middle: 'Antiquissima vero *ad se advocandi* (well-known from Homer) vi recte explicuit Hermannus' (E.). Hermann is followed by Tournier (even in closely connecting καλούμενον with φωνήσατ' *invocantem alloquimini*) [1]), Masqueray, Dain-Mazon. If Brunck's conjecture κακούμενον is accepted (Campbell, Jebb, Pearson, Webster), I am not inclined to follow Webster in regarding all the adjectives as predicates to be connected with κακούμενον but should prefer to take δύστηνον, μόνον, ἐρῆμον ὧδε κἄφιλον κακούμενον as the three adjuncts of ἄνδρα; the last of the three being the most impressive and to be rendered, for instance, thus: '(a man) thus in his forsakenness and friendlessness wasting away'.

εἴπερ: 'if indeed'.—Even now, after this pathetic appeal, he remains without answer.

230, 1. ἀλλ': 'come now . . .'.

ἐμέ / ὑμῶν ἁμαρτεῖν τοῦτό γ': 'that I am disappointed, in regard to this at least, on your part' (Jebb's excellent interpretative rendering). ἁμαρτάνειν amounts to οὐ τυγχάνειν.

τοῦτό γ': the getting, at least, of an answer.

232, 3. ἀλλ': 'well . . .'.

---

[1]) This would be founded on a reinterpretation of the Homeric formula καί μιν φωνήσας ἔπεα πτερόεντα προσηύδα.

The tense curtness of Neoptolemus' answer, in striking contrast with the other's expansiveness and urgency, is on the one hand expressive of his ἀπορία at the confrontation with the pitiable human being he is about to deceive, and on the other of the restraint arising from his preoccupation with the question how to proceed with the task before him. Not a word of pity, nor of horror at what he sees, not a single expression of simple humanity. His behaviour is like that of a young colonial officer confronted with a potential enemy in the wilderness.—For the wording of 233 cf. Eur. *Heracl.* 134 Ἀργεῖός εἰμι· τοῦτο γὰρ θέλεις μαθεῖν.

234, 5. ὦ φίλτατον φώνημα: cf. 224. It refers both to the fact that the utterance is in Greek and that they are Greeks.

λαβεῖν / πρόσφθεγμα τοιοῦδ' ἀνδρός: 'to be addressed by', cf. 1066, 7.

φεῦ τὸ ... λαβεῖν: on the inf. with the article in emotional exclamations see K.-G. II 46.3.

φεῦ: not of grief or anger [1]), but of astonishment or even joy; see L.-Sc. s.v. II.

καὶ: 'so much as', 'at all'; Denniston *G.P.*² 294 tries to catch the meaning by rendering 'to think that' but that covers only the exclamation as such.

τοιοῦδ' ἀνδρός: according to Campbell only referring to his being a Greek; different Jebb: 'not merely a Greek, but one of such gentle breeding as is announced by the stranger's mien and speech'. This can only be accepted if 'gentle' is to be taken as meaning 'well-born' and if, preferably, 'and speech' is left out.

ἐν χρόνῳ μακρῷ: 'after a long time'. Cf. Eur. *Hel.* 629 ἐν μακρᾷ φλογὶ φαεσφόρῳ, *Phoen.* 305.

236, 7. τίς ... τίς ... χρεία: either τίς belongs to χρεία; it is a misappreciation of Philoctetes' exuberant way of speaking to want to alter the text (τί σ' Wakefield, τίς ὢν ... προσέσχες Cavallin); 'what need ...'.

προσέσχε: causative, lit. 'made you land here'. The normal use of προσέχειν (with ναῦν to be understood, as a rule, cf. κατέχειν) 244.

προσήγαγεν: either 'to Lemnos' and then we have a ὕστερον πρότερον or 'to me' (perhaps better; this is preferred by Jebb. It might contain a dramatic irony, for προσάγω in a military sense is very common for 'bring up' for the attack, 'move on towards' *e.g.* μηχανὰς πόλει Thuc. II 76.4—see L.-Sc. *s.v.* I 6 and for metaphoric uses 7, and cf. 'seemingly intransitive' use *ib.* II).

---

[1]) Schn.-N.-Radermacher's comment is wrong.

τίς ὁρμή: ὁρμή amounts either to 'enterprise' (cf. *El.* 1510 with schol.) or to ἐπιθυμία.

τίς ἀνέμων ὁ φίλτατος: τίς ἄνεμος ὅς τῶν ἀνέμων ὁ (*the*) φίλτατος ἐστίν.

238. γέγωνέ: on γέγωνε imper. of γεγώνω (= γέγωνα) see Groeneboom ad *Prom.* 193.

239, 41. γένος ... τῆς περιρρύτου / Σκύρου: γένος is acc. of respect and the phrase amounts to: 'I am a native of' (Dutch: 'geboortig uit').

αὐδῶμαι δὲ παῖς / 'Αχιλλέως Νεοπτόλεμος: cf. *Trach.* 1106 ὁ τοῦ κατ' ἄστρα Ζηνὸς αὐδηθεὶς γόνος. 'I am called by name Achilles' son Neoptolemus'. I am inclined to leave out the comma after 'Αχιλλέως, cf. 4. Or we may regard the phrase as a condensation of: 'I am Achilles' son, my name is Neoptolemus'. For the metre see note ad 4.

οἶσθα δή: this reading (A) strikes me as more natural than the much better attested οἶσθ' ἤδη.

242-44. ὤ ... ὤ ... / ὤ: the repetition is as suggestive of emotion as the four times repeated τίς 236, 7.

φιλτάτου: cf. 224, 234, 237.

The friendship between Philoctetes and Achilles is one of the fundamental data of Odysseus' μηχάνημα, so much we may easily infer (it wins the trust of Philoctetes in the young man), and also one of the causes of its failing (for Neoptolemus' φύσις, inherited from his father, prevails in the end over his readiness to perpetrate the fraud, confronted as he is with somebody whose standards of conduct are his father's, and so his).

Philoctetes shows himself entirely cognizant of the circumstances of Neoptolemus' birth (and the poet will have assumed the same knowledge in his audience.—Webster reminds us of Euripides' *Scyrians*) [1]). The hearer will remember that Scyros is not far from Philoctetes' country.

ὤ φίλης χθονός: not dependent on παῖ, but genit. of origin referring to τῆς περιρρύτου Σκύρου.

τοῦ: *illius.*

τίνι / στόλῳ: 'on what mission', 'on what errand'. The dative is causal with a final tinge.

προσέσχες: see note ad 236.

πόθεν πλέων: on a par with τίνι στόλῳ.

245. τοι δὴ τανῦν γε: Buttmann's division instead of δῆτα νῦν is

[1]) But Sophocles also wrote a play Σκύριοι, see Introduction p. 7 n. 1.

generally accepted; δῆτα, indeed, in this sentence would be out of place. Webster is right in feeling 'reluctant admission' in the combination τοι δή, comparing *O.T.* 1171 κείνου γέ τοι δὴ παῖς ἐκλήζεθ'. If this is correct the tone of expression belongs to the fraud. γε exclusively emphasizes τανῦν.

246, 7. οὐ γὰρ δὴ ... γ': 'certainly not at any rate', see *G.P.*[2] p. 243. What Philoctetes says is based on his knowledge both that this was not the case and also that it could not have been, in view of Neoptolemus' youth. But we had better not speculate on the interesting question of Neoptolemus' age at the beginning of the Trojan war.

κατ' ἀρχὴν ... στόλου: construe στόλου with ἀρχήν.

248. Here Neoptolemus starts on his course of deceit, in which he will persevere as far as l. 895. In order to convince the other of his total ignorance, he puts to him a question, which will render him aghast. The question is cruel for it cannot but convey to Philoctetes the idea that in the course of years all memory of him, and of his miseries, has become entirely lost.

τοῦδε τοῦ πόνου: πόνος *labor*, amounting to πόνος μάχης, πόλεμος, as often in Homer.

249. μ' ὄντινα εἰσορᾷς: admirable condensation of ὅστις εἰμὶ ἐγὼ ὃν εἰσορᾷς.

γὰρ: 'Sometimes a γάρ question, forming the answer to a preceding question, conveys a surprised recognition of the grounds which occasioned that question' (Denniston, *G.P.*[2] pp. 78, 9; the same holds good for γάρ in the next line).

250. κάτοιδ' ... εἶδον: an instance of the fact that εἶδον and οἶδα were felt as belonging to the same root. For οἶσθα ... κάτοιδα cf. *Ant.* 1063 sqq..

251, 2. οὐδ' ... κλέος: LΛGR have οὐδ' ὄνομ' οὐδὲ τῶν ἐμῶν κακῶν κλέος, A οὔνομ'. Many edd. have corrected L's reading, rejecting A's on the ground that the epic form οὔνομα does not occur elsewhere in Tragedy. But it is the common form in the Herodotus transmission. There are other rare instances of epicisms and ionisms in Sophocles besides the numerous common ones. So I side with the Budé-editors who choose A's reading. Ed. Fraenkel (*o.l.* p. 49) prefers Erfurdt's οὐδ' ὄνομ' ἄρ' οὐδέ.

διωλλύμην: during all these years.

253. ὡς ... ἴσθι: 'I know nothing, be assured of that'. ὡς with participle dependent on verba sentiendi is common, stressing the viewpoint to be taken by the person addressed, if the verb is in the imperative.

254-316. Now Philoctetes embarks on the story of his miseries. This comes in a perfectly natural way after Neoptolemus' declaration of his ignorance. The hearer gets a moving picture of Philoctetes' past and present condition, of the way he has experienced what his comrades have done to him, of his unfair treatment. To Neoptolemus the story offers an easy starting-point for contriving the deceit in accordance with Odysseus' precepts (319-321 ∼ 58 sqq.).

254-56. πικρὸς: 'offensive', *invisus*. In this passive meaning rare. See ad 510.

οἴκαδε / μηδ᾽ Ἑλλάδος γῆς μηδαμοῦ: 'to Malis nor to Greece anywhere' (we may think of continental Greece or of 'Greece' in a still wider sense). The alteration into μηδαμοῖ (Blaydes, Pearson) smoothes the inconcinnity but is nevertheless very dubious: the word does not occur in Tragedy, no more than does οὐδαμοῖ, and adverbs in -ου are often found with verbs of motion. που, if not altered into πω, has to be taken in the sense of 'methinks' (Campbell), μηδαμοῦ που (local) is not Greek. μη- is used because the relative clause implies the idea 'if, so it seems, it is true that'; ('how the gods hate me, if' Webster).

257-59. γελῶσι σῖγ᾽ ἔχοντες: not quite 'laugh in their sleeve', but 'laugh <at my fate> while they keep silent about it'.

τέθηλε: for the metaphoric use cf. *El.* 260. Diseases (corporeal and spiritual, also of the 'body politic') are often designated in terms of 'morbid growth').

ἐπὶ μεῖζον ἔρχεται: 'gets worse', 'grows rampant', *grassatur*, 'festers'. For the phrase (also in its connection with τέθηλε) cf. P. Oxy. 2805.11 (*Niobe*) ἐπὶ μέγα τόδε φλ[ύει κα]κόν (Barrett apud Carden, *The Papyrus Fragments of Sophocles*, pp. 176, 182, 3). *In bonam partem* Eur. *Hec.* 380.

260-70. Follows an enormous, pathos-loaded sentence, introduced by addressing Neoptolemus solemnly as Achilles' son, in which the revelation of Philoctetes' identity, and his undoing by the shameful treatment received at the hands of the Atreidae and Odysseus while suffering from the terrible wound, are packed together.

261-63. ὅδ᾽: implying both 'here' (before you) and 'now' [1]).

---

[1]) In *El.* 1351 ἦ κεῖνος οὗτος ὅν one can be in doubt whether κεῖνος or οὗτος is the subject, here ὅδε is the subject together with ἐγώ.

ὃν κλύεις ... / ... ὄντα: on the construction cf. K.-G. I p. 360 Anm. 8, II pp. 51, 2. On κλύειν = audivisse cf. K.-G. I p. 135.

δεσπότην ὅπλων: cf. L.-Sc. s.v. δεσπότης II 1, s.v. ἄναξ IV.

ὃν (261) ... ὃν (263): the construction is curious because the first ὃν has as its antecedent κεῖνος, the second ὁ ... Φιλοκτήτης which is in apposition to κεῖνος. The effect is that of an adversative asyndeton of the two relative clauses with actually one and the same antecedent and, stylistically, of an anaphoric pattern expressive of emotion. This emotional effect is immediately enhanced by the syntactic enjambment of οἱ / δισσοὶ στρατηγοί. This form of syntactic enjambment (article / noun) is rare, but generally speaking comparable instances abound in Sophocles, often, but by no means always, expressive of emotion [1]).

264-67. οἱ / δισσοὶ ... ἄναξ: here for the first time Philoctetes mentions the culprits responsible for his misery, as often afterwards.

Κεφαλλήνων ἄναξ: in accordance with Il. II 631 sqq..

ἔρριψαν: with emotional force (cf. supra 5 ἐξέθηκ').

ὧδ': sicut videtis (cf. 228) (but local meaning is possible).

ἀγρίᾳ / νόσῳ: here and again in τῆς ἀνδροφθόρου / ... ἐχίδνης the syntactic enjambment has emotional force; the overflow of his feelings is to be perceived in the overflow of the syntactic units in relation to the metre.

ἀγρίᾳ: see note ad 173.

τῆς ἀνδροφθόρου / ... ἐχίδνης: τῆς (Auratus) is better than τῆδ' (Musgrave); τῆσδ' mss is not impossible (the νόσος is felt as the everlasting presence of the ἔχιδνα), but less probable in view of the aorist participle πληγέντ'.

πληγέντ': subordinate to καταφθίνοντα.

ἀγρίῳ χαράγματι: I entirely agree with Webster (contra Campbell and Pearson) in rejecting φοινίῳ (from Eustath. opusc. 324.60): ἀγρίῳ is 'picked up' from 265, as ἐρῆμον 269, and ᾤχοντο 273 from 269. The 'unpleasantness' of the repetition derives from a bias based on a superficial rhetoric rule.

χαράγματι: 'bite', but properly the imprinted mark or brand.

268-70. ξὺν ᾗ: referring to νόσῳ, his only companion.

προθέντες: used of 'exposing' (a child) Hdt. I 112.3, of 'laying out' (a corpse) ib. V. 8, also of 'throwing to' (the dogs) Hom. Il.

---

[1]) This is a subject that ought to be studied within a larger frame of reference.

XXIV 409, Eur. *El.* 896. Eur. *Phoen.* 803 has τὸν θανάτῳ προτεθέντα (Oedipus).

ἐρῆμον: emphasized by its place in verse and sentence.

ἡνίκ' . . . / . . . στόλῳ: see ad 8. One could imagine that we may reconstruct the supposed facts as follows: Before arriving at the coast of Troy the fleet had moored at Chryse; there Philoctetes was bitten by the snake. Once before Troy, Philoctetes' wound prevented the Achaeans from offerings. Therefore a number of ships, with the Atreidae, Odysseus, and Philoctetes aboard, sailed to Chryse in order to placate the goddess. When this did not abate Philoctetes' sufferings, they sailed for Lemnos and left him there. This is no more than a reconstruction. Otherwise we have to suppose that Philoctetes himself never reached Troy and was immediately transported from Chryse (where the fleet of the Achaeans had put in before arriving at the coast of Troy) to Lemnos. The text here is in favour of that interpretation but, on the other hand, how then are we to understand Philoctetes' conversance and familiarity with the heroes before Troy? It is to be noted that, according to Apollod. *epit.* III 26-28, Philoctetes was bitten by a *hydros* that came from the altar of Apollo at Tenedos when the Achaeans were offering to Apollo after the death of Tenes by the hand of Achilles, and that it does not clearly appear from that text whether Philoctetes was directly transported from Tenedos to Lemnos (by Odysseus) or whether the second half of § 27 is to be regarded as an anticipation. It is, however, a fact that nothing in the mythographic tradition nor in Quintus lends any support to a reconstruction as attempted above. So we had better give it up, and assume that according to Sophocles Philoctetes had not arrived before Troy. After all, the stay at Aulis had been long.

ποντίας / Χρύσης: *i.e.* the isle of Chryse.

κατέσχον: 3. pers. plur. (not 1. pers. sing., as D.-M. will have it and mentioned as alternative by Campbell).

ναυβάτῃ στόλῳ: the fleet or part of it.

271-73. ἄσμενοί μ' ὡς εἶδον . . . εὕδοντ' ἐπ' ἀκτῆς,: 'when to their joy they saw me lying asleep on the shore'. ἄσμενοι has to go with εἶδον, μ' in the first instance with εἶδον and of course also with λιπόντες. I prefer to put the comma after ἀκτῆς, not after εὕδοντ' (Webster), and certainly not after πέτρᾳ (or πέτρῳ) (many edd., but not Radermacher), and I assume the Achaeans to have lifted Philoctetes, sleeping, into the cave. I am convinced that the words bear this interpretation (κατὰ τὸ σιωπώμενον) and even that it is necessary: (1) it would be strange,—if the poet's intention was to express that Philoctetes was lying asleep in the cave, or at any rate some distance above the shore—for him to have used the words ἐπ' ἀκτῆς ἐν κατηρεφεῖ πέτρᾳ—in that order—. Nor can ἐπ' ἀκτῆς mean: above (over) the shore. (2) Besides, we should bear in mind that we are meant to understand, in all probability, that the sleep of Philoctetes has come over him after an 'attack' of his disease, just as it does in the play itself. Now there is the problem of ἐκ πολλοῦ σάλου. Webster (as G. Hermann before him) takes the phrase as referring to an attack of his disease; this is possible [1]) though far from certain. I think that we have to understand (with the majority of edd.) 'after a stormy voyage' but that even so an attack, caused by the tossing of the ship, is implied. It would be strange to imagine the crippled Philoctetes clambering up to the cave instead of immediately falling asleep on the shore after the exhausting voyage. If we put the comma after ἀκτῆς (in the caesura), ἐπ' ἀκτῆς alone belongs to εὔδοντ' and ἐν κατηρεφεῖ π. to λιπόντες. The κατηρεφὴς πέτρα(-ος) cannot be other than Philoctetes' present abode, cf. 16 sqq.

πέτρᾳ: πέτρῳ mss; instances of πέτρος 'cave' (or the like) are not found whereas πέτρα is often so used since Homer (so elsewhere in this play). It may be that πέτρος could be used here because of the epithet κατηρεφής. (I note that in L.-Sc. s.v. πέτρα the reading πέτρῳ is rejected, whereas it is accepted s.v. κατηρεφής; the conjecture πέτρᾳ (Blaydes) is adopted by Jebb, Pearson, Webster, and by Campbell in *Paral. Soph.*, not by Radermacher and D.-M.. The mistake, if mistake there is, could easily have arisen from a confusion in minuscule (αι, ωι)) [2]).

273-75. οἷα φωτὶ δυσμόρῳ: as <good enough> for a poor wretch.

προθέντες: here as since Homer of meals 'set before', cf. *Ai.* 1294, *Ant.* 775, slightly zeugmatically with ῥάκη, and so enhancing the sneering bitterness of the tone, also present in βορᾶς (cf. Denniston ad Eur. *El.* 425).

οἷ' αὐτοῖς τύχοι: καταρᾶται Σ, cf. 315. Perhaps better a semicolon before οἷα (D.-M., but without the transposition of 273, 274—Desrousseaux,—which is needless).

---

[1]) Cf. Pl. *Leg.* 923 b ἐν νόσοις ἢ γήρᾳ σαλεύειν, and *O.T.* 23, *El.* 1074.

[2]) It is to be noted that Sophocles and Herodotus use ταφή instead of τάφος *sepulcrum.*

276-78. τέκνον: here, 260, 284, 300, 307, ὦ παῖ 315, signals of the 'illocutionary' character of Philoctetes' rhesis.

ποίαν μ' ἀνάστασιν ... / ... <ἀνα>στῆναι: grammatically comparable is Eur. *Bacch.* 925, ὁ τὴν Ἰνοῦς στάσιν / ... ἑστάναι. ἀνάστασις 'rising up from sleep' is not common, but ἀνίσταμαι is. The anaphora ποίαν ... ποῖ' ... ποῖ' enhances the pathos. (cf. also *El.* 266).

ποῖ' ἐκδακρῦσαι, ποῖ' ἀποιμῶξαι κακά: the most natural interpretation is to take ποῖ' (1) as cognate (internal) acc. = ποῖα δάκρυα and ποῖ' (2) with κακά as acc. of the object 'what woes I lamented'. (But a case can be made either for ποῖα ... κακά as cognate (= κακὰς οἰμωγὰς) with ἀποιμῶξαι or for connecting κακά with the first ποῖ' as well; then we twice have an acc. of the object).

279-82. μὲν ... / ... δ': on the place of μὲν see in general Denniston *G.P.*[2] pp. 372 and 586; Jebb is obviously right in stating that here as in 1136 'the irregular place of μέν is due to the writer having begun as if he intended to repeat the participle of ὁράω'.

ἂς ἔχων ἐναυστόλουν: Here we are informed that Philoctetes' ships were present when the Achaeans sailed for Lemnos (seven ships according to *Il.* II 719). These words, on the whole, corroborate the tradional interpretation of 268-270, as preferred above.

ἔντοπον: more vivid than *e.g.* παρόντα.

οὐχ ὅστις ... οὐδ' ὅστις: again a pathetic anaphora.

ἀρκέσειεν ... / ... συλλάβοιτο: the (present or) aorist opt. with final force in a relative clause (after a secondary tense), though not common in Attic, has to be acknowledged; it is, after all, not a strange phenomenon in view of the many final clauses with an optative. (I for one am even of the opinion that subjunctives with final force in relative clauses are sometimes found, at least in poetry).

ἀρκέσειεν: *auxilio esset* (as often in poetry). Sc. ἐμοί.

νόσου / κάμνοντι συλλάβοιτο: συλλαμβάνομαί τινί τινος = 'assist a person in a thing'. Cf. Eur. *Med.* 946; the active is so used in Ar. *Vesp.* 733.

283, 4. οὐδὲν ... παρόν: οὐδὲν παρὸν πλὴν <τοῦ> ἀνιᾶσθαι.

εὐμάρειαν: 'opportunity', 'provision for'. εὐμαρεῖν does not differ much from εὐπορεῖν, cf. Bacch. I 175 τὸ δὲ πάντων εὐμαρεῖν [1]) οὐδὲν γλυκὺ θνατοῖσιν. The word recurs 704 ὅθεν εὐμάρει' ὑπάρχοι πόρου.

---

1) 'i.e. πάντα πρόχειρα ἔχειν' B. Snell, *a.l.*.

Somewhat different *Trach*. 193 (*facilitas*); εὐμαρής is fairly common in Lyr. and Trag.. On the etymology see Chantraine *Dict. Ét. s.v.* μάρη (probably plur. of μάρος; Eur. *Her*. 18 and 81 has ἐξευμαρίζω).

285-299. Description of Philoctetes' Robinsonesque existence on Lemnos. The poet enters into his imagined condition, and the picture owes something to the vivid curiosity about primitive peoples and the condition of primitive man, the origins of civilization, which we find in the logographi, Herodotus, the early sophists, Aeschylus' *Prometheus*.

285. χρόνος . . . διὰ χρόνου προύβαινέ μοι: since διὰ χρόνου normally means 'after a lapse of time' it seems to me that Jebb is right in interpreting: lapse of time proceeded after lapse of time > 'So time went on for me, season by season'. Not χρόνος = 'time experienced by Philoctetes', διὰ χρόνου 'advancing through χρόνος' = 'general time' (Webster).

285-87. μὲν (285) . . . / καὶ. (κἄδει): *G.P.*² p. 374. καὶ suggests that the need manifested itself continuously with the continuous progress of time (it amounts almost to καὶ ἅμα).

τι: an understatement, amounting to: 'everything the need of which arose time and again' ¹). ('The sense is nearly ἕκαστόν τι', Jebb).

διακονεῖσθαι: (ἔδει με) ἐμαυτῷ ἐξυπηρετεῖσθαι Σ.

287-89. μὲν: probably in correlation with τ' 292 (μέν . . . τε is common, *G.P.*² p. 374 sq.), whereas δὲ continues the description of the food-supply. But μὲν . . . δὲ can also be regarded as marking the two phases of this foraging.

τὰ σύμξορα: 'what was suitable'.

ἐξηύρισκε: 'procured', cf. *Trach*. 25 μή μοι τὸ κάλλος ἄλγος ἐξεύροι ποτέ. We can divide τόξον τόδε 'ξηύρισκε or τόδ' ἐξηύρισκε (L has εὕρισκε). The bow is spoken of as a comrade (mark the effect of αὐτὸς 290).

ὑποπτέρους: implying 'not to be caught without the aid of the bow'.

289-92. πρὸς . . . τοῦθ': to be connected with ἄν . . . εἰλυόμην, pathetically repeated at the end of the sentence, there to be connected with the participle; τάλας with the subject, δύστηνον ²)

---

¹) Cf. the idiomatic Dutch: 'er is altijd *iets*' (lit. there is always something, sc. that has to be done, that has to be provided for).

²) Canter's conjecture has to be accepted, cf. 1377 and Campbell in *Paralip. Soph.*, p. 203.

5

with the object reinforce each other. The repetition of ἄν emphasizes the suggestion of repeated laboriousness.

νευροσπαδὴς ἄτρακτος: ἄτρακτος 'spindle' and 'arrow', of uncertain etymology; 'arrow' Aesch. *fr.* 139 N.² (*Myrmid.*) πληγέντ' ἀτράκτῳ τοξικῷ, *Trach.* 714 τὸν γὰρ βαλόντ' ἄτρακτον (arrow of Heracles that wounded Chiron), [Eur.] *Rhes.* 312 ἀτράκτων τοξόται. Quoting the words of a Laconian πολλοῦ ἂν ἄξιον εἶναι τὸν ἄτρακτον, εἰ τοὺς ἀγαθοὺς διεγίγνωσκε, Thucydides (IV 40.2) feels the need to explain 'λέγων τὸν ὀιστόν'. Still more obscure is the etymology of ἠλακάτη 'distaff' which, according to schol. and Hesych., also means 'arrow' in the compound χρυσηλάκατος. It would seem that ἄτρακτος 'arrow' is a metaphor, perhaps Laconian in origin, perhaps borrowed from choral lyric, (metaphors used to designate weapons borrowed from domestic or handicraft terms are found in every language). See Chantraine *s.vv.* ἄτρακτος and ἠλακάτη. νευροσπαδὴς 'drawn back with the string'. For -σπαδὴς cp. λιθοσπαδὴς *Ant.* 1216, νεοσπαδὴς and νεοσπάς resp. Aesch. *Eum.* 42, *Ant.* 1201, ὀδυνοσπάς 'racked by pain' Aesch. *fr.* 361 N.² (and other compounds in -σπάς in later poetry).

ἄν ... / εἰλυόμην: for the iterative use of past tenses of the indicative with ἄν, rare in Tragedy, see Goodwin, *G.M.T.* §§ 162, 249, Pearson ad Eur. *Phoen.* 401. The instances listed by Bruhn, *Anhang* § 117, are not all of them relevant.

εἰλυόμην: 'I crawled', cf. 702. Fr. 'ramper'.

292-95. καί (292): probably in correlation with καί (293).

πάγου χυθέντος: 'when frost had spread'.

ἐμηχανώμην: every simple thing had to be devised by τὸ μαχανόεν τέχνας.

295-97. ἐκτρίβων: A's reading, preferred by edd.. I am not so sure that ἐκθλίβων LGR has to be rejected; it would mean 'squeezing' a stone by means of stones. I do not quite see how ἐκτρίβων, if the correct reading, came to be altered into ἐκθλίβων; inversely ἐκτρίβων (*s.l.* in L) can easily be regarded as an intrusive gloss. Jebb himself, while rejecting ἐκθλίβων, remarks: 'The use of two stones would suggest concussion rather than friction'. θλίβω and compounds do not occur in Tragedy, but is that a serious objection in a technical description?

ἔφην': the aorist, because the momentary character of the action (although a repeated action) has to be expressed. (Very good note in Campbell).

ἄφαντον φῶς: the light (of the fire) hitherto hidden and invisible [1]). In φῶς the idea of salvation is implied, as is made explicit in the relative clause.

ὃ καὶ σῴζει μ’ ἀεί: 'and that it is which preserves me' (Denniston, G.P.², p. 295).

298, 9. The end of the sentence makes clear that it is not meant as a general truth.

γὰρ οὖν: 'οὖν adds to γάρ the idea of importance or essentiality' (G.P.², p. 446).

πυρὸς μέτα: to be connected in the first instance with the subject. Mazon's rendering is correct: 'Dès que j'ai du feu, le gîte où je loge m'assure le reste — moins la guérison'.

300. φέρ’ . . . μάθῃς: the only instance of the second person of the subjunctive after φέρε in an affirmative exhortation. If not a corruption (but why would anybody have bothered to alter μάθε into μάθῃς) it would seem that the poet used it because he had in mind the normal φέρ’ εἴπω or φράσω or διδάξω (Campbell) rather than the normal prohibitive use (μὴ μάθῃς). Most modern edd. retain μάθῃς (Radermacher does not); it is defended by J. Wackernagel, Vorl. üb. Syntax I p. 234 and by Ed. Fraenkel, o.l. p. 51, rejected by Schw.-Debr. II p. 316.4; accepted with misgivings by Goodwin, G.M.T. § 258, and by K.-G. I 220 Anm. 2.

301-03. ὅποι: antecedent: 'a town', 'a place'.

ἐξεμπολήσει κέρδος: subject <τις>; (such a place that) 'one can drive there a gainful trade' (L.-Sc.). Future indicative in a consecutive-final clause, where Latin uses the subjunctive.

ξενώσεται: future middle with passive meaning.

304-06. Here, as between 300 and 301, between 303 and 304, again between 306 and 307, the asyndeton lends a breathless and at the same time abrupt quality to the style of the passage, suggestive of a *stretto* in the enumeration of his miseries.

ἐνθάδε: = δεῦρο, as often. The line has a sinister (as if referring to a passage to Hades) and scornful ring.

οὖν: 'proceeding to a new point', (G.P.², p. 426), introducing a modification (Campbell).

ἔσχε: κατέσχε.

τάχ’: τάχα in its modal meaning without ἄν is rare in the language of Tragedy. I do not believe that any alteration is called for nor

---

[1]) quaerit pars semina flammae / abstrusa in venis silicis Verg. *Aen.* VI 6, 7.

that the aorist indicative here has a 'timeless' character [1]). What the words convey is this: 'it happened indeed—*as is only natural*—that somebody (Mazon renders: 'tel ou tel') put in against his will'. 'Perhaps' does not fully render the meaning of τάχα in this context; rather does it suggest that such a thing was likely to happen.

τάδε: = τοιάδε, τοιαῦτα, as very often: 'such things as the necessity of putting in at an isle like Lemnos' or 'such things as the unexpectedness of some one's putting in etc.'. (See end of this note). πολλά predicative, amounting to 'often'.

ἐν τῷ μακρῷ ... ἀνθρώπων χρόνῳ: 'in the long course of men's lifetime' (not: 'the time during which men have existed' Campbell). The idea that anything may happen in the long course of time is expressed in similar terms by Hdt. V 9.3 γένοιτο δ' ἂν πᾶν ἐν τῷ μακρῷ χρόνῳ, I 32.2 ἐν γὰρ τῷ μακρῷ χρόνῳ πολλὰ μὲν ἔστι ἰδεῖν τὰ μή τις ἐθέλει, πολλὰ δὲ καὶ παθεῖν [2]), followed by ἐς γὰρ ἑβδομήκοντα ἔτεα οὖρον τῆς ζόης ἀνθρώπῳ προτίθημι. The problem is whether the phrase refers to Philoctetes' own lifetime or to the sailors' (as Jebb and others understand it); in favour of the latter is the plural, of the former vs. 235, and perhaps also *O.C.* 7, 8 στέργειν γὰρ αἱ πάθαι με χὠ χρόνος ξυνὼν / μακρὸς διδάσκει.

307-09. οὗτοι: referring to τις 305. Thus Eur. *Or.* 315 βροτοῖσι refers to the indefinite 2. pers. sing. in 314.

λόγοις / ἐλεοῦσι μέν: contrasting with ἐκεῖνο δ' ... θέλει / σῶσαί μ' ἐς οἴκους 310, 11.

ἐλεοῦσι ... / προσέδοσαν ... / ... θέλει (310): the opposition between present and aorist is to be understood as follows: always when such people have arrived they show pity in words (and it has happened that they gave me '(something)' or 'it happens that they give me etc.') but never is anybody willing etc.. οἰκτίραντες may be rendered by: 'acting in a moment of compassion', 'driven by an impulse of compassion'.

που: 'perhaps', 'haply' (*G.P.*[2], p. 494); this, just as προσ- in προσ-έδοσαν—in addition <to their words of pity>—, has a scornful ring.

τι καὶ βορᾶς μέρος: cf. 274.

τινα στολήν: some piece of raiment.

310-13. ἐκεῖνο δ': emphatically announcing σῶσαί μ' ἐς οἴκους.

θέλει: if we want to supply an infinitive it should be δοῦναι rather than ποιῆσαι.

---

[1]) Though it does not matter much whether we regard it as such or not.
[2]) Cf. J. de Romilly, *Le Temps dans la Tragédie grecque* (1971), p. 87.

βόσκων τὴν ἀδηφάγον νόσον: time and again we meet instances of the personification of the illness (cf. ad 268).

ἀδηφάγον: 'greedy', lit. 'eating one's fill'. Cf. Aesch. *fr.* 253 N.² and Eur. *fr.* 792 N.² φαγέδαινα (both from Ar. *Poet.* 1458 b, 23). Figurative uses in Lys., Com., and probably in Soph. *fr.* 976 (where see Pearson) ἀδηφαγοῦσα.

314-16. ἥ τ' 'Οδυσσέως βία: Webster is probably right in assuming that the phrase suggests Odysseus' *violence*. Cp. Kitto's translation in *Form and Meaning* p. 115. Others refuse to hear more in it than an epicism.

οἷς: mss, if retained αὐτοῖς means 'themselves'. Many edd. adopt Porson's οἵ' (rejected by Ed. Fraenkel *o.l.* p. 51), οἵ' αὐτοῖς τύχοι 275 does not seem sufficient reason for adopting it.

ἀντίποιν' ἐμοῦ: 'retribution for me', 'for my sufferings'. Predicative, if Porson's reading is accepted. — 'By Greek standards, a most reasonable prayer' (Kitto, *o.l. ib.*).

317, 8. The Coryphaeus, referring to 307 sqq., and in keeping with his instructions (τὸ παρὸν θεραπεύειν 149), discharges the two trimeters traditional after a long rhesis; in τοῖς ἀφιγμένοις ἴσα ξένοις ἐποικτίρειν some irony is perhaps to be perceived.

319-21. τοῖσδε μάρτυς ἐν λόγοις: at the utterance of these words <feeling myself> their (or: your) witness > 'in respect of these words a witness'. Perhaps *Ichn.* 34 is comparable.

ἐγὼ δὲ καὐτός: joining up with the Coryphaeus' ἔοικα κἀγώ. ('Et je témoigne à mon tour' Mazon). I do not think that Campbell is right in stating that καί goes with the whole sentence.

συντυχών: the genitive is uncommon, but defensible if we take συν- as meaning 'in like manner as you', with Campbell and *pace* Jebb. Cp. v. Wilamowitz 'denn erfahren hab' auch ich', Mazon 'pour avoir moi-même trouvé des méchants dans les Atrides et le puissant Ulysse'.

βίας: see note ad 314.

322-23. πανωλέθροις: cf. πάνωλει 1357.

παθών: for having *suffered* <injuries from those quarters>. But the sole παθών at the end of the verse is much more effective than a more explicit wording.

324-26. θυμῷ: picks up θυμοῦσθαι.

θυμῷ γένοιτο χεῖρα πληρῶσαί ποτε: thus the codd.. Edd. read θυμὸν ... χειρὶ (Lambinus). Webster remarks: 'the change is perhaps not necessary', translating 'to fill my hand with fury'. But if we retain the transmitted text it seems better to follow Σ and Lloyd-Jones (Cl. Rev. N.S. XIV. 2. (1964), p. 130) interpreting εἴθε γένοιτό μοι ὠργισμένῳ ('my θυμός = 'me in my anger' Lloyd-Jones) ὅρμησις κατ' αὐτῶν καὶ τὴν δύναμιν ἐνδείξασθαι. χεῖρα, then, amounts to δύναμιν [1]), and we are reminded of El. 455 'Ορέστην ἐξ ὑπερτέρας χερὸς ἐχθροῖσιν ... ζῶντ' ἐπεμβῆναι ποδί, El. 1090 ζώης μοι καθύπερθεν χερὶ [καὶ] πλούτῳ τε τῶν ἐχθρῶν, (1092) ὅσον νῦν ὑπὸ χέρα ναίεις. πληρῶσαι: 'fulfil'.

αἱ Μυκῆναι ... ἡ Σπάρτη θ' ... / χἠ Σκῦρος: cf. Andromache addressing Hermione Eur. Andr. 209 sq. σὺ δ' ἦν τι κνισθῇς, ἡ Λάκαινα μὲν πόλις / μέγ' ἐστί, τὴν δὲ Σκῦρον οὐδαμοῦ τίθης. Cf. also the proverbial phrase 'Αρχὴ Σκυρία: παροιμία ἐπὶ τῶν εὐτελῶν καὶ μηδὲν λυσιτελὲς ἐχόντων· παρόσον πετρώδης καὶ λυπρά ἐστιν ἡ Σκῦρος (Zenob. Cent. I 32, Paroem. Gr. I p. 11).

327, 8. εὖ γ': 'bravo', more or less a colloquialism, not else-where—without a verbal form—in Tragedy. Ed. Fraenkel (o.l. p. 52) compares ναίχι O.T. 684.

γάρ: cf. G.P.[2] p. 82.

τίνος ... / ... ἐγκαλῶν ἐλήλυθας: a pregnant construction in which the anger at the (supposed) infliction of injury has taken the place of the injury itself. Webster's paraphrase is correct: 'what, which caused this mighty anger, do you charge them with?' i.e. τί, τοῦ μεγάλου χόλου αἴτιον ὄν, ἐγκαλεῖς;

ὧδε: pace Jebb and others I am inclined to take this with ἐλήλυθας ('hither'), but 'thus' (with the participial clause) is possible; it makes, however, ἐλήλυθας all but redundant (cf. Campbell, who interprets ὧδε in the same way as Jebb).

Pearson's ἐκκαλῶν and Broadhead's ἐγκοτῶν (Tragica, 1968, p. 99) had better be left out of account.

329-31. ἐξερῶ, μόλις δ' ἐρῶ: what the words—in this case, of course, dissembling words—convey belongs to the τόπος that the report of past sufferings or injuries renovates the affliction, of which the oldest example is Od. IX 12 σοὶ δ' ἐμὰ κήδεα θυμὸς ἐπε-τράπετο στονόεντα / εἴρεσθ', ὄφρ' ἔτι μᾶλλον ὀδυρόμενος στεναχίζω, and the most famous 'infandum, regina, iubes renovare dolorem'.

ἐξελωβήθην: only here (Soph. uses or forms many compounds with ἐκ-), but λωβάομαι, λωβητός, λώβη, λωβητήρ belong to the common stock of his vocabulary.

---

[1]) Σ, however, χεῖρα τὴν πρᾶξιν, evidently with the meaning 'exaction of vengeance', 'retribution', cf. Eur. I.A. 272.

μολών: after my arrival in Troy.

ἐπεὶ . . . θανεῖν,: γὰρ introduces the cause for his coming to Troy. For the main sentence the hearer has to wait till 343. His words are interrupted by Philoctetes' οἴμοι on hearing of Achilles' death.

ἔσχε μοῖρ' Ἀχιλλέα θανεῖν: lit. 'fate overtook Achilles to die', i.e. (in Campbell's words) 'the fate of death overtook Achilles'; θανεῖν is epexegetic infinitive.

333. τόδ'· ἦ τέθνηχ' ὁ Πηλέως γόνος;: this (L) is more forceful than τόδ', εἰ τέθνηχ' ὁ Πηλέως γόνος (GRA).

334, 5. In the *Iliad* the dying Hector foretells Achilles his death through the agency of Paris and Apollo (XXII 359 sq.); the prediction of his horse Xanthus: ἀλλὰ σοὶ αὐτῷ / μόρσιμόν ἐστι θεῷ τε καὶ ἀνέρι ἶφι δαμῆναι (XIX 416 sq.) amounts to the same, whereas in Achilles' report of his mother's prophecy we hear λαιψηροῖς ὀλέεσθαι Ἀπόλλωνος βελέεσσιν [1]) (XXI 278). In Proclus' *Chrestomathy* 192 (Severyns) we read: Ἀχιλλεύς . . . ὑπὸ Πάριδος ἀναιρεῖται καὶ Ἀπόλλωνος (according to the *Aethiopis*). Apollo alone is responsible for Achilles' death according to Quintus III 60 sqq.; 'c'est la tradition la plus répandue' (Vian, Quintus t. I p. 91 n 3). Vian refers to Aesch. *fr.* 350 N² (= 284 a M.), Soph. *Phil.* 334 sq., Pind. *Pyth.* III 101, Hor. *Carm.* IV 6 3-8, but none of these really supports this view, nor do I believe that *Il.* XXI 278 is really at variance with the other two Homeric passages. As regards our passage, the wording seems to me unclear on purpose, but not without an allusion to the version in which Paris, it is true, may have shot the arrow, but it was directed by Apollo. Jebb, however, is right in stating that there is, in this case, no difference between ὕπο and ἐκ. Achilles' death, of course, seemed the more glorious the less the rôle of a human agent was explicitly mentioned.

ὕπο: ἀπὸ κοινοῦ. Both ὕπο and ἐκ can be understood both of the direct and the remote agent.

τοξευτός . . . δαμείς: amounting to τοξεύματι δαμείς.

336-38. ἀλλ': 'well'. 'A sympathetic reaction to the previous speaker's words . . .' (*G.P.*² p. 19).

μέν: lends an assentient emphasis to εὐγενής.

ἐλέγχω . . . στένω: deliberative subjunctives (the construction is mistakenly listed among indirect questions following verbs of fearing in *G.M.T.* § 376).

---

[1]) Cp. K. Reinhardt, *Die Ilias und ihr Dichter*, p. 33.

ἐλέγχω: 'question'. Nothing proves more clearly than these words that the poet wishes us to understand that Philoctetes by his isolation has not forgotten that 'lacrimae rerum' exist also in respect of others.

339-40. μὲν: cf. *G.P.*² pp. 380 and 382 (III): contrasted idea expressed, with words denoting opinion, appearance, or probability. Cf., in Soph., with δοκῶ *El.* 547, *Ai.* 56, with εἰκάσαι *O.T.* 82, *O.C.* 1677.

καὶ: 'even', > 'actually'.

τῶν πέλας: 'd'autrui'.

341, 2. τοιγαροῦν: = διὰ ταῦτα καί.

αὖθις πάλιν: this redundant phrase recurs often in Soph., even αὖθις αὖ πάλιν occurs twice (*infra* 952, *O.C.* 1418). πάλιν conveys the notion 'going back to', αὖθις rather that of *iterum*. The phrase refers to 229-331.

τὸ σὸν ... / ... πρᾶγμ', ὅτῳ σ' ἐνύβρισαν: the reading ὅπως ἐνύβρισαν (*fere* GRQ), preferred by Pearson, seems to me *a lectio facilior et deterior* (cf. v. Wilamowitz, D.L.Z. 45 (1924) 2316 = *Kl. Schr.* I p. 462). Radermacher speaks of a 'Breviloquenz' in the wording: = τὸ σὸν φράσον ... μοι (καὶ φράσον τὸ πρᾶγμα, ὅτῳ σ' ἐνύβρισαν); Webster's 'how you fared, namely how (but ὅτῳ would yield 'wherein') they did violence to you' amounts to about the same. It remains to be seen whether the accusative of the person with ἐνυβρίζω is acceptable: Eur. *El.* 68 is no case in point, Kaibel *Epigr. Gr.* 195.1 (= 1370.1 Peek), quoted by Jebb, is very late. Jebb is right in rejecting any influence of ἐν- on the dative ὅτῳ; for the force of ἐν- he refers to ἐγγελᾶν, but ἐγγελᾶν is always construed with the dative [1]). Perhaps we have to assume a mistake deriving from *scriptio plena* σοι ἐνύβρισαν, where σοι 'νύβρισαν or (better [2])) σοὐνύβρισαν ought to be written. Otherwise the accusative is analogous to the acc. with synonymous verbs, or ἐν- merely reinforces the verbum simplex, often construed with the acc. of the person.

343-47. After the interruption 331, 2 Neoptolemus' sentence is continued. But note that in Greek this is brought about more smoothly than would be easy in a modern translation.—On this instance of the periodic style see the relevant remarks in Webster's

---

[1]) Similarly ἐμπαίζω, ἐγχάσκω, ἐγκαλέω.

[2]) Because aphaeresis of ἐν is very rare: cf. Ed. Fraenkel ad Eur. *Phoen.* 21 (*Zu den Phoenissen des Euripides*, Sitzber.-München, 1965, 1, p. 6).

Introduction to Sophocles[1], p. 155. On the 'false tone' of Neoptolemus' report see Reinhardt, *Sophokles*[1], p. 279 n. 181. On Neoptolemus 'odious position as a false friend', Bowra, *Sophoclean Tragedy*[1], p. 274. On the (unanswerable) question whether or not the facts of the story are partly 'true' cp. K. Alt, *Schicksal und* φύσις *im Philoktet des Sophokles* (Hermes 89, 1961, pp. 150, 1 = Wege der Forschung XCV, *Sophokles*, 1967, p. 426).

ἦλθον ... μέτα: 'came to fetch'. μετέρχομαι *arcessitum eo* is Homeric.

ποικιλοστόλῳ: certainly not an *epitheton ornans*; the ship is adorned because of the solemn occasion. It is dubious if in -στόλῳ the 'prow' is meant. See Groeneboom ad Aesch. *Pers.* 408 (στόλος 'equipment'); it seems best to interpret (with Campbell) = σὺν ποικιλίαις ἐσταλμένη 'decked out with ornament'.

δῖος: Homeric, as a title (thus only here in Soph., never in Aesch. or Eur.); a sarcastic tinge on the part of Neoptolemus does not seem impossible [1]).

χὠ τροφεύς ... πατρός: Phoenix, well-known from the *Iliad*, in particular from IX. As far as we know Sophocles does not follow a tradition (for Philostr. *Imag.* 1 can be based on Sophocles).

μάτην: *falso*, cf. *El.* 63, 1298.

γίγνοιτ': strictly oblique, replacing γίγνεται in direct discourse.

τὰ πέργαμα: in Hom. only ἡ πέργαμος, in Soph. only neutr. plur., in Eur. both forms occur. In Aesch. *Prom.* 956 πέργαμα is used of the *arx deorum*. First occurrence of πέργαμα Τροίης in Stesich. 15.3 P. (= 32.3 B.) cf. *infra* 353, 611. Ibycus 1.8 P. has Πέρ]γαμον ... ταλαπείριο[ν

348-51. οὐ πολὺν / χρόνον μ' ἐπέσχον μή με ναυστολεῖν ταχύ: lit. 'they did not cause me to delay a long time from sailing in haste', *i.e.* 'they caused me to sail immediately in haste'. ἐννέποντες is certainly not a participle absolute or pendens, nor is ἐπέσχον 1. p. sing., as is still assumed by Mazon (as earlier by v. Wilamowitz); see Jebb's objections. The comparative lack of clarity in the expression derives from its indirectness. 'The mind is dwelling on a fact or supposition, reverts to what is opposite or correlative, and

---

[1]) Cf. M. Lechner, *De Sophocle poeta* 'Ομηρικωτάτῳ, Progr. Erlangen 1859, p. 24: 'cum quadam ironia', quoted by L. Bergson, *L'épithète ornementale dans Eschyle, Sophocle, et Euripide*, 1956, pp. 55, 6. Bergson contests Lechner's view, wrongly, I think.

is thus led to refine upon the direct and natural mode of expression'
(Campbell, *Essay on Language*, § 42 a, p. 79). Instead of μή, μὴ οὐ
would be normal. For the two με's cf. *O.C.* 1278, 9. ταχύ, more or
less redundant, reinforces the idea expressed by οὐ πολὺν χρόνον.

μάλιστα μὲν: answered by ἔπειτα μέντοι 352.

οὐ γὰρ εἰδόμην: ζῶντα (Σ). This on the assumption that, after the
birth of Neoptolemus, Achilles returned to Phthia never to come
back to Scyros (the same can be deduced from *Il.* XI 765-782 and
XIX 331 sq.).

352, 3. ὁ λόγος καλός: καλὸς is predicative; ὁ λόγος the 'consideration' founded on their promise. The words may be rendered by
'the attractiveness of the consideration'. Since a εἰ clause follows it
seems better to regard αἱρήσοιμ' as the oblique form of αἱρήσω
rather than of αἱρήσεις (as Webster will have it), and λόγος as
Neoptolemus' 'consideration', 'reason' rather than as the others'
'argument', 'promise': the latter would be the case if the text had
ὡς or ὅτι instead of εἰ.

τἀπὶ Τροίᾳ πέργαμ': 'arcem supereminentem Troiam'.
ἰών: 'when I went'.

354-56. ἦν δ' ... / κἀγώ: cf. *O.T.* 717, 8, *G.P.*[2] p. 293 (10).

πικρὸν [1]): because of Achilles' tomb there, or because of the
pretended disappointments which lay in wait for him before Troy.

οὐρίῳ πλάτῃ: condensed for: οὔρῳ καὶ πλάτῃ.

356-58. It is immaterial whether or not we have to suppose that
Neoptolemus' story thus far is 'true'; at any rate the detail of
356-58 belongs to the deceit: the emphasis on Neoptolemus'
likeness to his father is for the purpose of winning Philoctetes'
trust in him. As far as we know this is the first instance of a well-
known τόπος but *fr. ad.* 363 N.[2] οὐ παῖς Ἀχιλλέως, ἀλλ' ἐκεῖνος
αὐτὸς εἶ (from Plut. *de adulat. et amico* c. 5, p. 50 c and *Vit. Alcib.*
c. 23) may come either from Sophocles' *Philoctetes in Troia* (Blaydes) or from his *Scyrii* (Pearson): see Radt *T.G.F.* IV p. 483. A
famous occurrence of the τόπος in Liv. XXI 4.2.

πάλιν: to be connected with ζῶντα.

359. ἔκειτ': 'lay dead'; either sc. buried (thus Jebb, but we

---

[1]) I cannot follow Dawe (*The Collation and Investigation of Manuscripts
of Aechylus*, p. 70), who speaking of *Sept.* 561, where πικροῦ is a *v.l.* for
πυκνοῦ, remarks: 'It is very likely that πικρόν at Soph. *Phil.* 355 owes its
presence to emendation'.

should expect some comment on this precipitate burial) or =
προὔκειτ' (the majority of commentators) — or there is intentional
ambiguity.

360-62. οὐ μακρῷ χρόνῳ: 'before long'. Cf. *O.C.* 1648 χρόνῳ βραχεῖ,
El. 1273 χρόνῳ μακρῷ. In the perspective of historical grammar these
datives are 'comitative'—instrumental rather than locative—temporal, cf. the common χρόνῳ 'after the course of (a long) time', *tandem.*

'Ατρείδας πρὸς φίλους, ὡς εἰκὸς ἦν: condensation of πρὸς 'Ατρείδας
ὡς πρὸς φίλους, ὥσπερ εἰκὸς ἦν αὐτοὺς εἶναι φίλους, as correctly
paraphrased by Campbell. RGQ have the interesting reading
προσφιλῶς 'amicably'. Should we prefer this [1]), then Ατρείδας has
to be construed as the personal object of ἀπήτουν and ὡς εἰκὸς ἦν
has to be regarded as adverbial adjunct with προσφιλῶς ἀπήτουν.
προσφιλῶς occurs at *El.* 442.

ὅσ' ἦν: sc. τοῦ πατρός.

363-66. τλημονέστατον λόγον: τλημονέστατον implies as it were
the indignant exclamation: 'how did they dare'. It amounts to
ἀναιδέστατον.

ἑλέσθαι: with its primary meaning 'take for yourself', 'take with
you'.

κρατύνει: = κρατεῖ, as often, particularly with Sophocles.

We cannot but admire the poet's ingenuity in making use of this
famous motif of the saga (Odysseus' winning of Achilles' armour)
in order to provide Neoptolemus with a plausible motive for his
feigned wrath. We must beware of imagining that in this false story
the circumstance of the armour's not being returned contains an
element of truth, it is rather that the falsehood has all the appearances of truth and so is the more false. On the other hand, the more
plausible the fictitious reason for his wrath, the easier will he find
himself in his rôle. This is true 'psychology' [2]).

367, 8. δακρύσας: ingressive aorist.

ἐξανίσταμαι: 'I rose', 'I started up'.

καταλγήσας: again ingressive (cf. 59), κατ' intensifying (not. 'sc.
κατ' αὐτῶν—Campbell—).

369, 70. ὦ σχέτλι': 'wretch' ('with a notion of contempt' L.-Sc.).
πρὸς τὸν 'Αγαμέμνονα Σ.

---

[1]) It had been conjectured by Bothe and is approved by Lloyd-Jones,
Gnomon 33 (1961), p. 545, and *dubitanter* by Ed. Fraenkel, *o.l.* p. 53.
[2]) Note that according to Proclus 217-218 (*Ilias Parva*) Odysseus delivered
Achilles' arms to Neoptolemus.

'τολμῆσατ': conveying the same idea as τλημονέστατον 363.

ἀντ' ἐμοῦ τινι: 'to some one instead of to me'; comparable with the genitive of comparison = ἤ followed by dative.

πρὶν μαθεῖν ἐμοῦ: lit. 'before having heard from me', sc. my views, my approval. The phrase amounts to 'without consulting me'.

371-73. ὁ δ' . . . 'Οδυσσεύς: 'but he, Odysseus'. A Homeric use; instances in Tragedy are listed in Pearson's note ad Eur. *Phoen.* 1128.

κυρεῖ: historic present. If we follow the mss in reading κύρει, the form without augment may be defended on the ground that it occurs in a narrative comparable to a Messenger's story, where such an epicism is not rare. Besides, Soph. could have used κύρει (present), for he has ἔκυρον (imperfect) *O.C.* 1159.

παρών: 'étant là', *i.e.* at the battle over Achilles' corpse. Cf. Proclus 193-195 Severijns, *Od.* V 309 sq., Ov. *Met.* XIII 284 sq..

374-76. ἤρασσον κακοῖς / τοῖς πᾶσιν: Neoptolemus strictly adheres to the instructions of Odysseus (64, 5). For the use of ἀράσσω cf. *Ai.* 725.

οὐδὲν ἐνδεὲς ποιούμενος: leaving nothing (of all possible abuse) unsaid (lit. 'wanting', 'incomplete').

εἰ ἀφαιρήσοιτό με: in *oratio recta* Neoptolemus must be supposed to have said something like: I shall always call you a villain, a fox etc., (or: κακὸς κακῶς ἀπόλοιο etc.), εἰ ἀφαιρήσῃ με τἀμὰ ὅπλα.

377, 8. ἐνθάδ' ἥκων: *eo adductus* (E.); 'at this pass' (Campbell). *O.T.* 687 and 1158 are not entirely comparable.

δύσοργος: 'quick to anger', used by Teucer speaking of Telamon *Ai.* 1017.

δηχθείς: cf. *Il.* V 493 δάκε δὲ φρένας "Εκτορι μῦθος, *Od.* VIII 185 θυμοδακὴς μῦθος; Theogn. 910 δάκνομαι ψυχήν; *Trach.* 254, *Ant.* 317.

πρὸς ἀξήκουσεν: 'should be joined in the first instance with δηχθείς (—cf. πρὸς ταῦτα—), and resumed with ἠμείψατο' (Campbell). ἐξ-, as so often, has intensifying force. For δηχθεὶς πρὸς cf. *Ai.* 1018 πρὸς οὐδὲν εἰς ἔριν θυμούμενος.

379-81. οὔ σ' ἔδει: ἀπεῖναι. For this Neoptolemus could easily have blamed himself and so the fictitious reproach supposed to come from Odysseus strikes us as natural.

ἐπειδὴ καί: καί 'in addition to everything else' > 'even' > 'actually'. Cf. *Trach.* 321, *O.T.* 412. Denniston, *G.P.*² p. 296 (2) sqq..

θρασυστομῶν: first occurrence Aesch. *Suppl.* 203, θρασύστομος Aesch. *Sept.* 612, *Ag.* 1399.

ταῦτ': τὰ ὅπλα.

382-84. τοιαῦτα . . . κακά: object of ἀκούσας and internal object of ἐξονειδισθείς (the easier since κακά = ὀνείδη). ἐξ- with the same function as in ἐξήκουσεν 378.

τητώμενος: this verb 'be deprived' (of) (only present), not found in Homer, once in Hes., not in Aesch., once in Pind., occurs five times in Soph., six times in Eur.

πρός . . . 'Οδυσσέως: up to the end he sticks to his instructions. κἀκ κακῶν belongs to the traditional disparagement of Odysseus, cf. 417.

385-88. ὡς: amounts to <τοσοῦτον> ὅσον.

τοὺς ἐν τέλει: τοὺς ἄρχοντας. Why this extenuation of Odysseus' culpability? Perhaps in order to make the hearer aware that Neoptolemus himself is wanting to extenuate his own immoral conduct. οἱ δ' ἀκοσμοῦντες / . . . / κακοί certainly can be regarded as a 'self-defence' of Neoptolemus (Webster), or at least as a dramatic irony shedding light on Neoptolemus' real position. M. D. Reeve, G.R.B.S. 14 (1973) 145 sqq. wants to cancel these lines. (See on these lines the very interesting discussion in *Due Seminari Romani di Eduard Fraenkel* pp. 53-55).

ἐστι . . . τῶν ἡγουμένων: 'depends upon the rulers'. πᾶσα and σύμπας function as adverbs: 'entirely', 'wholly'.

οἱ ἀκοσμοῦντες: the offenders, those who encroach upon legal and moral laws and rules.

389, 90. There is all the more reason to read some measure of ambiguity into the four preceding lines because in these two the ambiguities are unmistakable. For Philoctetes λόγος λέλεκται πᾶς means: 'you have the whole story' [1]), for Chorus and audience: 'I have finished the (prescribed) programme'. The double-entendre of the next sentence is not in need of any comment.

391-402. The Chorus θεραπεύει τὸ παρὸν with a vengeance. They invoke the Asiatic mountain mother Cybele, identified with Earth and Rhea. (The Μήτηρ θεῶν had her sanctuary in Athens from at least the beginning of the Vth century, see Nilsson, *G.G.R.* I² p. 726; not long before the *Philoctetes* Euripides composed the remarkable syncretistic choral song *Hel.* 1301 sqq., wherein Eleusinian and Idacan cult-elements are contaminated, cf. Kannicht *a.l.*, pp. 338, 9). They had invoked her also when the Atreidae

---

[1]) Instances of this and related formulae at the end of a speech are listed by Ed. Fraenkel in *Zu den Phoenissen des Euripides*, p. 52, n. 1.

committed their offence against Neoptolemus—thus the Chorus in order to enhance the credibility of Neoptolemus' story. A tremendous goddess is called on as a witness, to further the deceit. Strong emotion is simulated by dochmiacs and syncopated or resolved iambics.

391. παμβῶτι: only here.

394. νέμεις: combines the notions 'inhabit' and 'rule' (Webster).

395. πότνι': reminiscent of her being πότνια θηρῶν.

399. ὅτε: insists on the preceding ὅτε.

παρεδίδοσαν: possibly, by the imperfect, the Chorus is supposed to avoid a downright lie (Webster).

400. ταυροκτόνων λεόντων ἔφεδρε: refers to her sitting on a throne decorated with 'bullslaughtering' lions, or possibly on < a chariot drawn by > lions.

402. σέβας ὑπέρτατον: in apposition to τεύχεα παρεδίδοσαν; the dative goes in the first instance with σέβας ὑπέρτατον (no comma after Λαρτίου). It would be strange if σέβας ὑπέρτατον, whether as an apposition to ἰὼ μάκαιρα or as a second vocative, referred to the goddess (Σ has both interpretations). σέβας can perfectly well mean: object of awe > object of honour, glory.

Λαρτίου: instead of Λαέρτου, again Λαερτίῳ 417 instead of Λαέρτῃ.

403, 4. σύμβολον σαφὲς / λύπης: their λύπη, experienced at the reported treatment, is as it were their *tessera hospitalis*, recognized by Philoctetes. λύπης is defining or explicative genitive.

405, 6. μοι προσᾴδεθ': you are in harmony with me, *i.e.* your story, experience is in harmony with mine, 'chimes in with' (L.-Sc.) mine. He addresses Neoptolemus and the Chorus; the plural cannot refer to 'you and your story' as Webster will have it.

407-09. ἔξοιδα ... / ... πανουργίας: ἔξοιδα γὰρ 'Οδυσσέα ὅτι πάντος ἂν λόγου κακοῦ γλώσσῃ θίγοι καὶ πάσης ἂν πανουργίας <χερσὶ> or <ἔργῳ>. The whole of the wording is somewhat zeugmatic; the idea <χερσὶ> or <ἔργῳ> is implied in πανουργίας. For θίγοι ... πανουργίας cf. Isyll. 5 (Powell) Αἰ δέ τις καλῶς προαχθεὶς θιγγάνοι πονηρίας. The antecedent of ἀφ' ἧς is πανουργίας.

μέλλοι: opt. by *attractio modi*. In the final relative clause the future ind. (ποιήσει) or its near equivalent μέλλει ποιεῖν would be normal (μή, μηδὲν is there the regular negation). (The possibility is not to be excluded that the relative clause in the optative — caused by θίγοι ἄν in the anteceding clause—replaces a relative clause of general or iterative meaning in the subjunctive with ἄν:

this seems to be von Wilamowitz' idea: 'Ich weiss, er ist zu jeder Schlechtigkeit / in Wort und Werk bereit, *wenn* er damit / sein ungerechtes Ziel erreichen kann').

ἐς τέλος: 'in the end'.

410. ἀλλ': ἀλλὰ <θαυμάζω> κτλ.

414. ἀλλ' ἦ: 'In ἀλλ' ἦ, ἀλλά puts an objection in interrogative form, giving lively expression to a feeling of surprise or incredulity' (*G.P.*², p. 27 (4)). Cf. *El.* 879. Ed. Fraenkel (*o.l.* pp. 56, 7) rejects ἀλλ' ἦ (ἀλλ' om. L) and accepts Seyffert's ἦ γάρ.

415. ὡς ... νόει: for the construction see K.-G. II p. 94 Anm. 5, cf. *supra* 253, *infra* 567, *Trach.* 289, *O.T.* 848 ἀλλ' ὡς φανέν γε τοὔπος ὧδ' ἐπίστασο.

416, 17. Odysseus and Diomedes are associates in a number of stories: the killing of Rhesus, the murder of Palamedes, the stealing of the Palladium, the bringing of Philoctetes from Lemnos. For this see 570.

οὑμπολητὸς Σισύφου Λαερτίῳ: Sisyphus' son, bought by Laertes. (He paid for Anticlea, pregnant by Sisyphus). Cf. *infra* 1311, *Ai.* 189, *fr.* 567 P.

418. τούσδε γὰρ μὴ ζῆν ἔδει: just because they *ought* not to be alive, *they* will not die. In the perverse world-order recurrently imagined by Philoctetes' frustrated and wounded mind the bad will thrive.

419, 20. οὐ δῆτ': θανοῦνται (referring to οὐ μὴ θάνωσι = a forceful οὐ θανοῦνται).

θάλλοντές: on the adjectival character of θάλλοντες see P. J. Aerts, *Periphrastica*, thesis Amsterdam 1965, p. 19. θάλλοντές εἰσι is not a mere periphrase of θάλλουσι. Jebb's translation is exact 'they are now prospering full greatly'.

421, 2. τί δ'; ὃς παλαιὸς κἀγαθὸς φίλος τ' ἐμός, Νέστωρ ὁ Πύλιος, ἔστιν; (A's reading): "'And what of him who is an old and good man, and a friend of mine, is he alive?'—seems unobjectionable" (Campbell). τί δ'; ὦ vel ὡ L, τί δ' ὁ GR may both be simple corruptions of an indistinctly written τί δ' ὅς. In that case this is an instance where A had a better source at its disposition (But, of course, A's reading, like the others', may be the product of corruption; many emendations have been proposed, none of them more convincing than A's reading. I had thought of: τί δ'; ('What?') ὁ <δὲ> παλαιὸς κτλ. ('But the good old man etc., is he alive?'). But the two δ's in succession are not attractive. Better is Dawe's χὠ (*Studies* III, p. 125).

422, 3. τά γε/κείνων κάκ': 'at least *their* evil designs'.

ἐξήρυκε: 'used to ward off'. Again a compound with ἐξ- (ἅπαξ).

424, 5. ὅσπερ ἦν γόνος: if we retain this reading we have to regard the words as an emphatic substitute for: his son, and to assume that Neoptolemus thought that perhaps Philoctetes did not know that. Many edd. prefer the conjecture ὃς παρῆν γόνος 'the son who was at his side'; they are possibly right. Ed. Fraenkel (*o.l.* p. 57) would put a *crux*.

426,7. δύ᾽ αὖ τώδ᾽ ἐξέδειξας: Porson's reading, based on Σᵞᵖ. 'Again you pointed out these two . . .', these two referring to Aiax and Antilochus, αὖ *i.e.* after having mentioned Achilles' death. The same three victims *par excellence* of the Trojan war on the Greek side are enumerated by Menelaus in Eur. *Hel.* 847-49. The mss reading δύο αὕτως δείν᾽ ἔλεξας is improbable: 'you spoke in the self-same way terrible things of two (men)'. Campbell's interpretation is too far-fetched: 'In those few words, you have told me a twofold calamity, (affecting those) of whom' (δύο neuter and the words referring to Antilochus and Nestor). But cf. τεθνᾶσ᾽ 429.

οἷν . . . ὀλωλότοιν: 'of whose death'. For the genitive *obiecti* cf. *O.C.* 307, *Ant.* 1182.

428-30. τί . . . δεῖ σκοπεῖν: the nearest parallel seems to me *O.T.* 964 φεῦ φεῦ, τί δῆτ᾽ ἄν, ὦ γύναι, σκοποῖτό τις / τὴν Πυθόμαντιν ἑστίαν, and the implied meaning is: 'Where can we look for a divine power upholding the moral order of the world'.

οἴδε: Achilles, Aiax, Antilochus.

ἔστιν αὖ: put a comma after αὖ (Campbell); αὖ = on the contrary.

κἀνταῦθ᾽ ἵνα: 'and that under such circumstances in which' [1]).

κἀνταῦθ᾽ follows the well-known idiom καὶ ταῦτα. (Cp. v. Wilamowitz' translation: 'und Odysseus lebt, / lebt grade jetzt, wo jeder wünschen muss, / dass er an ihrer Statt im Grabe läge'). I do not believe in a double-entendre hidden in κἀνταῦθ᾽ ('even here', which to Philoctetes means 'alive' but to the audience 'on Lemnos'—Webster; the idea is to be found in older commentaries—Schn.-N.-Raderm. for instance—and has been, rightly, rejected by Jebb).

431, 2. σοφός: 'clever' *i.m.p.*, > 'tricky', 'crafty'.

ἐμποδίζονται: 'are thwarted'. Jebb thinks that the metaphor in παλαιστής is continued ('tripped up') but I cannot find instances of such a use.—The sentence is an unmistakable instance of dramatic

---

[1]) For ἵνα of 'circumstances' see L.-Sc. s.v. A II 1.

irony ('Il ne croyait pas si bien dire'). Cf. Bowra, *Sophoclean Tragedy*[1], p. 269.

433, 4. γὰρ: *G.P.*[2], p. 82 (2) (II).

ἐνταῦθα: 'under these circumstances'. The words amount to: 'was not Patroclus there to afford you his support'.

τὰ φίλτατα: surely implying Achilles' and Patroclus' erotic relation, absent from Homer, but well-known from Aeschylus' *Myrmidons*.

435-37. τεθνηκὼς ἦν: 'was *dead*'.

τοῦτ' ἐκδιδάξω·: this (general) truth; semi-colon after ἐκδιδάξω.

πόλεμος ... / ... ἀεί: Cf. *fr.* 724 P. τοὺς εὐγενεῖς γὰρ κἀγαθούς, ὦ παῖ, φιλεῖ / Ἄρης ἐναίρειν· οἱ δὲ τῇ γλώσσῃ θρασεῖς / φεύγοντες ἄτας ἐκτός εἰσι τῶν κακῶν· Ἄρης γὰρ οὐδὲν τῶν κακῶν λωτίζεται (?), and other parallels quoted by Pearson and Bowra, *Sophoclean Tragedy*[1], p. 277 n. 2.

438, 9. κατ' αὐτὸ τοῦτό γε: 'in connection with this very point' (Campbell).

ἀναξίου ... φωτὸς: for the genitive cf. 426, 7. 'λείπει ἡ περί', the ancients would say.

ἐξερήσομαι: just as in ἐκδιδάξω (436), and very often, the future contains a desiderative element. So Jebb's 'I will ask' is entirely justified.

τί ... κυρεῖ: 'how he fares'. That κυρεῖ is intrans. is confirmed by 444.

441. ποίου ... ἐρεῖς: *i.e.* τίς ἂν εἴη οὗτος περὶ οὗ ἐρεῖς πλὴν 'Οδυσσεύς;

442-44. The portraiture of Thersites closely follows the epic one of *Il.* II.

ὃς οὐκ ἂν εἵλετ' εἰσάπαξ εἰπεῖν, ὅπου / μηδεὶς ἐῴη: ἂν εἵλετ' may be regarded either as a potential of the past or as an iterative, the aorist in itself marking each moment, ἂν the frequency of these moments (see Goodwin, *G.M.T.* § 249 [1])). But the iterative interpretation seems preferable. 'He would never be content with speaking once, where everybody would not allow him to speak <at all>'. This appears to have been the interpretation on which the not very clear scholion is based: ἀντὶ ἃ οὐκ ἤθελέν τις ἅπαξ ἀκοῦσαι, ταῦτα πολλάκις ἔλεγεν. Difference between εἰσάπαξ and ἅπαξ is, here at least, hardly perceptible. For Θερσίτης τις cf. Eur. *I.T.* 531 Κάλχας τις.

---

[1]) Schw.-Debr. II 350 δ).

445. τοῦτο παρὰ ἱστορίαν Σ. Follows the story of Thersites' death by the hand of Achilles because he had mutilated the corpse of Penthesileia. I am inclined to believe that Sophocles makes Neoptolemus tell this half-lie because it tallies with the survival of the worst, without himself wanting to go against this epic tradition. Cp. v. Wilamowitz' intelligent remark, *Einleitung Übersetzung* p. 20 n. 1.

446, 7. ἔμελλ': 'he would'. For Plato's objections against such views cf. *Leg.* 899 d sqq..

οὐδέν πω κακόν: Sud. *s.v.* παλιντριβῆ, seems better than οὐδέπω κακόν mss. The abstract wording οὐδέν . . . κακόν instead of οὐδείς . . . κακός lends a contemptuous ring to the phrase.

περιστέλλουσιν: 'wrap up', 'protect'.

448-50. παλιντριβῆ: τετριμμένα τοῖς κακοῖς (Σ), 'rubbed again and again' > 'knavish', cf. τρῖμμα 'a practised knave' (L.-Sc.) Ar. *Nub.* 260, *Av.* 431, τρίβων 'old hand', 'rogue' (L.-Sc.) Ar. *Nub.* 869 περίτριμμα δικῶν 'pettifogger' Ar. *Nub.* 447.

ἀναστρέφοντες: 'turn back', surely referring to Sisyphus.

ἀποστέλλουσ': εἰς "Αιδην, *ad inferos detrudunt* (E.).

451, 2. ποῦ χρὴ τίθεσθαι ταῦτα: if we have pondered Ellendt's rendering of τίθεσθαι in this sentence: (item significat) *cogitantem et iudicantem aliquo quasi loco censere et numerare*, we shall accept without more ado Campbell's paraphrase: 'What is one to make of these things?' 'What place assign them in thought?'

ποῦ δ' αἰνεῖν: in close connection with the preceding words: 'what place can we find for their approval?' > 'How can we approve them?'

τὰ θεῖ' ἐπαινῶν[1].: 'wanting to praise the divine government'. ἐπαινῶν is surely conative. The idea 'as a pious man should' is implied. Jens-Uwe Schmidt, *Sophokles. Philoktet* (1973) p. 96, is certainly right in speaking of a 'Notruf der Verzweiflung', and it is more interesting to remark how natural these exclamations are represented as occurring to a man in such straits of fate as depicted, than to speculate on the unanswerable question how much in these lines is due to the poet's own experience (cf. Kitto, *Form and Meaning*, p. 116, Kirkwood, *Sophoclean Drama*, pp. 265, 270), nor should we speculate too much on Sophocles' 'theology' in connection with these lines.

---

[1] ἐρευνῶν Schneidewin; retained by Radermacher. This does away with the difficulty of the text, but also with the meaningful paradox.

453-55. μέν: *solitarium* and emphatic.

γένεθλον: a fairly solemn word for *proles*.

Οἰταίου: reminds the hearer of the connection of Poeas and Philoctetes with Heracles and his death. The Oeta is the mountain of Malis. Cf. 479, 490, 664, 729, 1430.

τό τ' Ἴλιον / καὶ τοὺς Ἀτρείδας φυλάξομαι: 'I will beware of Ilium and Atreus' sons'.

τηλόθεν ... / ... εἰσορῶν: lit. 'by looking at them from afar', *i.e.* 'not heeding them'. Cf. on the one hand *O.T.* 794-6 τὴν Κορινθίαν / ἄστροις τὸ λοιπὸν ἐκμετρούμενος χθόνα / ἔφευγον, on the other Eur. *Hipp.* 102 πρόσωθεν αὐτὴν ἁγνὸς ὢν ἀσπάζομαι.

456-58. ὅπου: *i.e.* παρ' οἷς, cf. Pearson ad *fr.* 191 P.; θ' is probably paratactic conjunction, not correlative with the two καί's in the next line. Perhaps G. Hermann's δ' is to be preferred.

δεινός: mss 'the clever man', referring to the type of Odysseus, is, in my opinion, surely right [1]); most edd. prefer Brunck's δειλός. In *Ant.* 326 τὰ δεινὰ κέρδη seems also better than τὰ δειλὰ κέρδη (Kuiper retains δεινὸς and δεινὰ in both places). For 'absolute' κρατεῖ cf. Denniston ad Eur. *El.* 537.

459-60. This feigned nostalgia is well-calculated to exasperate Philoctetes' all too real and vehement desire for going home.

461-63. μεταστήσειαν: 'set free of'. Cf. Eur. *I.T.* 991-93 θέλω δ' ἅπερ σύ, σέ τε μεταστῆσαι πόνων / νοσοῦντά τ' οἶκον ... / ὀρθῶσαι.

ὡς αὐτὸς θέλεις: either referring to the fact or to the manner of being cured.

464, 5. πλοῦν ἡμῖν εἴκῃ: διδῶ, συγχωρήσῃ Σ. Meaning and construction seem certain, but no certain parallels are available.

466, 7. γάρ: 'Yes, for ...'.

μὴ 'ξ ἀπόπτου μᾶλλον ἢ 'γγύθεν: *i.e.* ἐγγύθεν μᾶλλον ἢ 'ξ ἀπόπτου. ἐξ ἀπόπτου amounts to 'at a distance'. The ship should not be ἄποπτος 'seen from a distance'.

468-506. Philoctetes' second long rhesis, containing his urgent appeal to be taken home. Since, as appears from 470 and still more clearly from 485, his conduct is in all respects formally that of a suppliant, we have to assume that, at least henceforth, he is on the same level as Neoptolemus, as is rightly remarked by Webster. But it is much more natural to imagine this to be the case from 229, 30 onwards; see n. ad 219.

---

[1]) Cf. E. M. Craik, *A Note on Sophokles' Philoktetes 456-458 and Antigone 323-326*, Mnemos. 1978, pp. 196, 7. I agree with her arguments.

468-70. σε ... / ... / ἱκέτης ἱκνοῦμαι: σε ἱκετεύω.

πρός τ' εἴ τί σοι ... προσφιλές: cf. *O.C.* 250.

470-72. μόνον, / ἐρῆμον: asyndeton, suggestive of urgency.

473, 4. ἐν παρέργῳ θοῦ με: 'regard me as a secondary task' (Jebb). Σ took θοῦ in a literal sense: οἷον οὐκ ἐν τετιμημένῳ μέρει τῆς νεὼς and so Campbell: 'stow me away as a supernumerary' (also in *Paralip. Soph.* p. 207). I cannot believe this; if Neoptolemus' primary ἔργον is his sailing home, taking Philoctetes on board is to be his πάρεργον (thus, in substance, Webster). There is dramatic irony in the words; for, if anything, Philoctetes is Neoptolemus' ἔργον. For ἐν παρέργῳ cf. Eur. *I.T.* 514, there with a genitive, cf. Eur. *Hel.* 925 πάρεργον δοῦσα τοῦτο τῆς τύχης; here τοῦ πλοῦ may be mentally suppled.

δυσχέρεια: 'disgust caused by a thing' (L.-Sc.). Cf. *infra* 900, 902.

φορήματος: this, referring to Philoctetes himself, is well rendered by 'cargo' by A. A. Long, *Language and Thought in Sophocles* (1968), p. 35 n. 29, though 'act of transporting' may also be the primary meaning (*id., ib.*).

ἔξοιδα: Kirkwood (*Sophoclean Drama*, p. 243 n. 23) draws a good parallel between 79-85 and 473-481. 'The phraseology of the two passages is so similar that the playwright seems to have intended to stress the contrast by verbal reminiscence'.

475, 6. τοι: marking a general maxim. It states the motive for acting as implied in ὅμως δὲ τλῆθι and its applicability in this case is made explicit in the next two lines.

476-78. ἐκλιπόντι τοῦτ': 'if you leave this out', 'if you omit to do it'. τοῦτ' refers to the deed of taking Philoctetes aboard, not to the general maxim.

οὐ καλόν: a litotes for αἰσχρόν. Cf. *Trach.* 453, 4 ὡς ἐλευθέρῳ/ ψευδεῖ καλεῖσθαι κὴρ πρόσεστιν οὐ καλή.

πλεῖστον εὐκλείας γέρας: = πλείστης εὐκλείας γέρας.

480-83. ἡμέρας ... μιᾶς: even in this respect the similarity to 79-85 (83!) is striking.

ὅπη θέλεις: ἐμβαλέσθαι. The alteration into ὅποι is not necessary, the less so if we regard ὅπη as an ionism.

ἄγων: either circumstantial ('take and thrust me' J.) or conditional: 'if you will but take me' (Campbell). In 488 ἔκσωσόν μ' ἄγων seems to amount to ἐκσῴζων μ' ἄγαγε.

ἀντλίαν: 'hold' (where cargo is stowed) [1].

---

[1] But properly speaking the place where the bilge-water is to be expected.

ἐς πρύμνην: since πρύμναν is metrically and πρύμναν θ᾽ syntactically (or stylistically) impossible, πρύμνην (Elmsley; the epic—Ionic ¹)—form) is indicated. Whoever wrote πρύμναν did so because he knew it was the normal Attic form. See n. ad 1451.

ὅπου: GR, but ὅποι LA is defensible (= ἐκεῖσε ὅπου), cf. Eur. *Hel.* 1607 ²).

484, 5. προσπίτνω σε γόνασι: Jebb and others interpret: 'I supplicate thee on my knees'. In view of the most characteristic feature of ἱκεσία, viz. the grasping of the other's knees (γουνόομαι, γουνάζομαι) Mazon's 'je tombe à tes genoux' (cp. v. Wilamowitz' 'sieh mich lahm, gebrechlich zu deinen Füssen liegen') is better; σε is, then, the object of the phrase προσπίτνω ... γόνασι = γουνάζομαι. προσπίτνω (προσπίπτω) can very well be construed with a dative.

ἀκράτωρ: κρατεῖν ἐμαυτοῦ οὐ δυνάμενος, *i.e.* having no control of my limbs. χωλός can be regarded as an explicative asyndeton.

486-89. ἐρῆμον ... χωρὶς ἀνθρώπων στίβου: cf. *Ant.* 773, where we have perhaps to read ἄγων ἐρῆμος (Antigone) ἔνθ᾽ ἂν ᾖ βροτῶν στίβου.

οἶκον τὸν σόν: Scyros.

Χαλκώδοντος: father of Elephenor, who led the Abantes of Euboea to Troy (*Il.* II 541, IV 464), of the same generation as Poeas, Peleus etc., and associate of Heracles against the Eleans (Paus. VIII 15.6).

490-92. It is better to place κἀκεῖθεν ... ἔσται between semicola, indicating that the words form a parenthesis, for ὡς δείξῃς can hardly depend on these words; thus the Budé editors. This parenthesis, of course, is more vivid than a relative clause introduced by ὅθεν περ (cf. *O.C.* 1226) would be.

Τραχινίαν τε δεράδα καὶ: Toup's correction of δειράδα. I cannot subscribe to Jebb's verdict ('bold'). Since δειρή, Attic δέρη can be used in a geographical sense = δειράς ('haute vallée', cf. Chantraine, *Dict. Ét. s.v.* δειράς) it would not be strange to find a form δεράς being used (or coined for the occasion). Its rareness would have caused the alteration despite the metre. I think Toup's conjecture much more convincing than either δειράδ᾽ ἠδ᾽ ἐς (Jebb) or δειράδ᾽

Cf. v. Leeuwen ad Ar. *Eq.* 434, quoting Cic. *ad Fam.* IX 15. 3. olim sedebamus in puppi et clavum tenebamus, nunc autem vix est in sentina locus.
¹) Normal in Hdt..
²) But see the doubts expressed by Kannicht *a.l.*.

ἢ τὸν (Pierson, Porson, Pearson, alii). Thus also Ed. Fraenkel (*o.l.* p. 59).

492-94. δείξῃς: cf. note ad *Ai*. 569.

παλαιὸν ἐξότου: this, Triclinius' reading, is the easiest remedy for the difficult παλαιὰν or πάλαι ἂν or παλαί' ἂν. παλαιὸν ἐξότου = παλαιός ἐστι χρόνος ἐξ ὅτου, cf. *Ai*. 600. It may be connected with δέδοικα or with μή μοι βεβήκῃ (= οἴχηται). I have thought of conjecturing πάλαι κἂν 'even perhaps long ago'; for fossilized κἂν cf. *El.* 1483 ἀλλά μοι πάρες κἂν σμικρὸν εἰπεῖν. If this is accepted, it has, of course, to be taken with μή μοι βεβήκῃ (or, perhaps, with the majority of the mss βεβήκοι), just as if we were to read παλαί' ἂν, as is done by Campbell [1]) but deemed impossible by Jebb.

494-96. τοῖς ἱγμένοις / ἔστελλον αὐτὸν: τοῖς ἱγμένοις instrumental dative of persons, just as at *Ant*. 164, 5 ὑμᾶς δ' ἐγὼ πομποῖσιν ἐκ πάντων δίχα / ἔστειλ' ἱκέσθαι. For στέλλειν amounting to μεταπέμπεσθαι or κελεύειν ('to urge') see also *supra* 60.

αὐτόστολον: K. A. Worp (*Miscellanea Tragica*, 1976, pp. 501-504) convincingly argues for taking αὐτόστολον as meaning 'a ship he would be able to sail without the assistance of a pilot / skipper'; he refers to P. Jand. inv. 616 + inv. 245 (Z.P.E. xx, 1976, pp. 157-165) ll. 6-9, an inscription from Myra *OGIS* II 572, ll. 41, 2, Mus. 255, *A.P.* VII 585. Thus the somewhat strained explications of αὐτόστολον and πέμψαντα can be dropped. Dawe (*Studies* III p. 125) conjectures αὖθις στόλον.

δόμους: Wunder, followed by many editors. (δόμοις mss, taken as a dative proper by Hermann: domui suae me sospitem reddere).

497-99. τὰ τῶν διακόνων: I do not believe that this = οἱ διάκονοι, nor that there is a sort of anacoluthon. We have to put a comma before τὰ and regard the phrase as a preceding apposition to … ποιούμενοι … ἤπειγον στόλον. Jebb's objection viz. that in such cases Greek has τὸ, not τὰ, is not valid for τὰ refers to both ἐν σμικρῷ μέρει ποιούμενοι and τὸν … στόλον ('they did the things that διάκονοι tend to do'). διάκονος here means 'messenger'.

ὡς εἰκός, οἶμαι,: οἶμαι enhances the bitterness of the tone. It has to be taken with ὡς εἰκός, not with the main sentence as Jebb seems to do.

τοὐμὸν … μέρος: LGR, this seems better than μέρει. The phrase amounts to: 'me and my lot', 'my fate'. For ἐν σμικρῷ … / ποιού-

---

[1]) He reads βεβήκῃ, and thinks that βεβήκοι is due to the preceding ἂν, 'which is thus shown to belong to an early tradition' (*Paral. Soph.*, p. 208).

μενοι Jebb compares Hdt. III 154.2 ἐν ἐλαφρῷ ποιησάμενος; other instances in L.-Sc. s.v. ποιέω V (but they read here ἐν σμικρῷ μέρει, as is done by Pearson and Radermacher; it is in Sud. s.v. διάκονος and A has μέρεις).

500-04. In Neoptolemus he sees a man who may be his πομπός and ἄγγελος in one, his πομπὸς αὐτάγγελος (or his ἄγγελος *αὐτόπομπος).

εἰσορῶν: for εἰσορῶ of mental vision cf. *Trach.* 1112, *El.* 584, 611, 997, Gow ad [Theocr.] 8.11.

σῶσον: picks up ἐκσῶσαι 496.

ὡς πάντα δεινά, κἀπικινδύνως βροτοῖς / κεῖται: perhaps better to construe δεινά sc. ἐστιν, not regarding δεινά as being on a par with ἐπικινδύνως both to be taken with κεῖται, as Jebb will have it. Then παθεῖν ... θάτερα is the subject of ἐπικινδύνως κεῖται. In these words the main emphasis lies on the second member, whereas the first has a concessive function, as is well noted by Webster. ἐπικίνδυνος properly means 'subject to risk' so that ἐπικινδύνως βροτοῖς κεῖται amounts to 'risk is inherent in the human condition'. The 'Fazit' of this wisdom is drawn in the last sentence (a sentence in the pregnant meaning) of the rhesis. Cf. E. Wolf, *Sentenz und Reflexion bei Sophokles* (1910), p. 46.

θάτερα: a well-known euphemism for τὰ κακά, τὰ φαῦλα.

504-06. ὁρᾶν: φοβεῖσθαι καὶ εὐλαβεῖσθαι. Campbell translates 'to be ware of'.

τὸν βίον: proleptic subject of λάθῃ.

507-18. Again, the Chorus θεραπεύει τὸ παρόν. It is immaterial whether the Chorus really feel pity, rather is this an altogether false question. The appeal to Neoptolemus' pity belongs to the deceit. As Karin Alt, *Schicksal und φύσις im Philoktet des Sophokles* (Hermes, 89, 1961 p. 153 = Wege der Forschung 95, 1967, *Sophokles*, pp. 429 sq.) puts it: 'Der Aufruf zum Mitleid bedeutet zugleich „Erhöre seine Bitte, nimm ihn mit" und „Bleibe ungerührt"; „Habe Mitleid" heisst in Wahrheit „Verschliesse dich dem Mitleid" — und doch scheint es für die Tragödie wichtig, dass hier vom Mitleid gesprochen wird'. Pity will arise in the breast of the sensitive hearer; later on in Neoptolemus' heart.

508, 9. δυσοίστων πόνων / ἄθλ': 'agonies consisting in toils hard to bear', cf. *Trach.* 506 ἄεθλ' ἀγώνων (in a literally agonistic context).

ὅσσα: Porson's emendation οἷα, accepted by many edd., does not seem to me really better; the comparative rarity of similar forms in Tragedy does not seem sufficient reason for alteration. See Collard ad Eur. *Suppl.* 58. For the accus. of a neuter plural pronoun with τύχοι cf. *O.C.* 1106 αἰτεῖς ἃ τεύξῃ, Eur. *Phoen.* 1666 οὐ γὰρ ἂν τύχοις τάδε.

510. πικρούς: '*invisos*', cf. 254, *Ai.* 1359 ἦ κάρτα πολλοὶ νῦν φίλοι καὖθις πικροί.

511-15. τὸ κείνων / κακὸν τῷδε κέρδος / μετατιθέμενος: the interpretation such as found *e.g.* in Campbell's commentary ('Converting their evil deed into a benefit for him') is not unsatisfactory provided we take τὸ κείνων κακὸν as referring to their pretended iniquity against Neoptolemus; κείνων is subjective genitive and μετατιθέμενος 'probably a book-making metaphor' (Webster): their debit in Neoptolemus' accounts is as it were to be converted into Philoctetes' credit. Σ's interpretation τὸ ἐκείνους λυποῦν τούτῳ κέρδος καὶ ὠφελίαν μεταποιῶν (κείνων objective genitive) seems a mistake. (The second scholion is perhaps a conflation of two interpretations).

515-18. ἔνθαπερ ἐπιμέμονεν: emphatically placed before πορεύσαιμ' and specified by ἐς δόμους; it is perhaps better to leave out the comma after ἐπιμέμονεν and put a comma after ἄν. ἐπιμέμονεν 'eagerly desires' is (for us) ἅπαξ εἰρημένον, forms of μέμονα do not occur in Soph..

πορεύσαιμ' ἄν: of course a courteous way of exhorting.

τὰν ... ἐκφυγών: because Philoctetes is a suppliant.

τὰν θεῶν: codd. have τὰν ἐκ θεῶν; the alteration is perhaps needless, for ◡ – – – ⌐ (θεῶν with synizesis) can answer ◡ – – ◡ – (reading Λαρτίου). (But ἐκ might have been an optical anticipation of ἐκ-, and ἐκ θεῶν ... ἐκφυγών seems somewhat cacophonic (admittedly an untrustworthy argument)).

519-21. τις εὐχερής: lit. 'as someone tolerant' (easy-going, compliant, implying some measure of rashness). For τις added to a predicative word Campbell compares *O.T.* 618, 9 ὅταν ταχύς τις οὑπιβουλεύων ... / χωρῇ. With παρῇς the words are well rendered by Jebb 'lest, as a spectator, thou are pliant'. Contextually there is an antithesis between παρῇς and ξυνουσία.

πλησθῇς τῆς νόσου ξυνουσίᾳ: the *genitivus rei* is normal with πίμπλημι, certainly in Sophocles, and when πίμπλαμαι means: 'be sated with'. So we had better take ξυνουσίᾳ as an instrumental dative functioning as a present participle 'through being with it'. For ξυνουσία cf. *O.C.* 63, where, as here, the ambiguity of the notion ξυνουσία is to be felt. (Of course, the alternative construction <τῇ> τῆς νόσου ξυνουσίᾳ is not to be excluded).

αὐτὸς τοῖς λόγοις τούτοις: 'identical with those words', *i.e.* 'standing by your promises'. Cf. *O.T.* 557; *Thuc.* II 61.2, III 38.1.

522, 3. τοῦτ᾽: emphatically placed first in the sentence belongs to τοὔνειδος.

524, 5. ἀλλ᾽ ... μέντοι: assentient, *G.P.*², p. 411 (2).

αἰσχρὰ: not different from αἰσχρόν, as often.

σοῦ ... | ... πονεῖν: construe σοῦ γέ μ᾽ ἐνδεέστερον <ὄντα> φανῆναι ξένῳ πονεῖν πρὸς τὸ καίριον. πονεῖν depends on ἐνδεέστερον, ξένῳ goes with πονεῖν or both with ἐνδεέστερον and πονεῖν. ξένῳ either = τῷ ξένῳ, or to a ξένος as Philoctetes is. πρὸς τὸ καίριον: *ad id quod opportunum est.*

526, 7. ἀλλ᾽ ... πλέωμεν: here ἀλλ᾽ with its normal use in an exhortation (= ἄγε δή, 'allons').

χἠ ναῦς γὰρ: καὶ ... γὰρ 'for in fact', *G.P.*², p. 111: not correlative with the following καὶ in κοὐκ (*contra* Campbell).

ἄξει κοὐκ ἀπαρνηθήσεται: ἀπαρνηθήσεται is to be regarded as deponent form instead of the normal (ἀπ)αρνήσεται; the ship is personified just like the Argo which is said to have refused to carry Heracles (Arist. *Polit.* III 13.16, 1284 a 24, 5). 'Das Schiff wird sich nicht weigern, ihn zu tragen' (v. Wil.). On the polarity of expression see Kirkwood *Soph. Dr.* p. 218.

528, 9. μόνον: cp. Latin *modo*; similarly *Trach.* 596 μόνον παρ᾽ ὑμῶν εὖ στεγοίμεθα.

ἔκ τε τῆσδε γῆς: τε Gernhard and the majority of modern editors since Dindorf. Mss are divided between ἐκ δὲ LAGR, and ἔκ γε AL^sl. ἔκ γε deserves, in my opinion more consideration than it has received; it would be a case lying between the emphatic and the limitative use of γε ('at least', 'in any case'). ἔκ γε τῆσδε γῆς occurs at *Trach.* 801.

βουλοίμεθα: optat. by *attractio modi*. 'Dass er—Neoptolemos—gewonnen zu haben glaubt, lässt er den Zuschauer deutlich erkennen' (v. Wil. *Einleitung* Übersetzung p. 21). Cf. Reinhardt's sensitive comment on this ambiguity (*Sophokles*¹, p. 186), Kirkwood *o.l.* pp. 259 sq..

530-32. ὦ ... | ... ναῦται: Against Webster's suggestion that all three could be nominatives we may allege the second person plural, referring it is true to φίλοι δὲ ναῦται in the first instance; but if this is vocative, the two others cannot but be vocatives too; so ἥδιστος ἀνήρ has to be regarded as a nominative form functioning as vocative, a not uncommon phenomenon. However, the border-line between exclamation and vocative is a shifting one.

φίλτατον ... ἦμαρ: cf. *El.* 1224, 1354.

ἥδιστος: *gratissimus.*

πῶς ἄν ... / ... γενοίμην: a well-known expression of wish (cp. *utinam*).

ἐμφανὴς / ... γενοίμην: amounts to '(how) could I clearly show'.

ὥς μ' ... προσφιλῆ: indirect question ('how ...') dependent on ἐμφανὴς γενοίμην.

προσφιλῆ: 'well-disposed', implying gratitude and obligation.

533-35. ἴωμεν: 'let us depart' (from Lemnos). This self-evident interpretation is made impossible if we follow Schneidewin and Pearson in reading γῆν instead of τὴν. ἴωμεν, then, has to be connected with εἰς οἴκησιν. But when Philoctetes and Neoptolemus actually enter the cave (674, 5) there is no mention of greeting the earth or the land, nor is there any merit in the reading of GR προσκύσοντε (if γῆν is written) for there is no need for entering the cave in order to greet the land. Unless more alterations (or the assumption of a lacuna) are desired, the greeting has to be referred to the cave itself, his dwelling-place. It would then seem that we should accept εἰσοίκησιν as an instance of Sophocles' tendency to coin and use -σις nouns in his later plays (cf. A. A. Long, *Language and Thought in Sophocles*, pp. 33, 4) and explain the word, preceded by ἄοικος, 'as an ironical extension of οἴκησις when Philoctetes applies it to his cave', as Long does. This seems better than Page's conjecture ἐξοίκησιν ('place of exile'), P.C.Ph.S. 6 (1960), p. 50. The apparently transmitted reading is vindicated by Campbell, Jebb, the Budé edd., and probably also by v. Wilamowitz.

ὥς με καὶ μάθῃς: according to Denniston *G.P.*[2], p. 298 (3) καὶ here expresses addition rather than emphasis: 'learn, as well as merely go'.

εὐκάρδιος: 'stout-hearted'; first occurrence *Ai.* 364, Eur. *Hec.* 549 has εὐκαρδίως. καρδία is common in Tragedy (κραδίη is the epic form, Hom. once has καρδίη). The exact meaning of εὐκάρδιος is to be illustrated by τέτλαθι δὴ κραδίη, as appears from τλῆναι τάδε 537.

536-38. ὄμμασιν ... θέαν / ... λαβόντα: a pathos-enhancing periphrasis of θεασάμενον. Blaydes' conjecture μόνον weakens the expressive force. Jebb is right, in my opinion, in rejecting a close connection between λαβόντα and τλῆναι; this would imply that τάδε should be taken as the object of θέαν λαβόντα—not impossible—, but it would seem more natural to take τλῆναι τάδε together.

προὔμαθον: either 'I learnt gradually', (many commentators), or 'j'ai appris de bonne heure' (Mazon).

στέργειν: 'acquiesce in', 'bear with', a fairly common use of the verb (cp. Dutch 'voor lief nemen' = 'put up with').

κακά (538): this v.l.—ΣL—instead of τάδε has to be accepted.

539-41. They are approaching the cave, The pseudo-ναύκληρος (cf. 128, 9) has entered, with another mariner of Neoptolemus' ship leading the way. This arrival comes expectedly for Neoptolemus, but not for the Chorus. (There is no intervention on the part of the Chorus during the scene). On the modest rôle of 'masquerade', embodied in the pseudo-merchant, see L. Radermacher, *Aristophanes' Frösche*[2] (1954), pp. 52, 3 (he 'ist sozusagen als Rudiment aus der Überlistungskomödie geblieben', id. *ib.*, p. 359; but we should remember that no play with Sinon as a character has survived. And the rôle of 'Überlisting' is certainly not negligible in Tragedy, especially not in Euripides' later plays).

ἐπίσχετον, μάθωμεν: 'wait (stop), let us learn (hear) what they have to say'; here the hortative is introduced by a real imperative, cf. Eur. *Hipp.* 567 ἐπίσχετ', αὐδὴν τῶν ἔσωθεν ἐκμάθω and Barrett *a.l.*.

ἀλλόθρους: 'a stranger', here and at *Trach.* 844 = ἀλλότριος. Its proper meaning (= ἀλλόφωνος) perhaps to be perceived in Aesch. *Suppl.* 973, *Ag.* 1200. The word does not occur in Eur.

ὦν μαθόντες: 'having learnt from them', sc. what they have to say.

αὖθις: 'afterwards' (as often).

542-46. τόνδε τὸν ξυνέμπορον: τὸν σὺν ἐμοὶ ἐν πόρῳ ὄντα, 'companion'. Not: 'fellow traveller with you' (Webster). It may be that the designation ἔμπορος referring to the pseudo-merchant (nowhere in the text) is due to the term ξυνέμπορος used here.

σε ποῦ κυρῶν εἴης: normal 'prolepsis' of the subject of a dependent question.

ἀντέκυρσα: σοί, i.e. 'our ways have crossed' (Campbell).

πέδον: 'land', i.e. coast.

547-50. οὐ πολλῷ στόλῳ: with small equipment, i.e. one ship and a not numerous crew.

ἀπ' Ἰλίου . . . / Πεπάρηθον: he is supposed to be a trader in wine for the army at Troy (cf. *Ilias* VII 467). Peparethus, half-way between Scyros and Malis, was famous for its wine (and other agrarian produce).

πλέων γάρ . . . / . . . / . . . ὡς ἤκουσα: amounts to πλέω γὰρ . . . ὡς δ' ἄκουσα. In terms of strict grammar πλέων belongs to the ὡς-clause.

τοὺς ναύτας ὅτι / . . . πάντες: proleptically = ὅτι πάντες οἱ ναῦται (all the seamen he is supposed to have met at the coast, *i.e.* the three mentioned in vs. 543).

συννεναυστοληκότες: Dobree's emendation of οἱ νεναυστοληκότες is very attractive; the meaning (with σοὶ as the personal pronoun) is much more to the point than that of the transmitted reading (with σοὶ either as the personal pronoun or as the possessive). The intention of these introductory words seems to be twofold: the man must effectuate the impression on Philoctetes' mind that he has a confidential message for Neoptolemus, and that really, apart from Neoptolemus' sailors, no one is nearby, that the coast, so to speak, is clear.

551, 2. σῖγα: what he means is made explicit by πρὶν φράσαιμί σοι; φράσαιμι remains without object; we have to understand 'my news'.

προστυχόντι τῶν ἴσων: Σ's interpretation is inept (ἀντὶ εὑρόντι τοὺς σοὺς ναύτας τοὺς ἐμοὶ ἴσους). Better Brunck's rendering [1]), accepted by many editors, 'consecuto quod aequum est', *i.e.* 'meritum praemium'. This locus communis of messengers belongs to the fraud; Neoptolemus promises his χάρις (557, 8), no mention is made of a reward, but that omission passes unnoticed. Jebb is right in pointing out that the words would be clearer, if they were to run ἔδοξέ μοι μὴ σῖγα τὸν πλοῦν ποιεῖσθαι, πρὶν φράσαιμι καὶ προστύχοιμι τῶν ἴσων. Nauck, Radermacher and Webster prefer: 'as I have the same lot as you', *i.e.* we have both anchored in Lemnos. 546 might be used in favour of this.

553-56. οὐδὲν σύ: asyndeton, suggestive of urgency.

ἅ . . . / . . . / . . . ἐξαργούμενα: expansive explication of the statement made in 553. 'You do not know, methinks, anything about your own affairs <not knowing> which νέα βουλεύματα . . .'.

ἀμφὶ σοῦ νέα: certain correction by Auratus of ἀμφὶ σ' οὕνεκα (σοῦ' νεκα).

ἐξαργούμενα: 'left undone'. Cf. *O.C.* 1605 κοὐκ ἦν ἔτ' οὐδὲν ἀργόν, *O.T.* 287 οὐκ ἐν ἀργοῖς, Eur. *Phoen.* 766 ἐν δ' ἐστὶν ἡμῖν ἀργόν; ἀργεῖσθαι 'to be left undone' Xen. *Cyr.* II 3.3.

557, 8. ἡ χάρις: as appears from προσφιλής, χάρις means the favour, the service (shown in, caused by his προμηθία); the words express lasting thankfulness on Neoptolemus' part.

---
[1]) But he read προστυχών τι.

559, 60. ἅπερ γ᾽ ἔλεξας: thus A and Marc. 467; γ᾽ is omitted in LAGR. The insertion of γ᾽ after ἅπερ is not very convincing, see *G.P.*², p. 123 (5). J. Jackson's (*Marg. Scaen.*, p. 44) proposal: ἅπερ δ᾽ ἔλεξας, ὡς μάθω, φράσον· τί μοι is possibly right.

ἀπ᾽ Ἀργείων: to be taken with βούλευμα.

ἔχεις: 'know' (or = ἔχεις φράσαι), cf. *Trach.* 318, *infra* 789; μοι has to be construed with it.

561, 2. φροῦδοι: sc. εἰσίν, but the wording is much more vivid without it; cf. *El.* 807 ἀλλ᾽ ἐγγελῶσα φροῦδος.

Φοῖνιξ ὁ πρέσβυς: his close relation to Achilles is well-known from *Il.* IX, cf. 344. He belonged to the dramatis personae of Soph. Ἀχιλλέως Ἐρασταί.

οἵ τε Θησέως κόροι: Acamas and Demophon, not mentioned in *Il.* or *Od.*; but they played a rôle in the Ἰλίου Πέρσις and are known to us from Euripides' *Heracleidae*. I am not so sure Jebb is right in posing that they are 'plausibly represented as foes of Neoptolemus, since their father Theseus was treacherously slain in Scyros by Lycomedes (Paus. I 17.6)'. For there cannot be any question of such enmity in the case of Phoenix [1]). Rather are they mentioned because they belong to Attic lore.

564. ἄκουσας . . . σοι: i.e. *fando audivi quae tibi nuntio.*

565, 6. οὕτω καθ᾽ ὁρμὴν: *tanto impetu, μετὰ τοσαύτης προθυμίας.*

567. ὡς . . . ἔτι: for the construction cf. *supra* 415.

568, 9. πρὸς τάδ᾽: Jebb prefers 'for this purpose' to 'in view of these facts' because of οὖν. Since Sophocles has no instances of πρὸς τάδ᾽ = πρὸς ταῦτα he is possibly right, though, then, τόδ᾽ would be more apposite. Therefore, and since I do not see why οὖν and πρὸς τάδ᾽ could not reinforce each other, I slightly prefer the other course.

αὐτάγγελος: *ipse nuntius*, to be taken with πλεῖν, not with ἦν ἑτοῖμος, as v. Wilamowitz seems to do ('Weswegen hat Odysseus sich nicht selbst dazu gemeldet?'). See Ellendt's comment.

570, 1. κεῖνος . . . ὁ Τυδέως τε παῖς: Odysseus and Diomedes, as in Euripides' play.

ἐπ᾽ ἄλλον ἄνδρ᾽: ἐπὶ combines the notions of *ad arcessendum* and of 'against'.

ἔστελλον: 'were making ready', without expressed object as *infra* 640; with πλοῦν *infra* 911, *Ai.* 1045. The coincidence with the

---

[1]) And compare Jebb's own correct vindication of λόγοις (563) against Nauck's δόλοις.

speaker's pseudo-departure is stressed by means of ἡνίχ' and the two imperfect forms.

572. ἄν: often (with Dobree) altered into αὖ. With ἄν two ways of interpretation are possible: with ἔπλει we may regard ἄν ἔπλει as a potential of the past; with πρὸς ποῖον ... τόνδε these words can be taken to mean: ποῖος ἄν εἴη πρὸς ὃν ἔπλει (thus Campbell, again in *Paralip. Soph.*, p. 210). (= ποῖος ἄν ἦν, past potential, would also be possible); cf. *O.T.* 523, 4, where ἄν belongs to βιασθὲν rather than to ἦλθε and *O.C.* 964, 5. Goodwin *G.M.T.* § 244, though translating 'who might this man have been to whom Ulysses was sailing' seems to take ἄν with ἔπλει as potential indicative expressing past possibility.

573, 4. ἦν δή τις: in order to avoid any suspicion of deceit the man has to simulate complete ignorance of Philoctetes' identity. On the other hand ἄν ... μέγα is designed to arouse the latter's curiosity and fear ('suspicion', says Webster, but not in the sense that he thought that the appearance of the ναύκληρος itself was a put-up job).

575. I presume that Neoptolemus, playing his rôle all too well [1]), does not heed the other's warning (cf. Jens-Uwe Schmidt, *Philoktet* - 1973 - p. 111). Masterly rendering of the verse by Campbell: 'Sir, you have the privilege of seeing here the famous Philoctetes', with the comment: 'Thus N. humours the feeling which Ph. had shown *supra* 261, 2'.

576, 7. The 'merchant', of course, speaks sotto voce; see Philoctetes' questions. In the fictitious situation Neoptolemus receives the advice to sail immediately in order to avoid a confrontation with Odysseus; the real intention, of course, is to urge him on to make off—with Philoctetes to Troy, and to intensify Philoctetes' craving to be taken on board by Neoptolemus.

σεαυτὸν ξυλλαβὼν: lit. 'packing yourself off', *i.e.* clear out, make off. Paley's conjecture ἔκπλευσον αὐτὸν ξυλλαβὼν, though clever, is rightly rejected by Campbell on the grounds that these words would be inopportune before Neoptolemus' avowal of friendship for Philoctetes; at 621 the case is altered.

578, 9. κατὰ σκότον: *clam* opp. ἐς φῶς *palam* 581.

διεμπολᾷ: 'is making traffic of me', implying the ideas of selling and betrayal. Cf. *infra* 978, *Ant.* 1036.

---

[1]) Not sotto voce as Ed. Fraenkel will have it (*o.l.* p. 60).

582-84. μή με διαβάλῃς στρατῷ: 'do not bring me into discredit with the army'.

λέγονθ': *i.e.* διὰ τὸ λέγειν.

πολλ' ... / ... πένης: πολλ' ... χρηστά γ' (perhaps θ' Dobree, Jebb) ἀπὸ κοινοῦ with δρῶν and ἀντιπάσχω; οἷ' ἀνὴρ πένης: οἷα χρηστὰ δρῶν ἀντιπάσχει ἀνὴρ πένης; 'as is natural in the case of one who is poor' (Campbell).

585, 6. ἐγὼ ... / ... στυγεῖ: by these words the 'merchant' knows that Neoptolemus is playing his part in accordance with instructions. So he can go ahead with carrying out his. The synaloephe in ἐγὼ εἰμ' is uncommon.

587, 8. κρύψαι πρὸς ἡμᾶς: instead of κρύψαι ἡμᾶς, the common construction in Attic; see Chr. Collard's comment ad Eur. *Suppl.* 296.

λόγον (or λόγων with Burges and many edd.) / ... μηδέν' ὢν ἀκήκοας: as Jebb remarks, λόγον μηδέν' ὢν can be taken either as λόγων μηδένα τούτων τῶν λόγων ὧν (or οὕς), or as μηδένα λόγον περὶ τούτων ἅ. With λόγων we have to construe: μηδένα λόγων ὧν ἀκήκοας. I have a slight preference for reading λόγων, as most edd. do.

589. 'Merely a piece of acting, like the feigned "aside" in 573, and with the same object—viz., to impress Philoctetes.' Thus, correctly, Jebb.

κἀγὼ: καὶ belongs to the whole sentence; the emphatic ἐγὼ implies 'without your warning'.

590. θήσομαι ... ποιοῦ: τίθεσθαι and ποιεῖσθαι here mean exactly the same. ποιοῦ λέγων: amounts to: you are welcome to it, if only you tell your story.

591-94. τῶδ' ὥπερ κλύεις: cf. 570.

διώμοτοι: 'bound by oath'; the perfect participle of ὄμνυμι and compounds is almost unfit for use in its inflected forms, at least in the trimeter.

ἦ μὴν: the common combination of particles for introducing an oath.

πρὸς ἰσχύος κράτος: on a par with λόγῳ πείσαντες.

595-97. οὗτος· ... / ... τάδε: Campbell regards οὗτος ... θατέρου as a parenthesis and δράσειν τάδε as a resumption of ταῦτα; this renders the construction needlessly difficult, δράσειν τάδε would have the effect of a somewhat lame addition.

598-600. τίνος ... / ... χάριν: construe τίνος δὲ πράγματος χάριν Ἀτρεῖδαι τοῦδ' ἄγαν οὕτω, χρόνῳ τοσῷδ', ἐπεστρέφοντο; The word order is strained so as to make the alliterating τίνος, τοῦδ', τοσῶδ' stand out in relief by their place in the verses.

χρόνῳ / τοσούτῳ: 'after *so* long a time'. Cf. the common χρόνῳ 'in process of time', 'after a (long) time'; διὰ χρόνου means about the same.

ἐπεστρέφοντο: lit. 'turn about' > 'turn the mind to', 'regard'. Cp. ἐπιστροφὴ 'attention paid to', 'regard'. The genitive as with μέλεσθαι, φροντίζειν and other *verba curandi*, K.-G. I 365.6.

εἶχον . . . ἐκβεβληκότες: I do not believe (*contra* W. J. Aerts, *Periphrastica*, thesis Amsterdam 1965, p. 158) that this is only a variation on the normal ἔχειν with aor. partic. Rather is the meaning 'were keeping as an outcast' (Webster). χρόνιον is predicative adjunct.

601, 2. τίς ὁ πόθος: τίς ἐστιν ὁ πόθος ὅς.

αὐτοὺς ἵκετ': for ἱκνέομαι 'come upon' with a person as object see the Homeric instances listed in L.-Sc. *s.v.* II 2: 'Αχιλλῆος ποθὴ ἵξεται υἷας 'Αχαιῶν *Il.* I 240 etc.

θεῶν βία / καὶ νέμεσις: constraint and vengeance from the gods; divine justice is regarded as constraining the Achaeans to fetch back Philoctetes, thus taking revenge for the injury he has suffered.

οἵπερ: ἧπερ (Dawe, *Studies* III p. 126) may be an improvement of the text. (ἧπερ Harl., εἵπερ U).

ἀμύνουσιν: 'repay', 'make pay for'; uncommon instead of the middle, but cf. *O.C.* 1128 and my note ad *O.T.* 107 on τιμωρεῖν.

603-21. The 'merchant' now tells the story of the capture of Helenus by Odysseus, of Helenus' prophecy and of Odysseus' promise to carry back Philoctetes. Since the 'merchant' is supposed to speak in accordance with Odysseus' instructions we may well ask why Sophocles made Odysseus picture himself in such an unfavourable light. This question may be answered as follows: (1) The unscrupulous manner in which he is said to have captured Helenus and his bragging promise in the matter of bringing back Philoctetes are calculated to strenghthen the latter's desire to fly with Neoptolemus at all costs. (2) Since this portraiture is in keeping with Philoctetes' own judgment of Odysseus and with Neoptolemus' deceitful story, it is supposed to enhance Philoctetes' trust in the young man, himself the victim of Odysseus' wile. But we may object: the arrival of the 'merchant' comes just at the moment when Philoctetes and Neoptolemus are about to depart, and it would be somewhat cheap to argue that Odysseus has lost patience. We should not forget that Neoptolemus at 539 has not yet carried out the main object of his instructions, viz. the capture of the bow. Now, without assuming—as some commentators do— that Odysseus is perfectly aware of the state of affairs (by spying from a hidden post of observation) [1]), we can surmise that it is indeed Odysseus' intention to hasten Philoctetes' departure, but still more to promote the capture of the bow by means of en- hancing Philoctetes' trust in Neoptolemus [2]). It is a fact that Neoptolemus' first step in this direction comes after the scene with the 'merchant'. (The attack of Philoctetes' sickness, of course, is not something Odysseus can be supposed to foresee). Another problem in the passage is raised by the story of the Helenus oracle. Are we to suppose that this is what Helenus 'really' said? I for one am inclined to answer: 'yes, but not all of it', and it is in accordance with Sophocles' often gradual unfolding of the facts that form the presuppositions of his μῦθοι that the hearer does not get acquainted with all their details before they become relevant to the dramatic structure [3]). It would, indeed, be inopportune to make mention at this point of Philoctetes' promised healing.

603. ἴσως γὰρ οὐκ ἀκήκοας: it would seem from 114, that Neoptol- emus is supposed not to know the whole truth about the Helenus oracle, but since ἴσως ... ἀκήκοας belongs to a speech of deceit, these words cannot be regarded as a confirmation of Neoptolemus' supposed ignorance there. If we want to absolve the poet of an oversight in this respect, we have to assume that he makes Neoptol- emus at 112, 114 'forget' what he is supposed to know already, in order to make the audience acquainted with some important presuppositions of the plot. In that case, what Neoptolemus may logically be supposed to have objected when he heard for the first time of the necessity to fetch Philoctetes (I mean, *extra drama*), he is made to object in the Prologue.

606-09. νυκτὸς ... / ... / δόλιος ... δέσμιον: the capture of Helenus is presented as a nocturnal assault by means of craft and violence.

ὁ πάντ' ἀκούων ... ἔπη: ἀκούων, as often = λεγόμενος.

λωβήτ': active: 'dishonourable' (Jebb's rendering).

---

[1]) Cf. 1013.
[2]) Let us not forget that the words of the 'merchant' are the words of somebody ποικίλως αὐδωμένου.
[3]) Cf. Kirkwood, *o.l.* pp. 79 sqq., Jens-Uwe Schmidt, *o.l.* 40 sqq..

δόλιος: predicative adjunct with εἷλε; its function does not differ from δόλοις, Housman's needless conjecture, adopted by Pearson.

ἔδειξε: cf. 492, 630. But it must be said that 'show', 'display' is here a better rendering in view of θήραν καλήν.

θήραν: 'prey'; the use of the word (not uncommon cf. L.-Sc. *s.v.* II) implies a metaphor and a metonymy.

Ἀχαιοῖς ἐς μέσον: amounts to the same as ἐν Ἀργείοις μέσοις 630.

610-13. τὰ τ' ἄλλα ... πάντα: it is a moot point whether these words are merely introductory to what follows or whether, by making the man speak thus, the poet wants us to understand that his rendering of the prophecy is incomplete. The audience will at least be reminded of the necessity of fetching Neoptolemus.

τἀπὶ Τροίᾳ πέργαμ': cf. 353. The hyperbaton, anticipating the object of πέρσοιεν, has the effect of seemingly placing τὰ ἄλλα πάντα and τἀπὶ Τροίᾳ πέργαμ' on a par, so that both can be felt as accusatives of respect.

πέρσοιεν: Helenus is supposed to have said οὐ μὴ πέρσετε (οὐ μὴ can take the future indic. as well as the subjunctive).

πείσαντες λόγῳ: in shrill contrast with Odysseus' reported words 617, 8.

614-16. ταῦθ': again hyperbaton. Needless to point out how much this stylistic device contributes to the vividness of the report.

δηλώσειν ἄγων: varying and echoing ἄγων / ἔδειξε 608, 9 and cf. 630.

617-19. οἴοιτο: on this use of the oblique optative, in a parenthetic sentence, not introduced by a subordinating conjunction, see K.-G. II 544 Anm. 2 and Goodwin *G.M.T.* § 675 (on εὕροι Aesch. *Ag.* 606 see Ed. Fraenkel, who—with Madvig and Cobet—rejects the possibility of an oblique optative there, and regards εὕροι as an optative of wish). Lys. XIII 9, quoted by Campbell, Jebb and others, offers a good parallel, but there λέγει ὅτι (functioning as a semi-colon) with a fut. inf. precedes οἴοιτο δέ.

μάλισθ': belongs to οἴοιτο: 'he thought it most likely'.

τούτων: with μὴ τυχών, the strongest instance of hyperbaton in this sequence.

κάρα / τέμνειν ἐφεῖτο τῷ θέλοντι: an almost burlesque expression of Odysseus' confidence, alluding to two passages in Homer: *Il.* II 259 μηκέτ' ἔπειτ' Ὀδυσῆϊ κάρη ὤμοισιν ἐπείη and *Od.* XVI 102 αὐτίκ' ἔπειτ' ἀπ' ἐμεῖο κάρη τάμοι ἀλλότριος φώς. The 'allusion' to Eur. *fr.* 706 N.[2] (assumed by Ed. Fraenkel, *o.l.* p. 61) is less clear in my opinion.

620, 1. ὦ παῖ: Σ has the foolish comment λείπει Ποίαντος.
τὸ σπεύδειν: cf. 576, 7.

καὐτῷ ... πέρι: 'both you yourself and anyone you care for'. I
side with Campbell and Webster rather than with Jebb ('both in
your own interest and in that of your friends'), but the difference is
slight. There is, however, nothing strange in the word order (σοι
καὐτῷ), since enclitics will be put near the beginning of a sentence.
Should we follow Jebb, then the words may be ambiguous and
κεῖ ... πέρι may be understood to refer seemingly to Philoctetes, in
'reality' to Odysseus. (But perhaps this is oversubtle). πέρι is
uncommon with κήδομαι.

622, 3. ἡ πᾶσα βλάβη: cf. *El.* 301 (Aegisthus) ὁ πάντ' ἄναλκις
οὗτος, ἡ πᾶσα βλάβη, *Inach.* P. Oxy 2369 fr. 1 col. I 24 τὸ πᾶν μύσος
(Carden p. 57); also *infra* 927.

στελεῖν: here 'fetch', 'bring' as at *O.T.* 860.

624, 5. γὰρ ὧδε: 'Philoctetes justifies the indignant credulity of
his question: "Why, in that case"' (Denniston *G.P.²*, p. 62). 'The
persuasion that has force to bring me back to Troy, would fetch me
from the dead' (Campbell).

ὥσπερ οὐκείνου πατήρ: Sisyphus, who θανὼν πρὸς φῶς ἀνῆλθεν (for
Sisyphus 'Odysseus' father' cf. 417).

626, 7. οὐκ οἶδ' ἐγὼ ταῦτ': in keeping with the humble rôle of a
lowly man refraining from meddling with the affairs of his 'betters'.

συμφέροι: 'help'.

628-30. ποτ' ἂν ... / ... δεῖξαι: = ὅτι ποτ' ἂν δείξειε.
λόγοισι μαλθακοῖς: *dictis blandientibus* (E.).
νεώς: ἀπὸ νεώς, cf. 613.
δεῖξαι ... ἐν 'Αργείοις μέσοις: echoing 608, 9 and 616.

631, 2. οὔ·: Jebb's defence of this forcible οὔ is clearly right.

τῆς ... / ... ἐχίδνης: cf. 266, 7. And for the intensified superlative
cf. Eur. *Med.* 1323.

ἄπουν: for the declension cf. K.-B. I 540, 1. Since in G ἄπουν is
correction of ἀπλοῦν and in R of ἄπλουν, de Marco [1]) assumes a *v.l.*
ἄπλουν.

633, 4. ἔστ' ... / τολμητά: i.e. he can be expected to say and
dare anything.

---

[1]) V. de Marco, *De scholiis in Sophoclis tragoedias veteribus*, Atti d. R. Ac.
dei Lincei, Mem. cl. di Sc. Mor., Stor. e Fil., Roma, VI (1937), p. 164.

καί: with the same function as *aussi* as first word of an inferential sentence. Mazon renders by 'c'est pourquoi'.

νῦν: goes with οἶδα.

635, 6. ὡς ... / ... ὁρίζῃ: Lambinus' correction (ὁρίζει mss) is necessary. Another possibility would be ὥσθ' ... / ... ὁρίζειν (Kuiper).

637, 8. ἤ τοι ... / ... ἤγαγεν: general truth, marked by τοι and gnomic aorist. Webster comments: 'Perhaps the elaboration of the maxim with the medical λήξαντος and ὕπνον looks forward to the disease scene'. Perhaps, and in that case the words would convey a dramatic irony of a sort, but the medical associations of λήξαντος and ὕπνον are vague. More important, in my opinion, is the fact that the sufferer is represented as looking forward to sleep after the strain and suspense of the present situation; this is in keeping with Philoctetes' sleep 271, 2, and, indeed, may point to the underlying idea that the attack of the disease, followed by sleep, is loosed by the tensions he has gone through.

639, 40. οὐκοῦν ... ἀνῇ / τότε στελοῦμεν· νῦν γὰρ ἀντιοστατεῖ: It would seem that Neoptolemus' objection against hastening to put to sea (quite apart from the unsolvable problem whether there 'really' is or is not a head-wind—east or west—) does not derive from moral scruples [1]) but from his ἀμηχανία: how can he put to sea—without the bow being in his possession.

τοὐκ πρῴρας: compare and contrast *infra* 1451.

ἀνῇ: *intr.* 'abate'; cf. Eur. *Or.* 227, 8 ὅταν ἀνῇ νόσος / μανιάς Σ, Chapouthier and others.

ἀντιοστατεῖ: only here, 'be contrary'. The wind is supposed to come from the west; this is confirmed by 642. At 464, 5 the same wind may be implied but Neoptolemus' words there have to be supposed to be spoken from the standpoint of reality, here from that of the fictitious situation. In both cases ambiguity is to be assumed. There is, of course, no ambiguity at 1451.

641. Philoctetes' riposte takes the character of a proverbial truth.

642. οὐκ, ἀλλά: 'not so, but on the contrary ...'.

ταῦτ': *i.e.* the difficulties of sailing caused by the adverse wind.

643, 4. οὐκ ἔστι ... ἐναντιούμενον: 'Seeräuber kennen keinen Gegenwind' (v. Wil.).

---

[1]) I do not agree with Webster *a.l.*; I do with Jens-Uwe Schmidt *o.l.* pp. 122, 3.

χάρπάσαι: cf. Tyrwhitt's all but certain conjecture χάρπαγὰς Aesch. *Ag.* 822. Ed. Fraenkel (*o.l.* p. 61) prefers Bergk's τι instead of τε.

645, 6. ἀλλ' ... χωρῶμεν: cf. 526.

λαβὼν: if sound, to be construed with <σὺ> implied in χωρῶμεν (K.-G. I 87 Anm. 2). λαβόνθ' Dobree (Webster agrees) introduces a not entirely unknown metrical enjambment, λαβεῖν (Page, Proc. Cambr. Phil. Soc. 6 - 1960 - p. 51) makes χωρῶμεν virtually mean: 'let us enter the cave'—not very probable in view of 526 and 637 [1]). Ed. Fraenkel (*o.l.* p. 61) assumes the sentence to be interrupted by Philoctetes.

647. ἔστιν ὧν δεῖ: amounting to the same as ἔστιν ὧν με χρεία καὶ πόθος ἔχει. ἀλλ' 'assentient', cf. *G.P.*[2], p. 20 (7).

καίπερ οὐ πολλῶν ἄπο: 'though not from a large store' (Webster).

648. ἔπι: Auratus instead of ἔνι mss, rightly defended by Jebb (Campbell's assumption of a partitive genitive is untenable; D.-M., reading ἔπι, note *in apparatu*: 'ἔνι codd., subaudito λαβεῖν, forsan melius'). Σ is not helpful: τί ἔχεις ὅπερ ἡ ἐμὴ ναῦς οὐκ ἔχει;

649, 50. φύλλον: 'herb', cf. 44, 698.

κοιμῶ: 'soothe', cf. *Il.* XVI 524 (τόδε καρτερὸν ἕλκος ἄκεσσαι,) κοίμησον δ' ὀδύνας.

πραΰνειν: here again the νόσος is felt as a θήρ, for πραΰνειν is used of the taming of wild animals; πρᾶος is the opposite of ἄγριος. The verb is not to be regarded as intransitive.

651. γάρ: turning to a new point (Jebb; *G.P.*[2] p. 82 (II)). We might punctuate τί γάρ; 'and then' (purely transitional *G.P.*[2] p. 83).

652, 3. εἴ ... / παρερρύηκεν: <ἐρῶ λαβεῖν>.

τόξων τῶνδ': it is simplest to take τόξα here as referring to the arrows, whereas in 654 the meaning is 'bow'. But, of course, τι τόξων τῶνδ' may also mean 'something belonging to these, my bow and arrows', *i.e.* some arrow.

ἀπημελημένον: 'entirely overlooked', 'without my having noticed by negligence'.

παρερρύηκεν: 'has slipped off' (we might supply: from the quiver).

ὡς λίπω μή: for the word order cf. 66, 7.

654. ἦ ... γάρ ...; : (is) 'indeed?' *G.P.*[2] 284, 5.

ἃ νῦν ἔχεις: not 'qui est tien maintenant' (Mazon) but 'which you are now holding'.

---

[1]) But he is right in rejecting J. Jackson's χωροῖς ἄν (*M.S.*, p. 242).

655. ταῦτ', οὐ γὰρ ἄλλ' ἔστ', ἀλλ' ἃ βαστάζω χεροῖν: thus GR, reading preferred by Jebb against οὐ γὰρ ἄλλα γ' ἔσθ', ἃ β.χ.A.LΛ have ἀλλ' ἐσθ' ἃ. A's text seems a correction of a text where ἀλλ' had been omitted by haplography; I do not believe that in ρ ἀλλ' had been inserted.

656, 7. ἆρ' ἔστιν ὥστε: *'fierine potest ut'*, see K.-G. II 11, 12 Anm. 9.

βαστάσαι: on the meaning of this verb: 'hold and poise', 'e.g. for careful examination' cf. Ed. Fraenkel ad Aesch. *Ag.* 35 (p. 22 with n. 2).

προσκύσαι θ' ὥσπερ θεόν: the bow, Heracles' gift, of course is sacred. But we have to bear in mind that Neoptolemus' respectful and reverent wording belongs to the fraud. So Jebb's note: 'This is the young soldier's reverence for a great weapon' does not, I am sure, do justice to the ambiguity of the passage. Cf. Jens-Uwe Schmidt, *o.l.* p. 125.

658, 9. κἄλλο τῶν ἐμῶν: 'anything else in my power' (Jebb) better than 'tout objet à moi' (Mazon).

ὁποῖον ἄν σοι ξυμφέρῃ: 'that is of a nature to accord with your desires' (Campbell).

660, 1. καὶ μὴν: 'yes indeed'.

ἐρῶ: sc. θέαν λαβεῖν, βαστάσαι, προσκύσαι.

πάρες: 'let it go'. I cannot believe in Webster's statement that: Neoptolemus' 'emotion is genuine', that he is not thinking of the success of Odysseus' plan, if he can get the bow. Rather is he depicted as playing his rôle all too well, because his sentiments in the non-fictitious situation would have been those he now feigns to feel. But this is not to deny that this ambiguity is a preparation for his reversal after the attack of Philoctetes' νόσος (but note that this reversal will not be instantaneously complete; otherwise he would have rendered the bow forthwith). That the poet does not mean us to understand that 660, 1 convey Neoptolemus' truly felt sentiments at this moment follows from the answer of Philoctetes: its self-evident painful dramatic irony disproves Webster's opinion.

662-66. ὁσιά ... θέμις: ὁσιά τε φωνεῖς: Neoptolemus' words are, thus Philoctetes, expressive of reverence, his request is entirely permissible.

ἔστι ... θέμις: directly referring to εἴ μοι θέμις, sc. λαβεῖν etc., sc. <σοι> / ὅς γ' (*quippe qui*).

ὅσ γ' ... / ... ὅς ... / ὅς ..., ὅς ... ὅς: this fourfold anaphora of ὅς is pathetically expressive of Philoctetes' thankfulness. And this outpouring is all based on delusion.

χθόν' Οἰταίαν μολεῖν: cf. 479.

πατέρα πρέσβυν: his fear of 493 has been forgotten.

πέρα: either adverb or preposition (on a par with ἔνερθεν)—it makes no difference:—'beyond' (or 'above') 'their reach', the result of ἀνέστησας ¹). In the dramatic context the words present us with a glaring tragic irony.

667-70. ταῦτα: the bow, subject of παρέσται.

δόντι δοῦναι: *i.e. ἐμοὶ δόντι ἀποδοῦναι.*

ἀρετῆς ἕκατι: on ἕκατι = ἕνεκα, χάριν with a *genitivus rei* (not epic), cf. M. Leumann, *Homerische Wörter*, 1950, p. 255; this use developed in choral lyrics, the word is exclusively poetic: hence the ā, also in dialogue, cf. G. Björck, *Das Alpha Impurum*, 1950, pp. 122, 3.

εὐεργετῶν: by kindling Heracles' pyre ²).

671-73. These lines cannot be spoken by Philoctetes, as mss will have it. If they are genuine they have to be attributed to Neoptolemus (the majority of modern editors, following Döderlein; in his edition Campbell regarded them as interpolated, but in *Paral. Soph.* p. 211 he declared himself convinced by Jebb's argument in favour of retaining them, adding: 'though it must be allowed that Neoptolemus is "daubing it" rather far'). Neoptolemus' three lines, if they are his, betray, on the one hand, the stiffness of ἀπορία, caused by the effusion of boundless thankfulness and trust on Philoctetes' part; on the other hand the words εὖ δρᾶν εὖ παθὼν 672 can not but refer to the promise regarding the bow (and so belong to the fraud, for they imply that Philoctetes will stand by his promise—and that is all he wants to attain).

φίλον: predicate belonging to the object of λαβὼν only.

674, 5. χωροῖς ἂν εἴσω: a courteous exhortation.

καὶ σέ γ' ... / ... λαβεῖν: By making Philoctetes speak these final words of the scene, the poet insists on the trust he puts in Neoptolemus. At the same time they prepare the spectator for the attack of Philoctetes' illness. It seems to me that Sophocles was aware of the fact that epileptics often experience a premonition of an attack ³) (that is, of course, not to say that Philoctetes is simply

---

¹) So I reject Pearson's text.
²) I cannot subscribe to the idea of interpolation of 668, 9, argued by Ed. Fraenkel, *o.l.* p. 63.
³) Cf. *De Morbo Sacro*, c. 12.

an epileptic, only that the manifestation of his sickness has much in common with an epileptic attack).

Stasimon 676-729, two antistrophic pairs

Only Ixion's fate was more wretched than Philoctetes', and he was a sinner against man and god (676-682), Philoctetes did not offend against anybody; how can he endure his unbearable life (683-690). Antistrophe α' and strophe β' elaborate on his miseries, antistrophe β' sings of his good fortune now that he has met the noble Neoptolemus and will return home, the scene of Heracles' burning and apotheosis. The song remains within the framework of the fraud but insists on the hero's pitiful and undeserved fate, and the Chorus, in antistrophe β', can be supposed to think of what will happen after Troy's fall: εὐδαίμων and in particular μέγας are easier to understand on that assumption.

The metre is a composition of iambic, dactylic and aeolic elements (cf. the parodos).

676. The strophe is introduced by an iambic trimeter, just as the first strophe of the parodos. The comparison of the hero's fate with that of a well-known figure of mythology [1] is a standing feature of choral lyrics. For the antithesis between the two compared cf. *e.g.* Lycurgus and Antigone in *Ant.* 955-965.

677, 8. As appears from 692, 3, probably sound, or nearly so, the transmitted text is corrupt. Jebb's *Appendix* offers an assortment of remedies. The text as restored in Jebb and Pearson (and with some variation in D.-M.) follows Schneidewin in leaving out Ἰξίονα, considered as intrusive gloss. Others prefer to regard δέσμιον as intrusive gloss. A recent attempt at restoration is J. Diggle's (Cl. Rev. N.S. XVI 3, 1966, p. 262), who proposes to write Ἰξίον' ἀν' ἄμπυκ' ἄδη<ν> δρομάδ' ὡς ἔλασεν, a clever combination of conjectures (ἀν' already Dindorf's idea); for the wrong division of ἄδη<ν> he compares *Rhes.* 480 (ἄδην ἐλαύνομεν); for ἄδην ἐλαύνειν the Homeric ἄδην ἐλάαν κακότητος.

πελάτης: *nomen agentis* derived from *πελα-: 'one who approaches', cf. 1164.

<τῶν>: this insertion (Porson), syntactically desirable, and metrically necessary, is generally accepted.

---

[1] Sophocles wrote a Tragedy *Ixion*, and so did Aeschylus and Euripides. See Radt *T.G.F.* 4, p. 267.

The elimination of δέσμιον renders κατὰ δρομάδ' ἄμπυκα or ἀν' ἄμπυκα ... δρομάδα difficult, whether we read ἔλαβεν, ἔβαλεν, or ἔλασεν, though perhaps not impossible (κατὰ and ἀνὰ for 'on' are anyhow uncommon) [1].

ἄμπυκα: ἄμπυξ = 'rim of wheel' > 'wheel', only here (ἄντυγα has been conjectured by Musgrave).

δή: mss (om. T) is left out by many editors; Diggle's solution is elegant.

ἔλαβεν: ἔλαβ' ὁ majority of mss, ἔβαλεν ὁ Vat. Palat. 287, preferred by Campbell, Jebb, Dain-Mazon and others. With Diggle's ἄδην, ἔλασεν is better than either, or rather necessary.

682. τοῦδ': ἢ τόνδε.

θνατῶν: goes with ἄλλον οὔτιν'.

683. ὃς οὔτε τι ῥέξας τιν', οὔτε νοσφίσας: οὔτε τι ῥέξας is Eustathius' reading 763.2, ably defended by M. D. Reeve, Cl. Rev. N.S. 21.3 (1971) p. 325 (οὔτ' ἔρξας τιν' codd., the second οὔτε codd., οὔτι Schneidewin, Jebb, Pearson); Reeve is right in attaching, in this case, more importance to Eustathius' authority than to the objection that elsewhere in Tragedy τι ῥέζειν is to be scanned τῐ ῥέζειν. The verse is then a trimeter, and 699 has to be altered accordingly, as has been proposed by J. Jackson, M.S., pp. 111, 2 (see below; Reeve's treatment of 683 improves upon Jackson's: ὃς οὔτι ῥέξας <οὔτιν'>, οὔτι νοσφίσας and is more convincing than T. C. W. Stinton's ὃς οὐ ῥέξας τιν', οὔτι νοσφίσας (J.H.S. 97 (1977) pp. 133-6)).

νοσφίσας: for νοσφίζω τινά τι 'deprive', see L.-Sc. s.v. II 2.

684, 5. ἀλλ' ἴσος ὢν ἴσοις ἀνήρ: 'righteous towards the righteous', or 'in the eyes of the righteous'. If we prefer ἔν γ' (G. Hermann) the words can also have both meanings, preferably the second [2]. Cp., then, ἐν δὲ τοῖσδ' ἴσος O.T. 677 (with my note).

ὤλλυθ' ὧδ' ἀναξίως: either here or in 701 or in both lines there is corruption. The metre of the transmitted words here runs: –ᴜ–ᴜ–ᴜ–, of 701 (ἕρπει γὰρ ἄλλοτ' ἄλλᾳ) ––ᴜ – ᴜ––. Perhaps we should read in 685 ἀτίμως (Erfurdt) and εἶρπε δ' (εἶρπε Bothe, δ' G. Hermann) in 701: then we have –ᴜ– ᴜ––. But there are many other possibilities, most of them as precarious as these or still more so. The most attractive seems to me ὤλλυτ' ἀνάξι' ὧδε (v. Wilamowitz, Gr. Vsk. p. 409 n. 1, Bergk's idea; οὕτως Burges), εἶρπε γὰρ ἄλλοτ' ἄλλᾳ in 701.

---

[1] One could surmise that the idea 'stretched out over' is conveyed by κατὰ or ἀνὰ, but with δέσμιον this is easier to grasp.

[2] For in that case γ' seems more meaningful.

686. τόδε δ' αὖ θαῦμά μ' ἔχει: this seems better than τόδε τοι κτλ. and is rightly preferred by J. Jackson, *M.S.*, p. 80, D.-M., Webster.

687, 8. ἀμφιπλάκτων ῥοδίων: 'the breakers dashing on both sides', ἀμφιπλάκτων active-intransitive rather than passive.

κλύων: a case of R having the right reading against the senseless κλύζων.

689, 90. κατέσχεν: 'kept his hold upon' (Jebb), '(comment) a-t-il pu conserver (pareille vie)' (Mazon). οὕτω belongs to πανδάκρυτον.

691. ἵν' αὐτὸς ἦν πρόσουρος: all things considered I think it best to retain this text and to interpret: 'where he was himself his own neighbour', an oxymoron. It is really relevant to compare Luc. *Tim.* 43, as has been often done: θεοῖς θυέτω καὶ εὐωχείσθω μόνος ἑαυτῷ γείτων καὶ ὅμορος. Campbell compares also Aesch. *Cho.* 866 μόνος ὢν ἔφεδρος, and so does Jebb. πρόσουρος is an ionism.

οὐκ ἔχων βάσιν: 'without power of movement' (Campbell).

692-95. τιν' ἐγχώρων: hardly different from τιν' ἔγχωρον. See note ad 1-3.

κακογείτονα: (as a) 'neighbour of his misery'. Σ goes astray in taking κακογείτονα with στόνον; another scholion by explaining οὐ μόνον ὅπου καλὸν οὐκ εἶχε γείτονα ἀλλ' οὐδὲ κακὸν κτλ..

παρ' ᾧ ... / ... αἱματηρόν: the hardest problem of these words is this: can στόνον ἀντίτυπον βαρυβρῶτ' αἱματηρόν be regarded as meaning: 'a lament for a plague that gnawed his flesh and drained his blood' (Jebb), can the epithets of the νόσος be given to the στόνος? Campbell taking τὰν from 696 (mss) before βαρυβρῶτ' (but his reading of 680 is unsatisfactory) [1]) and regarding <τὰν> βαρυβρῶτ' (sc. νόσον) αἱματηρόν as object obtains a construction with ἀποκλαύσειεν consisting of an object proper and a 'cognate' accusative. The same is suggested by Webster (without inserting the article; βαρυβρώς would be a noun, comparable to βουβρώς τις *Il.* XXIV 532 as proposed by L. J. D. Richardson, Hermathena 95 (1961) p. 64). It is, however, true that Aesch. *Sept.* 348-50 βλαχαὶ δ' αἱματόεσσαι τῶν ἐπιμαστιδίων ἀρτιτρεφεῖς βρέμονται is, up to a point, comparable, and cf. Eur. *El.* 752 φόνιον οἰμωγήν.

στόνον ἀντίτυπον: a lament <that would have been> echoed, <that would have found> response. Cf. 1460, where the meaning is literal.

---

[1]) Better in *Paral. Soph.* p. 211: λόγῳ μὲν ἐξήκουσ', ὄπωπα δ' οὐ μάλα / τὸν πελάταν λέκτρων ποτὲ τῶν Διὸς / ἄν' ἄμπυκα δὴ δρομάδα / δέσμιον ὡς ἔβαλεν / παγκρατὴς Κρόνου παῖς.

ἀποκλαύσειεν: theopt. as in 281.

αἱματηρόν: the form is not to be alleged against Campbell's idea: cf. Eur. *Or.* 962 αἱματηρὸν ἄταν.

696-700. ὃς τὰν: G. Hermann and many edd.; οὐδ' ὃς τὰν mss: either οὐδ' or τὰν has to go.

αἱμάδα: 'gush of blood' (only here).

ἐνθήρου: wherein the θήρ (his νόσος) is housed. See my paper Mnem. Ser IV I 3 (1948), pp. 198-204. Another instance of a comparable ἐν- compound in μανίαισιν . . . ἐναύλοις Eur. *Her.* 878, 9 (?).

κατευνάσειεν . . . ἐμπέσοι: If we follow J. Jackson (*M.S.* p. 113) in supplying after ἐμπέσοι <πόθος>, κατεύνασειεν is to be derived from κατευνάζω and ἑλεῖν (700, mss) can be retained, Cf. κοιμῶ 650. We have then to follow either Jackson or Reeve in their restorations of 683. In 700 Page's ἔκ τι γᾶς ¹) (P.C.Ph.S. 1960, 52, accepted by Webster) seems the best solution. As to εἴ τις ἐμπέσοι πόθος . . . ἑλεῖν I remark (against Webster's objection) that the πόθος must be Philoctetes', and that the service of the supposed γείτων would have consisted in the fetching and applying of the herbs. This is in keeping with what follows, particularly so if we retain γὰρ in 701 ²). Further I observe that πόθος is as good a subject of ἐμπίπτειν as νόσος.

701-06. εἶρπε γὰρ ἄλλοτ' ἄλλᾳ: see ad 685 and ad 696-700.

εἶρπε . . . ἄν: iterative.

τότ': may have double function: it refers back to εἴ . . . ἑλεῖν and announces ἀνίκ' . . . ἄτα. If we have to make a choice, I should prefer the backward reference.

εἰλυόμενος: cf. 291.

ὅθεν . . . ὑπάρχοι: <ἐκεῖσ'> ὅθεν κτλ.. εὐμάρεια 'means of comfort'.

πόρου: Wakefield's conjecture (mss divided between πόρον and πόρων) in order to connect it with εὐμάρεια, but involving the dubious shortening of -ου, in a choriambic dimeter. If we retain πόρον it would either be internal accusative with εἶρπε . . . εἰλυόμενος and 'antecedent' of ὅθεν . . . ὑπάρχοι, or has to belong to the clause with ἀνίκ' (hyperbaton of a common type, comma before πόρον): then we have to interpret, with Campbell, 'at such time as his wearing trouble left him free to move' ('πόρον = possibility of locomotion'). With πόρου, ἐξανείη has its expected meaning of 'slackening'.

---

¹) ἔκ τε γᾶς mss.
²) Or take Hermann's δ' = γάρ.

707-11. φορβάν: predicative adjunct.

ἱερᾶς γᾶς σπόρον: periphrasis = 'corn'.

ἄλλων: partitive as object.

τῶν: the genit. of the relative by attraction; νέμεσθαι τι 'feed on'.

ἀλφησταί: probably = σιτοφάγοι, whereas in Aesch. *Sept.* 769 the word seems to be derived from ἀλφάνω, see Groeneboom *ad locum*, Chantraine, *Dict. Ét. s.v.*.

πτανῶν πτανοῖς ἀνύσειε Α(Q): πτανῶν ἀνύσειε πτανοῖς LΛGR: πτανοῖς ἰοῖς ἀνύσειε Brunck, multi. Perhaps no alteration is needed, if we interpret (with Campbell) either: 'From his winged arrows by means of winged birds' or 'with winged shafts he contrived a sustenance consisting of winged birds'. Campbell *Paral. Soph.* p. 214 repeats his second interpretation and compares πτανά = ὄρνιθες Eur *Ion* 903: ἔρρει πτανοῖς ἁρπασθεὶς θοίνα παῖς μοι. πτανός is used by Philoctetes of his bow and arrows (πτανῶν ἀπ' ἐμῶν ὅπλων 1109) as well as of the birds he shot (ὦ πταναὶ θῆραι = πτανὰ ἃ ἐθήρασα 1146). Again the words remind the audience of Philoctetes' own report 287 sqq.. πτανῶν πτανοῖς forms a schema, somewhat artificial perhaps, but no more so than σμικρὸς προσήκεις ὄγκος ἐν σμικρῷ κύτει *El.* 1142, ὁ δυσφιλὴς γέρων γέροντι συγκατῴκηκεν πίνος (πόνος) *O.C.* 1258, ἄνακτ' ἄνακτι ταῦθ' ὁρῶντ' . . . Φοίβῳ Τειρεσίαν *O.T.* 284, 5.

712-15. ὅς: κατὰ σύνεσιν, for ψυχά amounts to 'the whole personality' (Webster).

οἰνοχύτου / πώματος: πώματος οἴνου κεχυμένου, a cup of wine. The genitive as with ἀπολαύω, τέρπομαι, κορέννυμαι etc.

δεκέτει χρόνῳ: surely better than δεκέτη χρόνον.

716, 17. λεύσσων . . . / . . . προσένωμα: probably λεύσσων στατὸν εἰς ὕδωρ ὅπου γνοίη, <εἰς τοῦτο> αἰεὶ προσένωμα ('intr'. see note ad 167, 8). The Chorus was not present at l. 21. στατὸν ὕδωρ: 'standing water', *stagnum*, unknown from elsewhere.

718-20. παιδὸς ὑπαντήσας: since ἀντάω takes the genitive of the person, this (exceptional) genitive with ὑπαντάω seems possible [1]); some editors prefer παιδὶ συναντήσας (Froehlich).

ἀνύσει: with predicative adjectives amounts to: 'come to be'. Intransitive ἀνύω and compounds can mean 'attain', 'reach a goal'. The idea 'in the end' is implied. ἐξέρχομαι *O.T.* 1084 is, up to a point, comparable and so is *evado*.

ἐκ κείνων: after those unhappy circumstances. ἐκ as in ἐκ πένητος πλούσιος and the like.

---

[1]) Possibly also on the analogy of τυχών.

721-26. πλήθει / πολλῶν μηνῶν: the dative as at 598.

πατρίαν ... αὐλάν: amounts to πατρίδα.

Μαλιάδων νυμφᾶν: on a par with Σπερχειοῦ, to be connected with ὄχθαις. If we take Μαλιάδων νυμφᾶν with αὐλάν, ὄχθας should be read. But the other course of interpretation seems preferable.

727-29. ἵν᾽ ... / ... παμφαής: πᾶσι(ν) does not scan and seems otiose. G. Hermann conjectured θεοῖς / πλάθει θεὸς θείῳ πυρὶ παμφαής and v. Wilamowitz (Die Καθαρμοί des Empedokles, Sitzber. Pr. Ak. der W., Phil.-Hist. Kl. 1929, p. 661 = Kl. Schr. I p. 520 with n. 1) preferred this reading, with πλάθη instead of πλάθει. Perhaps Schneidewin's θεὸς / πλάθει θεοῖς etc. is slightly better. πλάθει, at any rate, does not need correction: a historic present as with the verbs of birth, death, marriage etc. seems even desirable, and conjecturing augmentless forms in choral lyrics is a hazardous affair. But it remains hard to understand how πᾶσι came into being [1]).

ὁ χάλκασπις ἀνήρ: Heracles as hoplite.

If we follow Schneidewin's conjecture it will not do closely to connect ἀνὴρ θεός (as is done by Radermacher), θεός has to be taken as predicative adjunct: '(he) approached the gods, himself a god ...'.

πλάθει: secondary present (suffix -θω) derived from *plā (cf. aor. πλῆτο, ἐπλάθην) 'approach'; the form sometimes in the lyrics of Tragedy.

It is, of course, important in view of Heracles' rôle at the end, that here a picture of Heracles' deification, in connection with Philoctetes' native soil, is sketched.

θείῳ πυρί: either of the pyre or of (Zeus') lightnings. Perhaps better the latter, cf. Apollod. II 7.7.12. Jebb will have it both ways.

That we should have to assume, with Jebb, Linforth (Philoctetes, The Play and the Man, Univ. of Calif. Publ. in Cl. Philol. 15.3, 1956, pp. 121-23) and others that the Chorus, on seeing Philoctetes and Neoptolemus leaving the cave, 'once more speaks language designed to support Neoptolemos' plan' is not to the point. There is no break in the song and, apart from its other functions, it remains, as a whole, within the framework of the fraud and so it

---

[1]) One might try θεοῖς / ἔπλαθε, πᾶς κτλ.

does not matter whether or not Philoctetes can hear the second antistrophe [1]).

Second Epeisodion 730-826

Neoptolemus and Philoctetes have descended from the cave; they are supposed to make for the ship, but it has to be borne in mind that Neoptolemus, though having won Philoctetes' trust, has not taken possession of the bow. He has not yet performed his instructions. But something unexpected happens: a violent attack of Philoctetes' illness.

730, 1. ἕρπ', εἰ θέλεις: after having reached the stage proper Philoctetes has come to a sudden standstill.

ἐξ οὐδενὸς / λόγου: 'for no reason' (L.-Sc. *s.v.* λόγος III 1).

ἀπόπληκτος: 'paralysed' (not: 'struck dumb', as in L.-Sc.). ἀπόπληκτος ἔχῃ: = ἀποπληξίᾳ κατέχῃ (Ellendt p. 294).

733, 4. τί ἔστιν: Sophocles admits hiatus after τί (see ad 100). παρεστώσης: probably = 'habitual'.

735. κουφίζειν: intr., 'to be relieved', medical term, Hipp. *Aph.* II 27. Intr. with ἄρουραν Hes. *Erg.* 463. An intransitive case also at Eur. *Hel.* 1555.

737. The reading is far from certain; οὕτως (A) is not in LGR. It would be possible to read with Cavallin: ἰὼ θεοί. Νε. τί θεοὺς ἀναστένων καλεῖς.

738, 9. σωτῆρας ... μολεῖν: Philoctetes' attempt at explaining away his outcry ἰὼ θεοί is immediately belied by his cries of pain.

740, 1. τί ποτε πέπονθας; : After these words a brief pause.

740 sqq. Webster makes the relevant remark that the frequency of resolutions in this emotional scene is about twice the average in this play.

φαίνῃ: with exactly the same meaning as δῆλος εἶ.

742-44. ἀπόλωλα: anapaest in first foot, as in 745 an 749. He has given up his futile attempts at dissimulating his misery.

παρ' ὑμῖν: 'when I am in your presence' (Webster). Dawe (*Studies* III, p. 127) proposes πρὸς ὑμᾶς.

ἀτταταῖ: exclamation of suffering, in our texts much rarer than παπαῖ and its derivations.

745. βρύκομαι: cf. *Trach.* 987 ἡ δ' αὖ μιαρὰ βρύκει. The segmentation of these verses is highly expressive.

---

[1]) Cf. O. Taplin, *The Stagecraft of Aeschylus,* p. 174 n. 3.

747, 8. πρόχειρον: cf. *El.* 1116. χεροῖν is dative: 'ready to your hands'.

εἰς ἄκρον πόδα: Jebb interprets as 'heel' (πτέρνα), others prefer to understand the whole foot, ἄκρον πόδα meaning the foot at the end of the leg (πούς, after all, can be used to denote the leg, just as χείρ the arm).

749, 50. ἀπάμησον: τὸν πόδα.

751, 2. νεοχμὸν ἐξαίφνης: to be taken closely together; νεοχμὸν *i.m.p.* just as often νέος, καινός.

ὅτου: genit. causae.

ἰυγὴν: ὀξεῖαν βοὴν Σ, cf. Hdt. IX 43.2 in an oracle of Bakis, ἰυγμός Aesch. *Cho.* 26, ἰύζω 'yell' of pain etc., fairly frequent in Tragedy.

σαυτοῦ: objective genitive with στόνον.

ποεῖς: altered by Jebb, Radermacher, Pearson into ποεῖ, *i.e.* ποῆ; στόνον ποιεῖσθαι, it is true, is the expected periphrasis of στένειν, but does not σαυτοῦ make a difference? I am much in doubt about the desirability of this slight alteration.

753, 4. The *personarum ordo*, as given in all modern texts, is certainly correct. But the question-marks after ὦ τέκνον and ὦ παῖ (Pearson and Webster: 'Philoctetes is starting a request': *either* 'do you know (what you promised)—do not desert me' *or* 'do you know the bow . . . keep it for me') are not convincing. Philoctetes says: 'you know—sc. the answer to τί . . . / . . . ποεῖς—, my son'. But Neoptolemus does not know and insists: τί ἔστιν and after οἶσθ' ὦ παῖ, again: τί σοί sc. ἔστιν; οὐκ οἶδα 'I do not know'. It is for the non-sufferer always all but impossible really to understand the other's agony. This painful dialogue is perfectly verisimilar.

755. γε: 'yes' . . .

τοὐπίσαγμα: 'the burden'. ἐπισάττω: 'pile a load upon'. τοὐπείσαγμα (ἐπ-εισ-αγ-μα) (LA) [1]) would mean 'access' or 'increase'; but the word occurs nowhere. Jebb, however, is somewhat dogmatic in stating that the word is not even conceivable. ἐπεισάγω 'bring in besides' is a common verb and the nouns κάταγμα and σύναγμα have existed: σύναγμα is a medical term, meaning 'collection', 'concretion' such as 'stone' or 'gravel' in the kidneys, L.-Sc. *s.v.* quoting Hipp. *Epid.* VI 3.7.. I reject τοὐπίσιγμα (Bergk, Pearson).

756. γὰρ: 'indeed'.

757. μὴ . . . προδῷς: Philoctetes, in the fictitious situation, can

---

[1]) Σ explains ἡ ἐπείσοδος, ἡ προσθήκη; the former seems to refer to ἐπείσαγμα, the latter to ἐπίσαγμα.

expect that Neoptolemus will get frightened at the sight of the attack and fearing the delay (for Neoptolemus himself is supposed to be pursued), will desert him.

758, 9. ἥκει ... / ... ἐξεπλήσθη: these words have been much discussed and often altered. I think they are sound and yield satisfactory sense. First of all I want to state that we had better discard the idea of a 'gnomic perfect' presented by ἥκει. The words, literally translated, mean: 'This (αὕτη = νόσος) has returned after a long interval, having, perhaps, been sated with its roamings'. So far I agree with Broadhead, *Tragica* p. 101, but he finds 'the sense quite unacceptable'. The reassurance for Neoptolemus is conveyed by διὰ χρόνου, implying that after this attack there will be again a long interval before the next one. The ὡς- clause elaborates the image of the νόσος as a roaming θήρ. Cf. Σ ἥκει ἡ νόσος ἴσως ὅτε ἐκορέσθη πλανωμένη· ὡς ἐπὶ θηρὸς δὲ ποιεῖται τὸν λόγον. (We have to discard also the idea that ἴσως ὡς ἐξέπλησθη could mean 'in no less strength than when it sated itself', Campbell (1) and repeated in *Paral. Soph.*, apparently accepted by van Groningen ad Theogn. 224, where he discusses ἴσως = equally) [1]). Radermacher's note on the roaming νόσος is still worth reading. πλάνοις has to be regarded as an instrumental dative within the ὡς-clause.

759, 60. ἐξεπλήσθη. Νε. ἰὼ ἰώ. The hiatus is exceptional, but there is change of speakers; the first ἰὼ has to be pronounced with synizesis. It seems better not to assume shortening of -η and of the first -ώ.

δύστηνε (760), predicative, and assimilated to the vocative participle.

διὰ πόνων πάντων: 'through the whole gamut of your toils' (see Webster's note).

δῆτα: repeated in 761 and in 762 is perfectly in keeping with the passionate style of this whole scene, with its many repetitions, exclamations, assonances; it ought not to raise suspicion. See on δῆτα in these three lines *G.P.*[2] pp. 277, 271, 276; its function is different in the three cases.

761. βούλῃ λάβωμαι: see K.-G. I 221.

τί: probably internal or adverbial accusative.

762. μὴ δῆτα τοῦτό γ᾽: 'no, certainly not *that*, I entreat you'.

---

[1] See the pertinent remarks on ἴσως in Greek Tragedy in ῎Ισως *dans la Tragédie grecque*, excellent study by J. Nuchelmans, in *Miscellanea Tragica*, 1976, pp. 225-247, esp. p. 228.

μοι: ethic dative and comparable with the dative with δέχομαι
sometimes in Homer.

764-66. ὥσπερ ἤτου μ' ἀρτίως: cf. 656, 7.

ἕως ἀνῇ: on the 'omission' of ἄν see Goodwin, *G.M.T.* § 620.
ἀνίημι 'give way', 'let go', 'slacken', cf. 639.

766-69. γὰρ οὖν: cf. note ad 298. A paraphrase of what is intended by γὰρ οὖν would run: 'for it is certain', 'you can be sure,
that'.

ὅταν περ: 'as soon as'.

ἐξίῃ: see notes ad 758, and, for the sleep, ad 272.

λῆξαι: subject τὸ κακόν.

εὕδειν: subject <μ'>.

769-73. τῷδε τῷ χρόνῳ: *i.e.* during the time of my sleep.

ἐφίεμαι: probably sc. σοι (though σε can be defended, cf. *Ai.* 112;
that the predicative adjuncts with μεθεῖναι are in the accusative is,
of course normal, whether we think of σοι or of σε).

ἑκόντα μήτ' ἄκοντα: μήθ' ἑκόντα μήτ' ἄκοντα. No need to read μηδ'
(with Eustathius). The following μήτε (LGR) can also be retained
though here μηδέ (A) may be the correct reading: the phrase may
mean 'not even in any wise', not on a par with ἑκόντα μήτ' ἄκοντα
but, as it were, by way of apposition (after all μηδέ τῳ τέχνῃ
amounts to the same as the Herodotean μηδεμιῇ τέχνῃ and cf.
πάσῃ τέχνῃ and the like).

μεθεῖναι: amounts to 'surrender', 'give up to'.

μὴ ... / ... γένῃ: We may well ask ourselves how this is to be
understood. Radermacher is right to compare curses in oath
formulae, well-known from inscriptions and the orators. Philoctetes will be destroyed by losing his bow and Neoptolemus by the
gods for betraying his πρόστροπος = his ἱκέτης.

κτείνας γένῃ: emphatic periphrasis = κτείνῃς, cf. *Ai.* 588.

774, 5. προνοίας: 'foresight', implying 'caution' (not: 'intention').

οὐ ... / ... κἀμοί: implying that he will hand it over to none other
than to Philoctetes. (And he will live up to this promise, even
before his conversion to Philoctetes' standpoint: Odysseus will
never be master of the bow). Neoptolemus is supposed to have
in mind the meaning of 115.

ξὺν τύχῃ δὲ πρόσφερε: ξὺν τύχῃ = ἀγαθῇ τύχῃ, πρόσφερε = δὸς
προσφέρων, cf. *El.* 1123.

776-78. τὸν φθόνον δὲ πρόσκυσον: on the concept φθόνος (θεῶν)
based on the fear of reprisals on the part of the gods for too great a

happiness fallen to the share of a mortal—a concept very much alive in Herodotus' thought—see E. R. Dodds, *The Greeks and the Irrational*, 1951, ch. II pp. 29 sqq.. But it seems to me less important in Sophocles than Dodds suggests: the explicit cases of φθόνος *invidia deorum* are rare, only here and at *El.* 1466. The possession of the bow, almost a divine being and at any rate representing a superhuman power and as such sacred, means great happiness and all the risks inherent in that. Hence πολύπον' 'causing pain and toil', as for Philoctetes himself and Heracles (in the case of the latter, we may think of his *labores* as well as of the cause of his death).

779-81. Neoptolemus' prayer, of course, is again as ambiguous as his lines 528, 9.

εὐσταλὴς: amounts to 'without impediments', 'undisturbed'.

ὅποι ποτὲ / θεὸς ... πορσύνεται: clearly Neoptolemus hopes that divine and human purpose (the στόλος to Troy which is being 'prepared' by Odysseus' design) will concur.

782. This line is corrupt; the attempts at regarding it as a dochmiac dimeter have not been successful. Desrousseaux' reading (adopted by D.-M.) Ἀλλὰ δέδοικ', ὦ παῖ, μή μ' ἀτελὴς εὐχῃ, assumes an elided μοι (impossible) and an improbable use of predicative ἀτελής (already in Campbell, but he regards μ' = με; I do not understand the accusative). Webster's μή μ' ἀτελὴς εὐχή, with <ἔχῃ> to be mentally supplied, is hardly convincing. Among the numerous old conjectures Wunder's δέδοικα δ', ὦ παῖ, μὴ ἀτελὴς (*i.e.* μὴ 'τελὴς) εὐχὴ <τύχη> (Pearson, Jens-Uwe Schmidt, p. 145 n. 1) is the most satisfactory. Among modern proposals R. H. Philp's, Cl. Rev. N.S. VIII, 1958, p. 220: ᾶ ᾶ ᾶ ᾶ (extra metrum) / δέδοικα δ' ὦ παῖ μὴ ἀτελὴς (*i.e.* 'τελὴς) εὐχὴ τύχη is an improvement on Wunder's, Broadhead's (*Tragica*, p. 178) μὴ ἀτελεῖς εὐχῃ <λιτάς> deserves mention, and Dawe's alternative for 'deletion' viz. ἀλλ' ἤδ' ἔοικε, παῖ, 'τελὴς εὐχὴ <τυχεῖν> (Proc. Cambr. Philol. Soc., 1968, p. 17) is very ingenious.

783, 4. στάζει ... φοίνιον ... / κηκῖον αἷμα: cf. 696, 7.

νέον: cf. 751.

785-88. The inserted bacchii (παπαῖ, φεῦ; προσέρπει) are by their rhythm suggestive of the sneaking evil, the prowling θήρ.

τόδ': vaguely referring to τι ... νέον, or to κακόν; cf. *Trach.* 1028-30, 1031 (τόδε referring to ἀγρία νόσος and its effects).

789. ἔχετε τὸ πρᾶγμα: 'Vous savez ce que c'est maintenant'

(Mazon). For ἔχω, used of mental possession, cf. L.-Sc. *s.v.* I 9, *supra* 560.

791, 2. ὦ ξένε Κεφαλλήν: for Κεφαλλήν cf. 264. If the phrase has a scornful tone (as some commentators feel it has) this is to be sought in ξένε rather than in Κεφαλλήν, expressing the absolute estrangement from a man who once was his comrade in arms.

σοῦ: depends on ἔχοιτ' 'cleave to' (Jebb).

στέρνων: with διαμπερὲς as sometimes in Homer.

793-95. ὦ διπλοῖ στρατηλάται: cf. 264. The second ὦ enhances the pathos.

πῶς ἂν ... / ... τρέφοιτε: just as *utinam* in Latin.

797, 8. ὦ θάνατε θάνατε: cf. *Ai.* 854, Aesch. *Phil.* fr. 255 N.².

πῶς ... / ... οὐ δύνᾳ μολεῖν ποτε: 'kannst du denn nicht endlich kommen'. (von Wilamowitz). δύνᾳ Porson, δύνῃ mss; Björck, *Das Alpha impurum*, pp. 150, 240 wants to retain the mss reading δύνῃ everywhere in dialogue.

799-801. Lemnos (ἀμιχθαλόεσσα *Il.* XXIV 753) has been volcanic, as its close relation with Hephaestus in itself makes sufficiently clear. Mount Mosychlos seems to have been a volcano (Antim. *fr.* 46 W.) (Neumann-Partsch, *Physikalische Geographie Griechenlands*, pp. 314 sqq.); Jebb's *Appendix* ad vs. 800, though still worth reading, has been superseded in many respects by the results of later excavations (Hephaestia and Poliochni, the Kabirion).

ἀλλὰ συλλαβὼν / τῷ ... πυρὶ / ἔμπρησον: the simplest interpretation is Jebb's: 'seize <me> and burn me up by means of (in) yonder fire famed as Lemnian' (Λημνίῳ ἀνακαλουμένῳ) ¹). Perhaps better (with Radermacher ²), Mazon, Webster) 'in yonder fire while you summon it up'. Σ (ἀνακαλουμένῳ· παρακαλοῦντι) seems to have in mind a very different construction: 'help (συλλαβὼν) me (τῷδ') who appeal to you, and burn me up with the Lemnian fire'. But this seems very strained. Meineke proposed ἀνακαλούμενον (accepted by Pearson) or ἀνακαλούμενος.

801-03. We cannot tell whether this connecting of the Oetaean pyre with the Lemnian fire is Sophocles' invention; for all we know it is.

ἐπηξίωσα: 'I deemed right'. The fact that Philoctetes draws a

---

¹) 'Lemnian flame' metaphorically used of fierce eyes is found in Bacch. XVIII 55, 6 Sn..

²) 'pack mich und verbrenn mich im hervorgerufenen Feuer dieser Insel'.

parallel between his own relation to Heracles and Neoptolemus' towards himself is the most impressive proof of his trust in him. Neoptolemus' sense of shame must be stirred by it to the highest degree; hence his silence expressive of his ἀμηχανία. With the symbol of Philoctetes' trust in his hands, the bow which is also the emblem of his mean triumph, he is standing there dumbfounded, lost in his thoughts and caught in the mazes of his false position. The scene, at this point, presents a highwatermark of Sophocles' subtlety in suggesting inner emotion by the simplest means. We have to assume a not too short pause before 804.

804, 5. τί φής, παῖ; / τί φής; τί σιγᾷς: the same rhythmic pattern as in 785, 6.

ποῦ ποτ' ὤν, τέκνον, κυρεῖς: sc. in your thoughts. At *El.* 1409 ποῦ ποτ' ὤν κυρεῖς; is literal.

806. ἀλγῶ ... κακά: this answer strikes me as sincere and evasive at the same time. Surely the impression made by the confrontation with Philoctetes' sufferings is real enough and the pity he feels will lead up to his 'conversion' (the relativeness of πάλαι does not allow us to surmise that the change in Neoptolemus' feelings has begun 'long before'), but he has as yet not reached the point of confessing the deepest cause of his embarrassment: for this we have to wait till 902, 3. He is misunderstood by Philoctetes who fears his departure may be provoked by aversion for the νόσος, as is well pointed out by Jens-Uwe Schmidt, *o.l.* p. 146.

τἀπὶ σοὶ ... κακά: 'the ills which lie on thee' (correctly, Jebb.) (We may compare *Ant.* 1140, 1 ὡς βιαίας ἔχεται πάνδημος πόλις ἐπὶ νόσου which amounts to ἐπὶ πόλει βιαία νόσος ἐστί).

807-09. καὶ θάρσος ἴσχ': 'have *courage*' Denniston, *G.P.* p.320 (6), better than Jebb's 'have good hope also' (as well as ἄλγος).

ἀντιάζω: 'supplicate', Soph., Eur., never in Attic prose.

μή με καταλίπῃς μόνον: cf. 789.

810-12. σαφῶς φρόνει: 'soyez-en sûr', sc. μενοῦντά με. σαφῶς is used with the *verba sentiendi* as well as with the *verba declarandi*.

οὐ μήν: on this exceptional case of emphatic μήν cf. *G.P.*[2] p. 331; Denniston rejects Jebb's explanation (adversative: <I should prefer a promise on oath>: however ...); v. Wilamowitz (*Anhang* in Schn.-N.-Radermacher) wants to write μέν. *O.C.* 650, very similar, has οὔτοι.

ἔνορκον θέσθαι: 'bind by oath', cf. ἔνορκον λαμβάνειν Aeschin. III 90. For ἔνορκος cf. *supra* 72.

ὡς: = ἴσθι ὡς.

οὐ θέμις . . . ἄτερ: ambiguous. Philoctetes is meant to understand that Neoptolemus is in duty bound not to desert him, his suppliant, but the words refer at the same time to their fated partnership in the fall of Troy.

813. ἔμβαλλε χειρὸς πίστιν: for this cf. *Trach.* 1181, *O.C.* 1632; Ar. *Nub.* 81 with Dover's note.

814, 5. ἐκεῖσε νῦν, ἐκεῖσε: opinions are divided as to the interpretation of these and the next lines. Jebb, von Wilamowitz (*Einl. Übers.* p. 25 n. 1), Radermacher think that Philoctetes wishes to return to the cave, Webster that he points to the volcano (if 799 sq. means 'throw me into the volcano') [1], D. B. Robinson (Cl.Qu. 1969, p. 41) that he 'wants to get to the cliff from which he could throw himself down, as he threatens to do again at 1000-1', Linforth (*o.l.* p. 124 with n. 22) that he tosses his arms to the sky, as if he would fly away from the earth into the upper air (a wish for 'Entrückung' as is well-known in particular from Euripides, cf. *Ion* 796-799, *Hipp.* 732-34). This last suggestion is ingenious, but still more convincing is Reinhardt's verdict: 'Schon das doppelte "dahin" weist auf kein diesseitiges Ziel mehr' (*Sophokles*[1], p. 191 and pp. 281, 2) [2]. Σ ad 814: διὰ τούτου νῦν ἔοικεν ὁ Φιλοκτήτης παραφρονεῖν ὑπὸ τῆς νόσου is in favour of Linforth's and Reinhardt's ideas. Neoptolemus, who has just grasped Philoctetes' hand (813), is at a loss what to do and does not relax his grip.

τὸν ἄνω κύκλον: the vault of the sky.

816-18. μέθες με: 'let me go', implying 'release me'.

ποῖ μεθῶ: 'where will you go if I release you' (Jebb, Mazon, Robinson). It is better not to regard ἐκεῖσε as strictly dependent on μέθες: just as in ποῖ μεθῶ the idea is: 'release me so that I can go . . .'. So the translation 'let me go' is correct provided that its ambiguity is taken into account.

ποτέ: *tandem aliquando*.

οὔ φημ' ἐάσειν: Neoptolemus is clearly apprehensive of a desperate act on Philoctetes' part.

προσθίγῃς: I am inclined to understand in προσ- the notion: 'still further'.

εἴ τι δὴ πλέον φρονεῖς [3]: not 'art more sane' (Jebb) but '(sup-

---

[1] The same idea is to be found in Campbell's comment.
[2] Approved by M. Pohlenz, *Erläuterungen*[2], p. 136.
[3] G. Hermann's all but certain reading.

posing that) you must know best' (Campbell), πλέον sc. ἐμοῦ [1]).
'Du musst es wissen' (v. Wilamowitz). Then Philoctetes sinks to the
earth. ('Der Hinaufbegehrende, zum Himmel Blickende ist Gegen-
satz zum Niedersinkenden', Reinhardt, *Sophokles*[1], p. 192).

819, 20. θανάσιμον: *moribundum*. Jebb prefers to take θανάσιμον
as proleptic; I do not quite see why, nor do I see why ὅπως ἔχω must
be taken as meaning 'forthwith'. I think that the admittedly
ambiguous wording is better rendered by Mazon: 'O Terre, ac-
cueille-moi mourant, tel que je suis là'.

ὀρθοῦσθαι: here also there is ambiguity, for ὀρθοῦσθαι can be
simply taken in the sense of: 'rising' (or even: 'standing upright')
but also in that of: 'being restored to health'. Here again Mazon's
rendering is outstanding: 'Le mal qui m'accable ne me permet plus
de me redresser'.—Σ ad 820 notes: εἰπὼν ἐκοιμήθη.

821, 22. οὐ μακροῦ χρόνου: 'before long' = οὐκ εἰς μακράν. Cf. *El.*
478.

ὑπτιάζεται: 'is falling back'.

τόδε: where in English one would say: 'look', 'behold'.

823-5. γέ τοι: 'at any rate' (τοι reinforcing γε: Denniston *G.P.*[2]
p. LIII remarks that the combination γέ τοι is common, whereas τέ
τοι—Buttmann's conjecture—tends to be avoided).

νιν πᾶν ... δέμας: καθ' ὅλον καὶ κατὰ μέρος. Radermacher quotes
from Hippocr. Προγνωστικά 6 οἱ δὲ ἰδρῶτες ἀγαθοί, ὁκόσοι διὰ παντὸς
τοῦ σώματος γινόμενοι ἀπέδειξαν τὸν ἄνθρωπον εὐπετέστερον φέροντα τὸ
νόσημα.

μέλαινα ... παρέρρωγεν ποδὸς / αἱμορραγὴς φλέψ: I do not think
Jebb is right in commenting 'φλέψ, not a vein of the body, but the
thin stream in which the blood issues'[2]). In substance v. Wilamowitz' free rendering: 'und an der Ferse sprang ihm Blut aus
einer Ader' seems to me quite correct. A vein has burst so that dark
blood bursts forth from near the heel of the foot (or the end of the
leg). Σ: νεῦρον (for νεῦρον ἔναιμον = vein, cf. L.-Sc. *s.v.* I b) ῥαγὲν
ἀπὸ τοῦ ἄκρου ποδὸς αἷμα ἀνίησιν. It would perhaps be preferable to
write πάρ' ἔρρωγεν.

825, 6. ὡς ἄν: final, normal in Homer, not uncommon in Tragedy. Goodwin, *G.M.T.* § 326.

---

[1]) Or πλέον τι means: κέρδος τι.
[2]) Thus also Webster.

Lyric interlude 827-838, 839-842, 843-854, 855-864

Lyrics consisting of one antistrophic pair followed by epode sung by the chorus, whereas Neoptolemus answers the Chorus' strophe in four hexameters. On such lyric dialogues, up to a point 'taking the place' of a 'stasimon' cf. O. Taplin, *The Stagecraft of Aeschylus* (1977) pp. 52 and 247 with note 3 for comparable examples. Although beginning in the fashion of a 'lullaby' (cf. J. Waern, *Greek lullabies*, Eranos 58, 1960, pp. 1-8), it is surely 'alles andere als ein Schlaflied'. . . 'vielmehr ein Lied der leisen, aber umso stärkeren Verführung zum Verrat' (K. Reinhardt, *Sophokles*[1], p. 192). On its possible connection with *Il.* XIV 230, 1 and some subtle inferences as to the rôle of Hypnos in the Heracles and the Philoctetes myth, see D. M. Jones, *The Sleep of Philoctetes*, Cl. Rev. 63, 1949, pp. 83-85.

On the metre of the strophic pair it may be said that the combination of dactylic, dochmiac and (syncopated) iambic elements is clear, and that a suggestive halting rhythm is brought about by the many 'dragged' closes. But in details there remain problems. Do we have to divide Ὕπν' . . . εὐαὲς ἡμῖν / (dactylic hexameter) [1]), ἔλθοις . . . ὦναξ / (dochmiac dimeter)—thus W. Kraus, *Strophengestaltung* pp. 163, 4,—or rather Ὕπν' . . . ἀλγέων / (prosodiac), εὐαὲς . . . ἔλθοις /, εὐαίων . . . ὦναξ—thus A. M. Dale, *Lyric Metres of Greek Drama*[1] p. 110—,? I am inclined to follow Kraus, because of the interrelation with Neoptolemus' hexameters, and because the dragged dochmiac dimeter seems a convincing proposal in this context, although for this there are no objective grounds. In favour of εὐαὲς . . . ἔλθοις –ᴗᴗ– ––– it can be argued that thus a colon admitting of aeolic interpretation in the antistrophic pair can be seen as announcing the aeolic cola in the epode.

827-29. ὀδύνας ἀδαής: 'unknowing of pain' (grief, distress), *i.e.* the sleeper does not feel his bodily pain or mental grief. This is reinforced by the second member of the invocation: on δ' without μὲν in anaphora cf. *G.P.*[2] p. 163 (2). For the idea cf. *fr.* 197 P. (201 g Radt) ἄπελθε· κινεῖς ὕπνον ἰατρὸν νόσου.

εὐαὲς: for the vocative by attraction instead of the nominative form cf. *supra* 760. The -α- is short, though compound adjectives deriving from the root of ἄημι have, as a rule, the α long. But its

---

[1]) Without μ' in the antistrophe (v. Wilamouritz, *Gr. Vsk.* p. 347, n. 1). Note that εὐαὲς is Hermann's conjecture for εὐαής.

verbal forms and other derivatives have ᾰ, so this quantity here is easily accounted for. Campbell is possibly correct in assuming an ambiguity in εὐαές: 'with kindly breath' and 'as with favouring gale' (to further our design). This would be perfectly in keeping with an ambiguity to be assumed in οὖρος 855 (but here only a literal meaning is accepted by Campbell).

εὐαίων: 'happy' > 'bringer of happiness'. Its repetition (Tricl.) seems plausible (cf. 845).

830, 1. ἀντέχοις: ἀντίσχοις Σ¹, not necessarily to be preferred.

ὄμμασι . . . / τάνδ' αἴγλαν: Exception has been made to αἴγλαν; among conjectures ἀχλύν has been repeatedly proposed (it has some measure of support in Σ), but the relative clause, then, is weak, as Jebb correctly observes and so also J. Diggle (Cl. Rev. 1966, p. 263); the latter, however, thinks that even with αἴγλαν, however interpreted, it is almost meaningless (and he proposes to read ὄμμασι δ' ἀντίσχοις τοῦδ' αἴγλαν, ὃς τέταται τανῦν). Here I venture to differ: αἴγλαν can only be retained if we retain ἆ κτλ. It has to be interpreted either as the serenity suggested by Philoctetes' closed eyes (for τέταται with 'light' as subject Jebb refers to Ant. 600) or as 'the dreamlight', — 'such as illuminates the visions that come in sleep' (Jebb) [1]). Webster makes the point that Aigla is Asclepius' daughter (cf. schol. Ar. Plut. 701); in the next verse Paion, 'healer', epitheton of Asclepius occurs). Σ κάτεχε τὸ ὁρατικόν . . . τῇ τοῦ ὕπνου ἀχλύι does not seem to interpret a text with ἀχλύν, but to attempt an interpretation κατ' ἀντίφρασιν (this gleam, which is only figuratively a φῶς, but materially the darkness of night brought on by sleep); this might be compared with Eur. fr. 386 a Snell (Phot. Berol. 89, 17) καὐτῷ δ' ἔπεισι νυκτὸς ἀμβλωπὸν σέλας. Not entirely to be ruled out.

832. ἴθι ἴθι μοι παιών: ∪∪∪∪‒ ‒‒ iamb., sp.; thus if the hiatus is accepted; otherwise ἴθ' ἴθι μοι παιήων (Dindorf, Radermacher) cret. mol.

παιών: either predicative adjunct or vocative (then better Παιών; v. Wilamowitz and Mazon have vocatives in their translations).

833-36. Since the responsion is defective, there must be some degree of corruption either in the strophe or in the antistrophe or in both. I think that on the whole the defective responsion is caused

---

[1]) 'Über seinen Lidern / liegt ein stiller Glanz, / Glanz von deinen Träumen' (von Wilamowitz).

rather by omissions in the antistrophe than by intrusions in the strophe, but a large margin of uncertainty remains: for the transmitted text does not yield nonsense, neither here nor there. So I prefer to retain the two δέ's in 834, accepting some supplements in 850. I reject van Herwerden's clever, but needless conjecture εὕδει 835 (instead of ἤδη), nor do I believe μενοῦμεν 836 to be corrupt: for ὧν ΛΑ in 852 yields good sense.

ὦ τέκνον . . . στάση / ποῖ δὲ βάση·: I prefer to put a semi-colon after βάση; πῶς . . . φροντίδος, then, is either a direct question or a question dependent on ὁρᾷς ἤδη;. But ὁρᾷς ἤδη can be interpreted either as a direct question or as a statement; in the latter case πῶς . . . φροντίδος had better be regarded as a direct question.

ποῦ στάση, / ποῖ δὲ βάση·: to be taken figuratively: 'which stand you will take, which course you will pursue'.

πῶς . . . / φροντίδος: 'was weiterhin zu besorgen' (Radermacher).

ὁρᾷς ἤδη: either ὁρᾷς ἤδη; i.e. 'are you already clear as to the course to follow?' or ὁρᾷς ἤδη. or ἤδη·: i.e. 'you already see the state of things': 'the situation is clear enough'.

πρὸς τί μενοῦμεν πράσσειν: certainly not dependent on ὁρᾷς ἤδη, as Radermacher will have it.

πρὸς τί: 'why', 'wherefore'.

μενοῦμεν: see ad 852. For the inf. with μένω cf. Aesch. Eum. 677, with Groeneboom's note.

837, 8. καιρός: perhaps to be written with a capital; at any rate, καιρὸς is personified. According to Ion of Chios Καιρὸς was Zeus' youngest son (Hymn to Καιρός, 38 v. Blumenthal); he had an altar near the entry of the stadion at Olympia. See W. Pötscher in Der kleine Pauly 14. kol. 48 (1967). On etymology and semasiology of the word, Chantraine Dict. Ét. s.v. The meaning here is best rendered by 'occasion', 'occasion favorable' and the use is well illustrated by El. 75 and Pind. Pyth. IX 78 ὁ δὲ καιρὸς παντὸς ἔχει κορυφάν, Eur. fr. 745 N.² τολμᾶν δὲ χρεών· ὁ γὰρ ἐν καιρῷ / μόχθος πολλὴν εὐδαιμονίαν / τίκτει θνητοῖσι τελευτῶν.

πάντων γνώμαν ἴσχων: γνώμη means 'judgment' > 'decision'; so: 'qui décide de tout' (καιρὸς often comes near to Latin discrimen).

<πολύ τι> πολύ: this supplement, in order to restore responsion, remains, of course very uncertain. Campbell's αἴσιον (after κράτος) deserves to be mentioned; it seems better not to tamper with 854.

πολύ: goes with κράτος: 'a mighty victory' (Webster), not = πολλάκις.

παρὰ πόδα: 'in a moment'; G. Hermann's *si statim utare* well renders what is implied.

The covert terms used by the Chorus imply an exhortation to depart with the bow and without Philoctetes; it is thus, at any rate, that they are understood by Neoptolemus. The latter protests in solemn hexameters suggestive of the oracle given by Helenus [1]. We remember that in the Prologue (112-116) it is not explicitly stated that Philoctetes himself has to go to Troy; Neoptolemus is instructed to capture the bow. But the 'Emporos' has spoken of the Helenus oracle (610-613), and Neoptolemus, loath to desert Philoctetes in his sleep and to make away with the bow, seizes upon the contents of the oracle in order to oppose the intimations of the Chorus. ('Faced with the unspeakable agony of the man he has come to pity and admire, he understands the real meaning of the prophecy of Helenos even though he has heard it only in the carefully calculated version of Odysseus' spokesman. It was not a promise of victory for the Greeks, with Philoctetes the instrument of their triumph; it was the recompense offered Philoctetes by the gods for all that he had suffered', B. M. W. Knox, *The Heroic Temper*, p. 131).

839, 40. ὅδε μὲν κλύει οὐδέν: implying: 'so we could make away with the bow unnoticed'.

θήραν / τήνδ' ... ἔχομεν τόξων: θήραν ἔχειν here does not mean θηρᾶν, as it does at *Ai.* 564 δυσμενῶν θήραν ἔχων. θήραν means 'capture' or even the 'booty' (with τόξων as an explicative genitive). Cf. *supra* 609.

841. τοῦδε γὰρ ὁ στέφανος: 'the crown of victory belongs to him'. Compare these generous words with *supra* 112,114.

τοῦτον: object of κομίζειν 'bring (back)', 'ramener' (Mazon).

842. κομπεῖν ... ὄνειδος: κομπεῖν ἀτελῆ σὺν ψεύδεσιν αἰσχρὸν ὄνειδός ἐστιν. 'To boast of what is unaccomplished and that with falsehoods, is a shameful disgrace'. Thus, in substance, Campbell, Jebb, Mazon [2]). This seems better than to take σὺν ψεύδεσιν = ψευδῶς with κομπεῖν. As appears from 845, 6 Neoptolemus has spoken his hexameters in a raised voice.

843. τάδε ... ὄψεται: 'will see to that' (Philoctetes' being brought to Troy).

---

[1]) Cf. C. M. Bowra, *Sophoclean Tragedy*[1], p. 281.
[2]) 'To boast of failure and lies together is disgrace indeed' (Kitto, *Form and Meaning*, p. 120).

844-46. ὧν: by attraction to λόγων. It may replace acc. or dative, ἀμείβομαι admitting of both constructions. If we take 827, 8 = 843, 44 as a hexameter there is something to be said for leaving out μ', for synaphy does not seem very probable (v. Wil. *Gr. Vsk.* p. 347 n. 1, W. Kraus, *Strophengestaltung* p. 163 n. 3).

βαιάν: 'soft' (very rare of sound or voice).

λόγων φάμαν: cf. Men. *Sicyon.* 369, 70 τίνος λόγου / . . . φήμην.

847, 8. πάντων: probably masculine, depending on ὕπνος (neuter is possible, as objective genitive depending on εὐδρακής).

εὐδρακής / ὕπνος ἄυπνος λεύσσειν: lit. 'a sleep that is no sleep quick-sighted'. λεύσσειν is epexegetic infinitive. The terms of sight involve all perception, because in opening his eyes the sleeper manifests his awareness of what is going on.

849-51. ὅ τι δύνᾳ μάκιστον: possibly this means no more than 'as far as possible', 'as far as it is in your power'. It is then adverbial adjunct to be connected with ἐξιδοῦ, or with λαθραίως, or with the whole main sentence.

But the clause can also be an anticipatory relative clause, taken up by κεῖνο . . . κεῖνο: 'the farthest-reaching thing you have in your power' (apparently v. Wilamowitz' interpretation: 'Und was am weitesten vorwärts uns bringen kann, dies eine, dies eine bitt' ich, dies lass uns tun, verstohlen, verstohlen uns tun'). This means: the making stealthily away with the bow.

In 850 the text remains uncertain; here I follow Pearson.

κεῖνο: object of πράξεις, if we accept ὅπως.

ἐξιδοῦ ὅπως πράξεις: ὅπως is the reading *s.l.* in L and Λ. ἐξιδοῦ with ὅπως is to be regarded as a *verbum curandi*. If we prefer the mss reading ὅτι (ὅ τι), κεῖνο has to be the object of ἐξιδοῦ and the antecedent of ὅτι. In my opinion the meaning of the words becomes poorer through this reading.

ἐξιδοῦ: ἐξ- reinforces the meaning of 'seeing to'. The shortening in an iambus, however, of -οῦ before ὅπως (or before ὅτι) is uncommon [1]. Should we conjecture ἐξιδέ γ' ὅπως? In uncials the corruption ΕΓ > ΟΥ would be possible. For γε in commands ('γε occasionally sharpens the tone of an imperative') see *G.P.*[2] 125 (7), where *El.* 345, 411 and *Phil.* 1003 are quoted.

852. οἶσθα γὰρ ὧν αὐδῶμαι·: ὧν is the reading of LΛ; I take it as neuter plural = <περὶ> τούτων ἃ or (better) ταῦτα <περὶ> ὧν and put a semi-colon after αὐδῶμαι; so the words announce what is

---

[1] Cf. W. J. W. Koster, *Traité de Métrique grecque*[2], 1953, p. 36.

conveyed by the next sentence. For the middle cf. 130. If we read ὅν L⁸¹Λ⁸¹GRA (this involves reading μένομεν 836) [1] it is pointless if ὅν refers to Philoctetes and ὅν must refer to Odysseus; but in that case τούτῳ in the next sentence must also refer to Odysseus and mean 'in regard to Odysseus'. This is Webster's interpretation, but I think it improbable.

853, 4. εἰ ταύταν τούτῳ γνώμαν ἴσχεις: 'if you stick to that purpose of yours' (referring to the implications of Neoptolemus' hexameters) 'for him' (Philoctetes, the dative being a dativus commodi; we might translate 'in the interest of that man'). ταύταν, it is true, is only in G, but the impossible forms ταὐτὰν, ταυτὰν may have their origin in the need for an easy regimen of τούτῳ. The same need gave rise to Dobree's ταὐτᾷ and other conjectures.

μάλα τοι . . . πάθη: 'then indeed (I warn you) there are inextricable troubles in store'. μάλα either to be connected with ἄπορα or strengthening the warning tone of the assertion (reinforcing τοι).

πυκινοῖς ἐνιδεῖν: lit. 'for shrewd observers to perceive'. 'Ce ne sont plus que des maux sans issue que doivent prévoir les gens avisés' (Mazon).

855-864. The epode combines aeolic elements (in a larger measure than the antistrophic pair, where they are scarce) with dactylic and iambic cola. The Chorus continues, in veiled terms as before, to insist on a swift departure with the bow and without Philoctetes.

855. οὖρος: figurative and so almost amounting to καιρός. If taken in a literal sense it would be all but irrelevant (Philoctetes would never be able to follow). (It would, however, not be at variance with 640, for there in the fictitious situation the wind, favourable for sailing to Troy would be the reverse for Philoctetes' return home).—Moreover, what the Chorus means by making away with the bow, without Philoctetes, has to be understood in the first instance as relating to handing on the bow to Odysseus.

859. ἀλεής: 'in the sun', 'in the warmth'. See Chantraine, *Dict. Ét. s.v. ἀλέα, ἀλέη.* The words form a parenthesis ('sleep in the sun is a sound sleep') and I cannot imagine why they should be an interpolation; the whole passage is somewhat at variance with 847, 8, but there the Chorus wants Neoptolemus to speak in a low voice, here they wish to urge him to take advantage of the occasion.

---

[1] Dawe, *Studies* III, p. 131 proposes ὅ γ', accepting Erfurdt's μένομεν at 836.

Metrically 857 is a hemiepes, 858 a reizianum with resolved base; there is no synaphy between the two, nor between 858 and 859.

861. τις ὡς: this, instead of ὡς τις, is a necessary correction. ᾿Αΐδᾳ πάρα κείμενος seems preferable to ᾿Αΐδᾳ παρακείμενος

862, 3. ὅρα, βλέπ᾽ εἰ: Seyffert's correction of ὁρᾷ, βλέπει (βλέπ᾽ εἰ G. Hermann) is necessary and satisfactory. I do not see why εἰ, though there seem to be no occurrences with βλέπω alone, could not depend on the emphatic ὅρα, βλέπε. The context [1]) makes clear that ὅρα ... φθέγγῃ means: 'we fear that your counsel (referring to 839 sqq.) is unseasonable' (thus correctly Jebb).

863, 4. τὸ δ᾽ ἁλώσιμον ἐμᾷ φροντίδι: possibly accusative of respect 'as far as my thoughts can understand'; or τὸ δ᾽ ἁλώσιμον ἐμᾷ φροντίδι = τὸ ... φροντίδι <τοῦτό ἐστιν>· (thus Schneidewin and K.-G. I 656).

ὁ μὴ φοβῶν: *i.e.* which is not attended with danger. I do not believe in Campbell's oversubtle: 'The best huntsman is he who does not scare the game' (*Paral. Soph.*, p. 219).

Third Epeisodion 865-1080

First scene, 865-974, Neoptolemus, Philoctetes, Chorus

865, 6. ἀφεστάναι φρενῶν: 'lose one's wits'. Perhaps not quite the same as ἐξεστάναι. Mazon's translation 'divaguer' seems to come near to the intended meaning.

867-81. Again as in 530 sqq. and in 622 sqq. Philoctetes' words are expressive of his effusive gratitude. Once again, and the more so after what has gone before, they must be supposed deeply to affect Neoptolemus' sense of his false position.

867, 8. ὦ φέγγος ... τό τ᾽ ... / ... οἰκούρημα: φέγγος is doubtless vocative, τό ... οἰκούρημα rather an exclamation, as appears from the article. The two are coordinated, though in addressing the light of day he does not, strictly speaking, address the οἰκούρημα. Webster's note is mistaken.

ἐλπίδων / ἄπιστον: *i.q.* ὑπὸ τῶν ἐλπίδων μου οὐ πιστευθέν.

οἰκούρημα: 'the staying and the watching'. On words on -μα in Sophocles cf. Long, *Language and Thought in Sophocles*, pp. 35-46 and for οἰκούρημα τῶνδε τῶν ξένων amounting to οἶδε οἱ ξένοι οἰκου-

---

[1]) Cf. K.-G. II p. 533. 14.

ροῦντες ¹) *ib.* p. 99, n. 127; on their frequent occurrences and various meanings in Tragedy see Chantraine, *Formation des Noms,* § 142.

869-71. τοῦτ' ἂν ἐξηύχησ': τοῦτ' is object of ἐξηύχησ', announcing the accus. cum inf. τλῆναί σε . . . μεῖναι. ἂν is best taken with ἐξηύχησ', together a past potential. αὐχέω, as often and in particular with Euripides, amounts to νομίζω, ἐλπίζω. The words obviously mean something like: 'I should not have trusted myself to hope'.

τἀμὰ πήματα: object of μεῖναι: 'await the end of my sufferings'.

872, 3. οὔκουν: 'Wherever, in Attic, γε is lacking after emphatic οὔκουν, it should probably be supplied' (Denniston, *G.P.*² 424, 5); so he suggested to read οὔκουν 'Ατρεῖδαί γ' αὖτ' (Cl. Rev. 1929, p. 118 and *G.P.*), comparing *e.g.* Reiske's τό γ', for τόδ', in *Ant.* 321 (which is widely accepted); αὖτ', referring to τἀμὰ πήματα, is certainly attractive.

εὐφόρως: the majority of edd. accept this conjecture (Brunck) instead of εὐπόρως; Paley, Kuiper (hesitatingly), D.-M. retain εὐπόρως, and it is defended by Ellendt. εὐπόρως 'easily' occurs in Xen. *Cyr.* I 6.9, εὐφόρως and its degrees of comparison are fairly frequent in medical writings. Neither adverb occurs elsewhere in Tragedy ²).

ἀγαθοί: for the sarcasm cf. *Ant.* 31 with note.

874-76. ἀλλ' . . . γὰρ: 'complex' use, cf. *G.P.*² 98, 9, *supra* 81.

εὐγενὴς . . . κἀξ εὐγενῶν: cf. Pl. *Gorg* 512 d 1 βελτίων . . . καὶ ἐκ βελτιόνων, see also *Ant.* 38.

ἐν εὐχερεῖ / ἔθου: For εὐχερής cf. *supra* 519. For τίθεσθαι ἐν *supra* 473, and the instances listed in L.-Sc. *s.v.* τίθημι B 3.

βοῆς . . . γέμων: cf. 9-11, 473, 4, 520. πλησθῆς 520 and γέμων here are comparable. For γέμειν cf. also *O.T.* 4.

877-81. κἀνάπαυλα δή: Jebb renders δή by 'at last' and this seems better than to regard δή as merely emphatic and to be combined with καί (cf. on καὶ . . . δή *G.P.*² 254).

σύ μ' αὐτὸς ἆρον: Philoctetes is still lying on his back.

κόπος: the 'fatigue' caused by the attack.

ἀπαλλάξῃ: 'release'.

ὁρμώμεθ' ἐς ναῦν: for the third time the intended departure to the ship will come to nought.

---

¹) Cf. Eur. *Or.* 928.
²) Dawe, *Studies* III, p. 131, suggests εὐφρόνως (εὐπόνως in K.—Laur. 31. 10—).

ἐπίσχωμεν τὸ πλεῖν: 'put off (the) sailing'. We may regard ἐπέχειν as transitive with the infinitive as object or as intransitive with epexegetic infinitive. For τὸ (and not τὸ μὴ) of K.-G. II 216 k.; Thuc. VII 33.3 ἐπέσχον τὸ εὐθέως τοῖς Ἀθηναίοις ἐπιχειρεῖν.

882-85. μέν: only emphasizing ἥδομαι. The apparent coolness of Neoptolemus' reply has to be understood in connection with his mental ἀπορία, as is well noted by von Wilamowitz (*Einleitung* p. 26). Others feel cordial sincerity in these words.

ἀνώδυνον: as a rule this is taken as predicative adjunct with both participles; then, βλέποντα and ἐμπνέοντα mean about the same. But Campbell ¹) makes a good case for taking ἀνώδυνον as adverbial neuter with βλέποντα 'looking as without pain', comparing Eur. *Alc.* 773, τί σεμνὸν καὶ πεφροντικὸς βλέπεις, and Pind. *Pyth.* II 20 δρακεῖσ' ἀσφαλές. In this way, it seems to me, the meaning of the whole line is fuller.

τὰ συμβόλαια: not different from σύμβολα and meaning 'symptoms'.

πρὸς τὰς παρούσας ξυμφορὰς: 'in view of the sufferings which have fallen to your lot' ('your ever-present sufferings').

σου: the reading σοι, much better attested, is unintelligible to me. Campbell's interpretation 'your commerce with the circumstances surrounding you' does not strike me as acceptable.

886-88. νῦν δ' αἶρε σεαυτόν: Jebb is right in assuming that Neoptolemus' 'hands ²) are now stretched forth to Philoctetes, ready to raise him'; this is clear from ὥσπερ νοεῖς 889. There is no question of a refusal on Neoptolemus' part. But he bethinks himself of another possibility.

τοῦ πόνου ... / ... δρᾶν: the Chorus' readiness has been made explicit in ll. 522, 3.

οὕτω ... δρᾶν: 'da wir die Fahrt beschlossen, du und ich' (v. Wilamowitz). The wording is deliberately vague.

889-92. αἰνῶ τάδ': polite refusal, *pace* Jebb. For Sophocles' use of αἰνῶ = παρίημι, παραιτοῦμαι cf. *fr.* 109 with Radt's apparatus. Cf. Plut. *de aud. poet.* 6.22 f.

καὶ: 'and <so>'. καὶ continues the idea, implied in αἰνῶ, that he does not want to be carried.

ὥσπερ νοεῖς: see ad 886.

---

¹) *Paralip. Soph.* p. 220.
²) Better 'hand', for we have to assume that he is holding the bow in his other hand. But cf. ad 1254-56 n. 1.

μὴ ... / ... δέοντος: for this fear cf. 482, 3.

πόνος: picks up τοῦ πόνου 887.

893. ἔσται τάδ᾽: Neoptolemus grasps Philoctetes' hand and helps him to stand up.

ἀντέχου: 'hold on to me'.

894. τό ... σύνηθες ἔθος: *i.e.* the fact that I always have to keep upright after such an attack. 'Une longue accoutumance saura me maintenir debout'. (Mazon).

ὀρθώσει: 'will keep me upright' (thus, correctly, Webster).

895. παπαῖ ... γε: τοὐνθένδε λέγε is the unmetrical reading of LAGR. J. Diggle (Cl. Rev. 1966, p. 263) proposes reading: παπαῖ· / τί δῆτα δρῶμ᾽ ἐγω<γε> τοὐν<τεῦ>θεν; λέγε. This is indubitably a clever conjectural reading; but would it not be strange for Neoptolemus in addressing Philoctetes to ask him, of all people, what he should do? There are, it is true, many trimeters in Sophocles ending in λέγε, but they do not support the idea of an expletive use, so to speak, of this imperative. Nor does it seem probable that he addresses the Chorus (he does so only at 974). Diggle does not touch on the problem raised by λέγε. All things considered I prefer to follow A's reading παπαῖ· τί δῆτα δρῶμ᾽ ἐγὼ τοὐνθένδε γε (or with Schaefer' supplement τί δῆτ᾽ ἄν, adopted by many editors).

δρῶμ᾽ <ἄν>: the insertion of ἄν, though plausible, is not strictly necessary, cf. Ant. 605. The form δρῶμι is exceptional in Attic.

τοὐνθένδε γε: Denniston renders by: *'next'*, but regards the text as uncertain. (*G.P.*² 116(1)). παπαῖ: expressive of mental suffering.

Neoptolemus' embarrassment must come as a complete surprise to Philoctetes. We have to assume that by now he is standing upright, ready for the departure. Further we have to bear in mind that Neoptolemus is on the point of reaping the fruit of his deceit. The bow is in his power. Philoctetes' trust in him is so complete that he does not even ask for it back. Neoptolemus has only to lead him to the shore and hand him over to Odysseus. Odysseus will see to the rest. He will have performed his task. But his real pity with the sufferer (we clearly see that the scene of the attack is central to the course of the action, a course indissolubly bound up with the evolution in Neoptolemus' mind) makes him acutely aware of the shameful character of the deceit, so greatly at variance with his own φύσις; by this awareness on the one hand, and on the other hand by his ambition and his sense of obligation to the Greek commanders, he is caught in an ἀπορία whence he will not emerge before having made up his mind about where his moral duty lies. For the moment he is only at the (very dramatic) beginning of a journey that will lead him to his ultimate choice.

896. ποῖ ... λόγῳ: Neoptolemus' words strike Philoctetes as a diversion, a wandering off course (cp. παρέκβασις). He asks for their intended meaning.

897. ὅποι ... ἔπος: what he wants to reveal is that Philoctetes has to sail to Troy (915). The best rendering I have come across is Campbell's: 'I know not which way to express what is so full of perplexity'. The wording remains within the same metaphoric strain as Philoctetes' question. The ἔπος is ἄπορον because no satisfactory way out of the moral embarrassment is to be found by means of words.

898. ἀπορεῖς δὲ τοῦ σύ;: 'you are at a loss? for what?' What Philoctetes fears is made explicit in 900 sq..

899. ἐνθάδε ... τοῦδε τοῦ πάθους: at such a point in this πάθος, *i.e.* ἀπορία, 'being at a loss'. 'embarrassment', sc. that I do not know what to say, (how to say what I ought to say). Neoptolemus' answer amounts to an emphatic restatement of 897. πάθος = 'mental state' (Webster's rendering). Jebb is right in rejecting Wunder's interpretation 'at such a point that I *must* speak', repeated by Campbell (1). But see *Paral. Soph.*, p. 220.

900, 1. οὐ δή: 'Soph. eight times has οὐ δή ..., to introduce a surprised or incredulous question' (*G.P.*[2] p. 223 (II)); cf. my note ad *El.* 1108.

δυσχέρεια: cf. 473. On the omission of the article cf. K.-G. I 607 k.

ὥστε: because the idea of 'effecting', 'bringing about' is implied in ἔπεισεν (A), cf. K.-G. II 8 Anm. 6 and 11 Anm. 9. But ἔπαισεν LGR is not impossible (thus Ed. Fraenkel, *o.l.* p. 64).

μ' ἄγειν ναύτην: 'as passenger'. Cf. the exact parallel Pl. *Ep.* VII 347 a ἆρά τις ἐθελήσει με ἄγειν ναύτην ὁρμώμενον ἐκ τῆς Διονυσίου οἰκίας.

902, 3. ἅπαντα δυσχέρεια: for the abstract predicate with the neuter pl. as subject commentators refer to *O.C.* 883 ἆρ' οὐχ ὕβρις τάδ'; Neoptolemus picks up the term δυσχέρεια, used by Philoctetes in referring to the loathsomeness of carrying his stinking body, and uses it with reverence to the loathsomeness of acting against his inner nature.

τὴν αὐτοῦ φύσιν: cf. 79, 88 sq., 874. Pohlenz, *Erl.*[2] p. 137, Kirkwood p. 243.

τὰ μὴ προσεικότα: sc. αὐτῷ or τῇ αὐτοῦ φύσει. Cf. *El.* 618.

904, 5. ἔξω τοῦ φυτεύσαντος: since Neoptolemus' (real) φύσις is determined by his father's (this is one of the determinants of the play's structure), there is nothing strange in this phrase. In what he supposedly is going to do (sc. to bring Philoctetes home, 'helping a noble man') there is nothing that falls 'outside' the pattern set by his father's example; this is expressed by the 'simple brachylogy' (Webster's term) 'outside your father'. The translation in L.-Sc. 'nothing unlike thy sire' is correct, and so is Mazon's 'rien qui soit indigne de ton père'.

906. αἰσχρὸς: 'base'; not common with personal subject.

πάλαι: from the use of πάλαι no conclusions can be drawn as to the moment when Neoptolemus became acutely aware of his predicament.

907. οὔκουν . . . γε: 'not . . . at any rate' sc. αἰσχρὸς φανῇ. Cf. ad 872, 3.

ὀκνῶ: 'I feel uneasy'.

Note the caesura media; the syllable preceding it is perispomene, as is very often the case. The rhythmical effect is suggestive of Philoctetes' contrasting feelings. δρᾷς occupies the same place in the verse as δρᾷ in 903.

908, 9. ὦ Ζεῦ, τί δράσω: here Neoptolemus' ἀμηχανία is expressed by the typically tragic formula known from Aeschylus, Sophocles and Euripides alike. Cf. *infra* 969, 1063, *O.C.* 1254; *Ai.* 809, 920, 1024; Aesch. *Cho.* 899, many instances in Euripides. See in general Snell *Aischylos und das Handeln im Drama*.

δεύτερον . . . κακός, / κρύπτων . . . ἐπῶν: there is no agreement at all among scholars as to the exact meaning of these words. Jebb's comment runs as follows: 'He has been base, first, as λέγων αἴσχιστ' ἐπῶν—telling the falsehood that he was sailing to Greece: next, as κρύπτων ἃ μὴ δεῖ—hiding the truth, that Ph. must go to Troy'. He translates: 'Must I be found twice a villain,—by disloyal silence, as well as by shameful speech'. Possibly this is correct, but his translation of δεύτερον and the distinction 'first' . . . 'next' in his comment may be misleading. The first time of his 'proving a villain' must refer both to his silence as to the real aim of his journey and to the 'falsehood that he was sailing to Greece' (and that he had quarrelled with the Greeks). If now he persists in this silence and this falsehood he will, for the second time, prove a villain[1]). δεύτερον has nothing to do with the bipartition κρύπτων θ' . . . καὶ

---

[1]) Similarly Radermacher.

λέγων. So I reject Webster's: 'he was first proved bad when he agreed to Odysseus' plan: confession to Philoctetes is the second time' (similarly Campbell). Mazon's translation is clear and correct: 'Dois-je être pris en faute une seconde fois, en cachant ce qu'il ne faut pas et en tenant un langage d'infâme?'

910, 11. κακὸς γνώμην: 'wanting in judgement'. In later Greek there existed the compound κακογνώμων. The same meaning is expressed by γνώμας λειπομένα σοφᾶς *El.* 473.

προδούς μ' ... κάκλιπὼν: the participles may be regarded as forming a hendiadys: 'treacherously leaving me behind'. τὸν πλοῦν does not belong to ἐκλιπὼν (L-Sc. *s.v.* ἐκλείπω 2. is mistaken) but to στελεῖν.

τὸν πλοῦν στελεῖν: somewhat emphatically: 'sail away'. Campbell correctly notes: 'the idea of the homeward voyage is so vividly present to Philoctetes' mind, that the only evil intention he can imagine in Neoptolemus is that of leaving him behind'.

912, 13. λιπὼν μὲν οὐκ ἔγωγε: sc. τὸν πλοῦν στελῶ.

λυπηρῶς δὲ μὴ / πέμπω σε μᾶλλον: 'but rather that I shall *convey* you *to your sorrow*'. Emphasis is thrown on λυπηρῶς (amounting to: 'that it will be to your sorrow that I convey you') and πέμπω by their placing. μὴ, because ἀνιῶμαι implies the idea of fear. The reading πέμπων (GR) is perhaps not to be rejected off-hand. Then we should construe: οὐκ ἀνιῶμαι μὴ λιπών σε <στέλλω τὸν πλοῦν> ἀλλὰ μᾶλλον λυπηρῶς σε πέμπων, or οὐκ ἀνιῶμαι ὅτι λιπών σε τὸν πλοῦν στελῶ, ἀλλὰ μὴ τὸν πλοῦν στέλλω λυπηρῶς σε πέμπων. Possibly Σ (οὐχ ὅτι καταλείψω σε ἄχθομαι ἀλλ' ὅτι λυπηρῶς καὶ οὐ κατὰ τὴν σὴν γνώμην μέλλω σε ἄγειν· ἐπὶ Τροίαν δέ φησιν) read πέμπων, but we cannot be sure.

915, 16. γὰρ: 'explanatory' γάρ, 'after an expression denoting the giving ... of information' (*G.P.*[2] p. 59 (2)). 'C'est que ...'.

στόλον: the fleet and the army.

917. τί εἶπας: the insertion of δ' (Jebb) is unnecessary, cf. *supra* 733.

918. ποῖον μάθημα;: cf. *Trach.* 427 ποίαν δόκησιν;.

919, 20. σῶσαι ... τοῦδ': κακοῦ τοῦδε: the νόσος [1]). Here for the first time this advantage of Philoctetes' return to the army is mentioned. This will be elaborated in 1326 sqq.: it will appear that it belongs to Helenus' prophecy. Cf. also 1378 sq. and 1424 (Hera-

---

[1]) But the wording is rather vague; one may also prefer to understand: 'this your miserable situation'.

cles). On the illogicality of Neoptolemus knowing the things he apparently cannot know and its necessity in view of Sophocles' dramatic design cf. Kitto, *Form and Meaning* pp. 127-135.

ξὺν σοί ... μολών: 1332 and 1335 might lead us to take τὰ Τροίας πεδία with μολών and <Τροίαν> as the object of πορθῆσαι. But this seems somewhat far-fetched, and we had perhaps better accept Jebb's: 'then go and ravage Troy's plains with thee'. ξὺν σοί belongs to πορθῆσαι (rather than to μολών) or to πορθῆσαι μολών.

921, 22. καί: for καί, not followed by an interrogative, introducing indignant (etc.) questions see *G.P.*² p. 311 II (a) and (b). *El* 1046 is a good parallel: καὶ τοῦτ' ἀληθές, οὐδὲ βουλεύσῃ πάλιν;

ἀληθῆ: there seems more to the use of ἀληθῆ than the label 'adverbial predicate' would lead us to suppose. Webster's periphrasis 'so that they will come true' seems correct.

πολλὴ ... / ... ἀνάγκη: τούτων, referring to ταῦτ', depends on κρατεῖ (sc. ὥστε οὕτω γενέσθαι). But it is hard to determine whether Neoptolemus here is supposed to think of the divine dispensation concerning Troy's fall, or of 'the compulsion on' him 'as a subordinate' (Webster). The two possibilities are not mutually exclusive.

καί: 'and therefore' (Campbell). He illustrates this 'slightly illative force' of καί with imperative by quoting Pl. *Gorg.* 449 c τούτου μὴν δεῖ, ὦ Γοργία· καί μοι ἐπίδειξιν αὐτοῦ τούτου ποίησαι.

923, 4. The resolutions, the shortness of the cola, the enjambment and the alliterations (λ, δ, τ) and assonances (ο, ω, α) are strikingly expressive of Philoctetes' violent emotion.

ὦ ξένε: after the many ὦ παῖ and τέκνον's (still in 914) this term is admirably calculated to express Philoctetes' feeling of estrangement. Note the recurrence of τέκνον in the pathetic verse 932.

925, 6. τῶν ... ἐν τέλει κλύειν: cf. *Ai.* 1352. οἱ ἐν τέλει *supra* 385, cf. *Ant.* 67.

τό ... ἔνδικον: refers to his duty as a subaltern towards his superiors. 'Duty' is a better translation than 'justice'.

τὸ συμφέρον: refers to the glory he will win.

927-962. Philoctetes' outburst of indignation is as vehement as his outpourings of gratitude were overwhelming. For Philoctetes, with Aiax and Oedipus (both in *O.T.* and in *O.C.*), as typically Sophoclean portrait of 'passionate' man, see J. C. Opstelten, *De Tragische Held bij Sophocles en zijn Dichter* in *De Antieke Tragedie*, 1947, pp. 71-73.

927, 8. ὦ πῦρ σύ: Neoptolemus is called πῦρ because of its destructive force; πῦρ = destructive force is to be perceived in epic phrases like καὶ εἰ πυρὶ χεῖρας ἔοικε *Il.* XX 371, μάρναντο δέμας πυρὸς αἰθομένοιο *Il.* XI 596, Ἕκτωρ πυρὸς αἰνὸν ἔχει μένος *Il.* XVII 565 and cp. Ar. *Lys.* 1015 οὐδὲν θηρίον γυναικὸς ἀμαχώτερον, οὐδὲ πῦρ, Eur. *Andr.* 271 ἐχίδνης καὶ πυρὸς περαιτέρω. Ar. *Eq.* 384 sq. ἦν ἄρα πυρός γ' ἕτερα θερμότερα καὶ λόγων / ἐν πόλει τῶν ἀναιδῶν ἀναιδέστεροι is relevant to our passage, because there θερμός (πῦρ) is associated with ἀναιδής (cf. Taillardat, *Les Images d'Aristophane*, § 313).

πᾶν δεῖμα: *qui totus terror es.* πᾶν is assimilated to the predicate[1]). δεῖμα amounts to 'monster'; cf. δεινὰ δειμάτων ἄχη Aesch. *Cho.* 586, δείματα θηρῶν Eur. *Her.* 700.

πανουργίας / δεινῆς τέχνημ' ἔχθιστον: 'exécrable modèle d'horrible perfidie' (Mazon). Note the contrast with 79, 80, 88 (cf. A. A. Long, *Language and Thought in Sophocles* pp. 116, 7). For the contemptuous use of the neuter in -μα cf. *Ant.* 756 δούλευμα, *Ai.* 381, 389 ἄλημα (cf. *Ant.* 320), *El.* 289 μίσημα. Climax is effectuated by the increasing size of the three vocativi, cf. *O.T.* 380, 1. I think that Jebb is right in rejecting the interpretation of τέχνημα = 'contriver' (*contra* Nauck and Webster).

930. τὸν προστρόπαιον: cf. Ed. Fraenkel ad *Ag.* 1587, quoting Otfrid Müller, *Aesch. Eumeniden*, p. 135: 'a προστρόπαιος, according to the primary meaning of the word, is like a ἱκέτης, one who turns towards another, beseeching him to take him in' etc. Cf. *Ai.* 1173 and πρόστροπον *supra* 773. But possibly the idea of *homo piacularis* (cf. 192 sqq., 1326 sqq.) is implied by a sort of dramatic irony. If not, it is simply synonym with τὸν ἱκέτην and the two reinforce each other.

ὦ σχέτλιε: 'wretch', as often in Tragedy.

931. ἀπεστέρηκας ... ἑλών: Jebb and Webster stress the difference in accentuation between βίος and βιός, 'so that no pun is intended or heard'. All the same there is much to be said for D. B. Robinson's discussion of the passage[2]) (taken together with 933 and 1282) in which, quoting Ar. *Plut.* 33, 4 τὸν ἐμὸν ... ἐκτετοξεῦσθαι βίον and Heracl. *fr.* 48 τῷ τόξῳ ὄνομα βίος, ἔργον δὲ θάνατος, he argues: 'We must consider the possibility that, without necessarily intending any direct echo of Heraclitus or allusion to his philosophy,

---

[1]) But Gow ad Theocr. 3. 18 thinks it probable that πᾶν, even with neuter nouns, was felt to be adverbial.

[2]) *Topics in Sophocles' Philoctetes*, Cl. Qu. N.S. XIX 1 (1969), pp. 43, 44.

Sophocles may have been displaying the same attitude to etymology as Heraclitus. He may have been hinting that for Philoctetes his τόξα = βιός was all too rightly named, since it was indeed his βίος, his means of livelihood'. This seems plausible.

τὸν βίον: for the uncommon accusative, caused by the parallelism with τὰ τόξ᾽ ἑλών see Kannicht ad Eur. *Hel.* 95.

932. The asyndeta (930/1, 931/2, 932/3, 933/4) are suggestive of breathless emotion and desperate frustration. So, likewise, the three resolutions in this verse, almost bursting out of bounds, and the two repetitions.

τέκνον: now that he takes recourse to supplication, the vocative τέκνον recurs.

933. τὸν βίον με μὴ ἀφέλῃς: LGR have μή μ᾽ ἀφέλῃς, metrically impossible, and a crasis μή μᾶφέλῃς (-ουα) is to be rejected; possible is μή μου 'φέλῃς A and others. Perhaps it is better to read με μὴ 'φέλῃς. Can ἀφαιρέω be used *and* construed with two accusativi as the much more common ἀφαιρέομαι? Sophocles has no other instances; Elmsley's με μὴ ἀφέλῃ (μὴ 'φέλῃ) has a chance of being correct. Men *Syc.* 252 μήπω μ᾽ ἀφέλῃς, but Reeve, followed by Kassel (ed. 1965), corrected into ἀφέλησθ', applauded by Ed. Fraenkel, *o.l.* p. 66. See Groeneboom ad Aesch. *Eum.* 360.

934, 5. προσφωνεῖ: transition to the third person, leading up to the invocation of the surroundings. At the end of the next pericope he turns again to Neoptolemus, passionately resuming ἀπόδος.

μεθήσων: τὰ τόξα, cf. 975. But the omission of the object has an effect well rendered by Mazon: 'mais il ne rendra rien' (lit. as 'some one who will never . . .'. ὡς is emphatically taken up by ὧδ᾽).

ὁρᾷ πάλιν: 'he averts his eyes'. Cf. Aesch. *Ag.* 777 παλιντρόποις ὄμμασι, *Suppl.* 173, 4 νῦν ἔχων παλίντροπον / ὄψιν ἐν λιταῖσιν, Eur. *Hec.* 343 πρόσωπον ἔμπαλιν / στρέφοντα.

936-39. Invocation of the surrounding nature with which he has been intimately conversant, just as Aiax in his utter distress *Ai.* 412 sqq..

λιμένες: 'bays', 'creeks' rather than 'harbours' (as is well remarked by Jebb).

προβλῆτες: well-known as adjective in Homer (with ἀκταί and the like); here, as in later authors, noun: 'headlands'. See ad 1455.

ὦ ξυνουσίαι / θηρῶν ὀρείων: 'concentrates our attention on the fact that the wild creatures of Lemnos form a fundamental part of Philoctetes' life' (Long, *o.l.* p. 111, who draws our attention to the meaningful exclamatory periphrases with abstract nouns here, 927, 8 and 952, quoting a number of other typical Sophoclean instances). Not: 'beasts crowding together' (Webster), but 'beasts with whom I dwell' (Jebb).

κατταρρῶγες: κατάρρώξ 'abruptus', 'praeceps', 'jagged', 'à pic': only here.

λέγω: subjunctive.

ἀνακλαίομαι: lit. 'I cry this aloud weeping'.

ὑμῖν ... / ... παροῦσι τοῖς εἰωθόσιν: παροῦσι is predicate, τοῖς εἰωθόσιν sc. παρεῖναι attribute to ὑμῖν [1]).

940, 1. οἷ' ἔργ' ... / ... ἄγει: Instead of writing either ὁμόσας γὰρ ἄξειν or μ' ἄγων the poet uses again asyndeton expressive of Philoctetes' agonizing indignation.

We might put either a colon or a comma after ἄγει.

942-44. προσθείς ... χεῖρα δεξιάν: 'having added the pledge of his hand' sc. to his oath (Jebb). Cf. 813. προσθείς is subordinated to λαβών; no question of a periphrastic construction λαβὼν ἔχει. Cf. fr. 472.1 P. ὅρκου δὲ προστεθέντος, and El. 47.

ἱερά ... τοῦ Ζηνὸς Ἡρακλέους: predicative (sc. ὄντα). Opinions are divided on the question, whether τοῦ Ζηνὸς Ἡρακλέους strictly depends on ἱερά ('sacred to'), or is to be regarded as a possessive genitive dependent on τόξα (sacra illa, quae quondam Herculis Iove prosati fuere E.). With the latter interpretation it is perhaps better to construe μου as ablatival genitive with λαβών (Webster).

καὶ θέλει: colon or full stop after θέλει. Webster, following Pearson, puts a comma, interpreting: 'he wishes it to appear to the Argives that'. This is surely impossible for φήνασθαι can not mean that. There is nothing against the asyndeton, on the contrary it is perfectly in harmony with the emotional, jerky style of this rhesis. As to φήνασθαι, this form does not occur elsewhere, but ἀπεφηνάμην is fairly common: the middle evidently means: 'show as his own', 'show as his trophy' [2]) (cf. the middle ἐπιδείκνυμαι). Cf. infra 1063, 4. (This interpretation is also possible with comma after θέλει and ὡς = ὅτι: 'will den Achaeern ihn als Beleg vorweisen, dass er mich, den starken Kämpfer überwältigte', v. Wilamowitz).

---

[1]) There is a very interesting discussion on 938, 9 in Due Seminari Romani di Eduard Fraenkel, pp. 66, 7. His students convince F. of the lines' authenticity!

[2]) Radermacher has the interesting note: φήνασθαι ostendere, nämlich τὰ τόξα, aber nicht tamquam praedam ... sondern tamquam mysterium. Perhaps too far-fetched.

945-47. ὡς: with ἑλών.

ἐκ βίας: with ἄγει.

ἐναίρων νεκρόν: cf. *Ant.* 1030 τὸν θανόντ' ἐπικτανεῖν. Possibly the verb ἐναίρω (rare in Soph.) is chosen because the bow is Neoptolemus' spoil.

καπνοῦ σκιάν, εἴδωλον ἄλλως: two phrases expressive of his utter impotence and debility. For καπνοῦ σκιά cf. Aesch. *fr.* 399 N.² τὸ γὰρ βρότειον σπέρμ' ἐφ' ἡμέραν φρονεῖ, / καὶ πιστὸν οὐδὲν μᾶλλον ἢ καπνοῦ σκιά, *Ant.* 1170. Both σκιά and καπνός (*Il.* XXIII 100) are easily associated with death and the dead, and so the first phrase prepares for the second (We cannot make out whether καπνοῦ σκιά properly means the shadow of smoke, or the shade (of a dead man) consisting of smoke).

εἴδωλον ἄλλως: 'merely a phantom'; cf. Eur. *Troad.* 476 ἀριθμὸν ἄλλως, *Hel.* 755 (μαντείας) βίου γὰρ ἄλλως δέλεαρ ηὑρέθη τόδε 'a mere bait'; Call. *Epigr.* 18.3 (Pf.) ἄλλως οὔνομα. (This is only a special case of ἄλλως 'otherwise than should be' < 'in vain'). We are reminded of *Ai.* 126, 7 οὐδὲν ἄλλο πλὴν / εἴδωλα . . . ἢ κούφην σκιάν. At Aesch. *Ag.* 839 εἴδωλον σκιᾶς 'denotes, as it were, the superlative of the unreal' (Ed. Fraenkel *a.l.*).

948. οὐδ' ἂν: εἷλεν.

950. <ἀλλ'> ἀπόδος: Turnebus <ἀλλ'> is far from certain. We might as well prefer ἀπόδος σύ γ Ven b. ἀλλὰ νῦν may be a case of 'limiting' ἀλλά ('now at least', cf. *Ant.* 552), but not necessarily so (cf. *G.P.*² p. 15).

ἐν σαυτοῦ γενοῦ: reading of A, preferred by Pearson for instance. The case for the genitive has received some corroboration from Men. *Sam.* 340 and *Asp.* 307, and see Colin Austin's note *ibidem*. The majority of edd. prefer to read ἐν σαυτῷ (LGR). I do not regard the question as settled. For ἐν αὐτῷ Jebb and others quote Xen. *An.* I 5.17 ἐν ἑαυτῷ ἐγένετο.

952, 3. The third address is to his wonted haunt, followed by an elaboration of the foreseeable misery of his life now that he is bereft of the bow, and ending in a renewed assault upon Neoptolemus: so the rhesis returns to its starting-point. —I think it possible that here Philoctetes returns to the entrance of the cave.

ὦ σχῆμα πέτρας δίπυλον: it is well observed by A. M. Dale ad *Alc.* 911 that periphrases with σχῆμα occur in emotional apostrophe[1]);

---

[1]) See Long *o.l.* p. 103 on the 'bitter and ironical' effect here: 'for a word appropriate to a palace is applied to a rock'. I am not sure that he is right.

other examples are Eur. *Andr.* 1 and *Hec.* 619. Here as at *Alc.* 911 the appearance of his haunt (as of the palace in *Alc.*) is as it were renewed 'through the strong feeling that sharpens his perception'. Mazon even goes so far as to translate 'O forme horrible de cette double porte ouverte dans le roc', borrowing the wording from Victor Hugo.

αὖθις αὖ πάλιν: emotional abundance of expression, not uncommon where the idea: 'again', 'once more', 'back' has to be made explicit.

ψιλός: bereft of the bow.

954. αὐανοῦμαι: indubitably the correct reading. Cf. *El.* 819. On the relation between 'drying up' and death cf. Onians, *The Origins of European Thought*, pp. 222 and pp. 255, 6, where he quotes schol. ad Ar. *Ran.* 194 (Αὐαίνου λίθος): ἀπὸ τοῦ αὔους τοὺς νεκροὺς εἶναι.

955-58. ὀρειβάτην: cf. ὀρεσσιβάτα *Ant.* 350.

τοισίδ': on this Ionic form, rare in Tragedy, see Ed. Fraenkel ad *Ag.* 520.

ὑφ' ὧν: Pearson followed Wunder in writing ἀφ', but Jebb's vindication of the mss text is valid ('Ph. is poetically saying that he had forced the beasts to become his τροφεῖς'). ὑφ' ὧν: <ἐκείνοις> or <τούτοις> ὑφ' ὧν.

καί μ' οὓς ἐθήρων . . . νῦν: the motif of the hunter hunted is central to Euripides' *Bacchae*. Here it is, I think, no more than a *concetto* prompted by the situation of the moment and leading up to the next two lines. The motif, however, recurs 1146 sqq.. I do not think 958 is an interpolation (Bergk, Ed. Fraenkel, *o.l.* p. 67).

959-60. φόνον . . . τείσω: It is certainly not far-fetched to derive this idea from the very ancient sense of guilt of the hunter towards his game, with which hunting rituals and taboos are connected (Burkert, *Homo Necans, passim*).

ῥύσιον: 'compensation'. On this word and its difficult semasiology cf. Ed. Fraenkel ad *Ag.* 534, Chantraine, *Dict. Ét. s.v.* ἐρύω.

πρός: by the agency of.

961, 2. ὄλοιο — μήπω: thus correctly printed by Jebb, Bruhn, D.-M.. 'May you perish—no, not yet, not before. . .'. Cf. *Trach.* 383, Eur. *Med.* 83.

γνώμην μετοίσεις: = μεταγνώσηι, 'change one's mind', implying 'repent', cf. 1270 καὶ μεταγνῶναι πάλιν, echoing Philoctetes' words here. This unmistakable echo and the natural interpretation of 1270

(v. Wilamowitz' free translation runs: 'Manchmal besinnt man sich auch eines bess'ren') make me demur at the habitual interpretations of καί in 961 (either with εἰ 'indeed' or with πάλιν 'even'); would it not be better to take καί with the whole clause: 'also' verging on 'still', 'for all that' (note that Jebb translates: 'till I see if thou wilt still change thy purpose').

πάλιν: I do not think that πάλιν is simply pleonastic. The fundamental meaning of πάλιν is *retro* rather than *rursus*. So in πάλιν the idea of 'drawing back from his purpose' is intended; it reinforces γνώμην μετοίσεις but adds to it an element of its own.

963, 4. ἐν σοί ... / ... ἐστί: 'it rests with you', very common in Hdt. and Tragedy.

καὶ τὸ πλεῖν ... / ... καὶ ... προσχωρεῖν: τὸ may be regarded as being used ἀπὸ κοινοῦ, or there is a slight variation of expression. Another matter is the question whether καὶ ... καὶ are disjunctive ('whether ... or') as the translations of Jebb, von Wilamowitz and Mazon imply, or purely and emphatically coordinative. It is, of course, true that emphatic coordination easily implies disjunction; cf. *O.C.* 1443, 4 ταῦτα δ' ἐν τῷ δαίμονι / καὶ τῇδε φῦναι χἀτέρᾳ (quoted by Denniston *G.P.*² 324, with the rendering 'whether ... or ...'). What the Coryphaeus wants to express must amount to: sail now to Troy or give in to Philoctetes' wishes (i.e. sail home taking him with you). But the alternative is not clearly and explicitly expressed.

ἤδη: best taken with πλεῖν: 'now', 'immediately' (thus Campbell and Webster).

965, 6. ἐμοὶ μέν: emphatic μέν 'solitarium'? But see end of this note. οὐ νῦν πρῶτον, ἀλλὰ καὶ πάλαι: 'Das πάλαι von 966 fällt schon dadurch heraus, dass seine lange Dauer so entschieden hervorgeheben ist: οὐ νῦν πρῶτον, ἀλλὰ καὶ πάλαι. Das ist hier auch besonders berechtigt, da der Zeitpunkt der ersten Sichtbarkeit des οἶκτος δεινός bis zum Beginn der Szene (730 ff.) zurückführt'. (Jens-Uwe Schmidt, *Sophokles-Philoktet* (1973) p. 171). It is not to be excluded that μέν presupposes an undelivered member with δέ, amounting to: 'but there is my loyalty to the Atreidae and Odysseus to be considered'. At any rate, notwithstanding his pity he has not as yet reached the point, where he sides with Philoctetes. His ἀμηχανία is the greater the stronger his pity grows.

967, 8. Philoctetes jumps at Neoptolemus' uttering of pity.

ἐλέησον: implies: show your pity by your deeds.

σαυτοῦ: objective genitive with ὄνειδος. GR have σαυτόν: 'do not let yourself become an object of reproach amongst men' (preferred by G. Hermann and Ed. Fraenkel *o.l.* p. 68).

ἐκκλέψας ἐμέ: 'through your deceiving me' (Campbell); cf. *supra* 55.

969, 70. Perfect expression of complete distraction. The wish for the past unattainable object, characteristic for this state of mind (cf. *O.T.* 1157), may be regarded as a first step towards renunciation of the promised glory.

971-73. Philoctetes attempts to take advantage of Neoptolemus' perplexity.

αἰσχρά: object of μαθών, receives emphasis by its position. Webster is quite right in rejecting οἵ' (Dindorf, Pearson): it is clear that <τὰ> αἰσχρά is object of δούς, and οἷς εἰκός is to be explained as = οἷς εἰκὸς τὰ αἰσχρὰ δοῦναι ('leave to').

ἔκπλει ... μεθείς: to all appearances Philoctetes has given up the idea of being taken home by Neoptolemus.

Second scene 974-1069, Odysseus, Phil., Neopt. (silent), Chorus.

974, 5. τί δρῶμεν, ἄνδρες;: Odysseus' subsequent words make it probable, that while asking this question, Neoptolemus makes a step in Philoctetes' direction. Thus, rightly I think, among others, Knox, *The Heroic Temper*, p. 133. Odysseus, at this critical moment, suddenly makes his appearance. He is supposed by a number of commentators to have kept in hiding at a look-out post not far from the place of action, but Webster, rightly I think, rejects this idea: 'Sophocles would have told us if he had arrived earlier'.

Odysseus arrives with attendants (983, 1003).

πάλιν: 'back', with εἶ.

μεθείς ... ἐμοί: Neoptolemus does not comply.

977. ἐμοῦ γ': on 'epexegetic' γε (giving 'force and urgency to an addition or supplement') see *G.P.*² pp. 138, 9.

978. πέπραμαι: cf. *Ant.* 1036 ἐξημπόλημαι.

979. ἀπονοσφίσας: ἀπονοσφίζω 'rob of'; there are a number of instances of νοσφίζω with this meaning and construction in Aesch., Eur., Pind., and cf. *infra* 1427; see also *supra* 683.

980. Odysseus is depicted as glorying in the successful deception and very sure of himself. His ultimate failure will be the more impressive.

981-83. αὐτοῖς: the bow. The great objection against interpreting αὐτοῖς as referring to Odysseus' attendants (not to speak of Neoptolemus and the Chorus) is this that, then, the need of Philoctetes-with-his-bow would be left out of account; 'if it is objected that the bow cannot be said to στείχειν, the answer is that στείχειν ἅμ' αὐτοῖς is merely a way of saying στείχειν ἅμα τοῖς τὰ τόξα φέρουσι' (Jebb).

στελοῦσι: Odysseus' attendants; 'ces gens te feront partir de force' (Mazon).

If this ellipse of the intended subject is not accepted, the best remedy of the text is perhaps J. Jackson's proposal στείχειν ὁμοῦ τοῖσδ' (the attendants), ἢ βίᾳ στελοῦσί σε. Then the objection mentioned above remains. Dawe's στελῶ σ' ἐγώ (*Studies* III, p. 132) is rather drastic.

984, 5. τολμήστατε: the objections against this form are illusory; cf. Schw.-Debr. I 249. -ηε- > η, cf. τιμῆντα, *Il.* XVIII 475.

ἐκ βίας ἄξουσιν: another way of saying βίᾳ στελοῦσιν.

986-88. τὸ ... σέλας / 'Ηφαιστότευκτον: cf. note ad 799-801.

δῆτ': on δῆτα in questions preceded by ταῦτα, εἶτα, ἔπειτα with a tone of indignation cf. the instances listed in *G.P.*[2] p. 272.

ἐκ τῶν σῶν: sc. precincts (or the like).

989, 90. ἵν' εἰδῇς: 'I tell you' (Campbell).

ὁ τῆσδε γῆς κρατῶν: τῆσδε γῆς: Lemnos. The phrase implies that Zeus is the higher authority over Hephaestus and local gods.

There is much disagreement on the interpretation of these lines. Kitto (*Form and Meaning* pp. 122, 3), quoting these words, adds: '"The dent you are!" we think ... If Sophocles wishes us to see in Philoctetes a man who is mistakenly opposing the will of the gods, he is setting about it in a very strange way'. Reinhardt (p. 196), on the other hand, comments 'wenn er—Odysseus—sich auf Zeus beruft, geschieht es keineswegs, damit die Situation ironisch der Berufung widerspräche' and he thinks that: 'in Odysseus das zielende Zupacken, in Philoktet die Stimme der verratenen und verletzten Menschlichkeit, beide in ihrem Recht < einander sinnfällig als gleichgewichtig gegenüberstehen >'. This, and the verdict: 'So sehr er—Philoctetes—als Leidender im Recht ist, so wenig ist er im Recht als Handelnder' are in my opinion 'überspitzt'. I should prefer to subscribe to Kirkwood's words referring to our passage: 'Ironically enough, it is this shifty opportunist who is in accord with the will of Zeus, to which the heroic individualist eventually submits' (Kirkwood, *o.l.* p. 149, and see also pp. 260, 1, on the 'irony' of the situation). But it should be remembered that Odysseus 'serves' the plan of Zeus in the wrong way.

991, 2. ὦ μῖσος: cf. *El.* 289 ὦ δύσθεον μίσημα; *Ant.* 760 ἄγετε τὸ μῖσος.

καί: 'actually'. Cf. *El.* 385 ἦ ταῦτα δή με καὶ βεβούλευνται ποιεῖν;

θεοὺς . . . τίθης: because, if Odysseus rightly appeals to Zeus, Zeus is responsible for Odysseus' fraud. The premise of Philoctetes' outcry is that the gods cannot be guilty of crime. Cf. Pl. *Resp.* II 382 a-e. See L. Schmidt, *Die Ethik der alten Griechen* II (1882) p. 407.

993. ἀληθεῖς: spoken from the conviction that the Helenus-oracle will come true; 'true prophets' is Jebb's translation.

πορευτέα: σοί, or σοί καὶ ἐμοί, or σοὶ ἅμ' ἡμῖν. But the necessity of the journey to Troy is the more forcibly expressed by the very laconism of the wording. This laconism is continued in the next line, admirably suggestive of the irreconcilability of the positions.

994. Φι.οὔ φημ'. Ὀδ. ἐγὼ δέ φημι: Jebb's vindication of Gernhard's reading is convincing, as Campbell recognized in *Paral. Soph.* p. 221.

995, 6. μὲν: *solitarium*; the implied contrast is self-evident: while *you* (Odysseus, the Atreidae) are born rulers.

σαφῶς: σαφῶς and ἄρα reinforce each other.

οὐδ': = ἀλλ' οὐκ.

997, 8. τοῖς ἀρίστοισιν: referring in the first place to Neoptolemus. (ἀριστεῦσιν G is a very plausible reading).

999, 1000. οὐδεποτέ γ': 'no, never'. I prefer to punctuate as follows: οὐδέποτέ γ', οὐδ' ἦν . . . κακόν,. The clause with ἕως is dependent on οὐδεποτέ γε <πείσομαι>. Or we have to assume that with ἕως (possibly better ἕως <δ'>) a new sentence begins, which is interrupted by Odysseus. Then a colon should be written after κακόν.

ἕως . . . βάθρον: I do not believe that Webster is right in thinking that Philoctetes has not moved from the opening of the cave since 730. If τόδ' αἰπεινὸν βάθρον refers to the platform before the cave, he will have returned to it at 952. But perhaps it is better to imagine that there was visible on the stage a steep cliff from which Philoctetes wants to throw himself (Cf. D. B. Robinson, Cl.Qu. 1969 p. 41; but it is not necessary to assume that in 814 this cliff is referred to). Others understand the phrase γῆς . . . βάθρον as referring to the whole rocky foundation of Lemnos: 'the island with its sheer cliffs, on which he is standing' (Jebb), 'this Lemnian steep' (Campbell), and cp. Mazon's translation,—but it fails to make clear how exactly we must understand the passage;—better, in my opinion, von Wilamowitz: 'noch ragt der Fels dort über jähem Abgrund'. (*Er wendet sich auf die Felsen zu*). γῆς can be interpreted as meaning: 'belonging to', 'formed by' this land. It is not even necessary (if 814 is left out of account) to think of a rock to be climbed: we can easily imagine that Philoctetes is supposed to approach the brink—level with the bottom of the stage—of a precipice. (By no means are we obliged to suppose that the stage is meant to be thought of as level with the sea; we are not on a beach).

1001, 2. ἐργασείεις: this desiderative also *Trach.* 1232.

κρᾶτ᾽: acc. sing. neuter; see Chantraine, *Morph. histor.*² p. 84. Frequent in Soph..

κρᾶτ᾽ ... | πέτρᾳ ... πεσών: πρὸς τῇ πέτρᾳ ἐναιμάξω τὴν κεφελήν μου ἄνωθεν πεσὼν ἀπὸ πέτρας (Σ). ἄνωθεν is adverb, πέτρας separative genitive, πέτρᾳ instrumental or locative dative. πίπτειν, as often, *ruere* rather than *cadere*.

1003. ξυλλάβετέ γ᾽ αὐτόν: on γε in commands see *G.P.*² p. 125 (7). But the correct reading is uncertain: LAGR have ξυλλάβετ᾽ αὐτόν, T ξυλλάβετε τοῦτον, evidently a conjecture. Bernhardy's conjecture ξυλλάβετον αὐτόν was adopted by Jebb. Campbell (comm. and *Paral. Soph.* p. 221) opts for the reading of A ('Ay, apprehend him'), supposing the attendants to have advanced of their own accord on seeing the intention of Philoctetes.

μὴ ᾽πὶ τῷδ᾽ ἔστω τάδε: μὴ ἔστω ἐπὶ τῷ Φιλοκτήτῃ ἡ ἐξουσία τοῦ κατακρημνίζεσθαι.

1004, 5. ὦ χεῖρες: cf. *Trach.* 1089 sqq.

ἐν χρείᾳ: 'for want of'. 'Now that I am bereft of'.

φίλης | νευρᾶς: cf. *infra* 1128 sqq.

συνθηρώμεναι: cf. *Ant.* 432, 3 σὺν δέ νιν | θηρώμεθα.

1006, 7. μηδὲν ὑγιὲς: on this, probably colloquial phrase see P. T. Stevens ad Eur. *Andr.* 448. In my opinion the use of μηδὲν is to be atributed to the tendency to use μή, where strong affect is involved (cf. the remark in K.-G. II 201 Anm. 3 and Schw.-Debr. II 594 (last six lines of the page)).

ἐλεύθερον: as often = ἐλευθέριον, cf. L.-Sc. *s.v.* II. (ἐλευθέριος does not occur in Tragedy except for τὸν ἐλευθέριον Ζῆνα *Rhes.* 358).

ὑπῆλθες: 'entrap' cf. *O.T.* 386 λάθρᾳ μ᾽ ὑπελθών, Eur. *Andr.* 435 οἴμοι· δόλῳ μ᾽ ὑπῆλθες, ἠπατήμεθα.

1008, 9. πρόβλημα: as a shield, a screen.

ἀνάξιον μὲν σοῦ, κατάξιον δ᾽ ἐμοῦ: 'caesura media' (but, as in the majority of cases, a perispomenon before the diaeresis). By this, by the rhyme and by the parallel structure of the two contrasting cola a lapidary effect is brought about. ἀνάξιον σοῦ amounts to: 'too good for you' and the meaning of κατάξιον δ' ἐμοῦ is defined by the antithesis. Cf. *Ant.* 518, *infra* 1021. The purport of the verse is well rendered by von Wilamowitz: 'Kein Schelm wie du, ein Ehrenmann wie ich'.

1010. Cf. *supra* 53 and 925.

1011, 2. δῆλος δὲ καὶ νῦν ἐστιν: Jebb attributes to καὶ νῦν the meaning 'already' ('though the time for remorse has been short'); others interpret 'encore à cette heure' (Mazon), 'jetzt noch' (v. Wilamowitz). Neither is convincing; Jebb does not give instances of the supposed usage. I think we should take καὶ as belonging to the whole clause and coming near to αὖ; or we might render by 'even' but without closely linking it with νῦν.

οἷς τ' . . . οἷς τ': τούτοις ἅ; the dative with ἀλγεινῶς φέρων as with the verba affectuum, ἄχθομαι and the like.

1013-15. διὰ μυχῶν βλέπουσ': Webster's 'looking through the innermost recesses of Neoptolemus' mind' seems more plausible than Jebb's 'ever peering from some ambush' (and similar interpretations); v. Wilamowitz' rendering 'Doch überall sieht deine Schurkenschlauheit / die schwache Stelle' apparently amounts to the same idea. For a metaphorical use of μυχός cf. Theocr. 29. 3 κἀγὼ μὲν τὰ φρένων ἐρέω κέατ' ἐν μύχῳ (Gow does not know other instances).

ἀφυῆ: 'by nature unsuited' sc. ἐν κακοῖς εἶναι σοφόν. Not: 'ungrown (and nevertheless unwilling)' suggested by Webster as an alternative. Possibly we should write ἀφυᾶ (the Attic form).

προυδίδαξεν: again, as in προὔμαθον, it is a moot point whether in προ- the notion 'gradually' is present, or whether it simply means 'beforehand' so that the verb means no more than 'instructed'.

Philoctetes' analysis is in agreement with the proceedings in the Prologue: cf. 26, 54, 93, 4, 86-9, 96-9, 109 sqq.. See Jens-Uwe Schmidt, *Sophokles-Philoktet*, pp. 184, 5 for a good discussion of the matter.

1016-18. συνδήσας: this does not mean that the attendants *have* fettered him. They are holding him by the arms till Odysseus commands them to release him 1054.

προυβάλου: much stronger than προθέντες 268, but cf. ἔρριψαν 265. Jebb quotes *Ai.* 829, 30 μὴ . . . / ῥιφθῶ κυσὶν πρόβλητος. The middle emphasizes Odysseus' responsibility.

ἄφιλον ἐρῆμον: cf. 228. On ἄπολιν see ad 1028.

ἐν ζῶσιν νεκρόν: cf. *Ant.* 920, 850-52; 1167 ἔμψυχον νεκρόν.

1019. καί: 'and indeed' (verging on 'and yet').

1020-24. ἀλλ' οὐ γάρ . . . μοι: cf. *G.P.*² pp. 98, 99. ἀλλ' belongs to the main sentence, γάρ to the dependent clause, which expresses the cause of what is conveyed by the main sentence introduced by ἀλλ'; the adversative function of ἀλλ' refers to the vainness, the unavailingness of the preceding words. The clause with γάρ immediately explains the adversative notion implied in ἀλλ'.

σὺ μὲν . . . ἐγὼ δ' . . .: 'caesura media', cf. *supra* 1009.

τοῦτ' αὖθ': internal accus. with ἀλγύνομαι, elaborated by the ὅτι-clause.

ὅτι ζῶ,: *Pace* Jebb I should say that a comma after ζῶ is desirable but (and here I agree with him) also one after τάλας. In my opinion σὺ μὲν . . . / . . . ζῶ together form a strong antithesis; τοῦτ' αὖθ' ὅτι ζῶ means 'just because of the fact that I am alive'. Then σὺν κακοῖς πολλοῖς τάλας is a development, not 'determinative' but rather 'digressive'. ὅτι ζῶ, σὺν . . . τάλας, seems to me a condensation of: ὅτι ζῶ, καὶ ταῦτα ζῶν σὺν κακοῖς πολλοῖς τάλας. This, again, is elaborated by means of the circumstantial participle γελώμενος. The painful clash between τάλας and γελώμενος is clearly perceivable.

1025-28. κλοπῇ τε κἀνάγκῃ: referring to Palamedes' ruse and the ensuing necessity for Odysseus to give up his madness. The story was told in the *Cypria* (Procl. *Chrestom.* 118 Severijns), alluded to in Aesch. *Ag.* 841, and was the argument of Sophocles' Ὀδυσσεὺς μαινόμενος.

ζυγείς: under the yoke of service under Agamemnon. Cf. Aesch. *l.c.*. But, regarding κλοπῇ τε κἀνάγκῃ as a hendiadys, we can also interpret: 'brought by means of ruse under the yoke of necessity'.

ἑπτὰ ναυσὶ ναυβάτην: lit. 'as a seafarer with seven ships' (cf. *Il.* II 718); ναυβάτην is an instance of rhetorical redundancy.

ἄτιμον ἔβαλον: ἔβαλον = ἐξέβαλον or προὔβαλον. ἄτιμον 'bereft of his τιμή, with all that this implies for an 'epic hero'; ἄπολιν 1018 does not in fact much differ from it in its purport, but has an anachronistic tinge.

Σ σὺ μέν, φησίν, ἐκείνους αἰτιᾷ, ἐκεῖνοι δὲ σέ. For ὡς σὺ φής cf. *supra* 6.

1029, 30. τί μ' ἄγετε; τί μ' ἀπάγεσθε: 'pourquoi m'emmener, pourquoi m'entraîner avec vous?' (Mazon) This seems better than Webster's 'why do you have me exported' for τί μ' ἀπάγεσθε.

οὐδέν εἰμι: cf. 1018 ἐν ζῶσιν νεκρόν.

ὑμῖν: 'as far as it rested with you'. Cf. *Ai.* 1128, Denniston ad Eur. *El.* 608.

1031-34. σοι: in your view.

πῶς θεοῖς ... / ... πῶς σπένδειν ἔτι: εὔξεσθ' is the mss reading, but it is very difficult to accept the infinitivi praesentis αἴθειν and σπένδειν as dependent on it; for, then, εὔξεσθ' must mean 'promise', 'vow' and we need the future (Campbell's vindication of the present, εὔχεσθαι meaning 'to vaunt' > 'promise' is not convincing). Pierson's ἔξεστ' (or ἔξεσθ' combined with the *v.l.* of G ὁμοῦ, thus Jebb) is accepted by many editors. Another way out, and a better one in my view, is to retain εὔξεσθ' ('pray'), to accept ὁμοῦ, to put a; after πλεύσαντος, a comma after ἱερά and to conjecture τ' ἔνι after σπένδειν: πῶς θεοῖς εὔξεσθ' ὁμοῦ πλεύσαντος; (ἐμοῦ is easily understood from the context) αἴθειν ἱερὰ πῶς σπένδειν τ' ἔνι; This was, in the first instance, proposed by Kuiper *in apparatu*, and then by Radermacher *in apparatu* (apparently independently of Kuiper; Pearson, in mentioning Radermacher's conjecture, forgot to add the latter's τ' before ἔνι). For Odysseus 'πρόφασις' (cf. Σ 1033) cf. *supra* 9 sqq.. The strained word order can be defended by the impassioned character of the passage. The elimination of the somewhat difficult ἔτι seems to me a gain.

πρόφασις: (falsely) alleged motive.

1035-39. ὀλεῖσθε δ': Brunck's certain conjecture; Jebb aptly compares Ar. *Thesm.* 887 κάκιστ' ἄρ' ἐξόλοιο, — κάξολεῖ γέ τοι.

θεοῖσιν εἰ δίκης μέλει. / ἔξοιδα δ' ὡς μέλει γ': cf. *Trach.* 809, 10: εἰ θέμις δ', ἐπεύχομαι· / θέμις δ', ἐπεί ...

ἐπεί: with the same function as γάρ.

κέντρον θεῖον ... ἐμοῦ: for κέντρον 'Antrieb der Leidenschaft' cf. Aesch. *Suppl.* 110. 'Dass Sophokles ἐμοῦ zufügt, als ob es ἐπιθυμία wäre, ist seine Kühnheit' (v. Wilamowitz, Übersetzung p. 113).

1040-42. ὦ πατρῷα γῆ: I do not believe that v. Wilamowitz is right in declaring that Philoctetes invokes his fatherland because the Atreidae have suffered when arriving home; rather would it seem that he is thinking of Mount Oeta and Zeus; ἐπόψιος, though here epithet of the gods in general, is special epithet of Zeus: see Pfeiffer's note ad Call. *fr.* 85.14. Cf. *El.* 175 Ζεύς, ὃς ἐφορᾷ πάντα καὶ κρατύνει. The verse is very similar to *El.* 67 ἀλλ', ὦ πατρῷα γῆ θεοί τ' ἐγχώριοι. I do not think that the Erinyes are meant.

ἀλλὰ τῷ χρόνῳ ποτε: cf. *El.* 1013; 411 ὦ θεοὶ πατρῷοι, συγγένεσθέ γ' ἀλλὰ νῦν.

κἄμ': 'καὶ in the protasis sometimes logically refers to the apodosis' *G.P.*[2] p. 304 (V). Without forcing the sense a translation 'if, indeed, you . . .' will do. At any rate, καὶ belongs to the verb, not to ἐμέ: 'wie ihr sonst der Leidenden euch erbarmt' (Schn.-N.-Raderm.) is wrong.

1043, 44. ὡς: for ὡς introducing the ground after an imperative at the end of a rhesis, see Ed. Fraenkel, *Zu den Phoenissen des Euripides*, p. 66.

ζῶ μὲν οἰκτρῶς: picking up 1022.

τῆς νόσου πεφευγέναι: *Od.* I 18 has οὐδ' ἔνθα πεφευγμένος ἦεν ἀέθλων, *Ant.* 488, 9 οὐκ ἀλύξετον / μόρου. Further it is clear that πεφευγέναι amounts to the same as ἀπηλλάχθαι, ἠλευθερῶσθαι.

1045, 6. βαρύς: <ἔστιν>. The meaning amounts to: bearing a heavy grudge. Cf. *Trach.* 1202 μενῶ σ' ἐγὼ / καὶ νέρθεν ὢν ἀραῖος εἰσαεὶ βαρύς; *Ai.* 656 μῆνιν βαρεῖαν, *Ant.* 767 νοῦς δ' ἔστι τηλικοῦτος ἀλγήσας βαρύς.

ὑπείκουσαν: transferred from the man to his words (Sophocles could have written ὑπείκοντος κακοῖς). The similarity in conception of Sophocles' inflexible protagonists clearly appears from the parallel *Ant.* 471, 2 δηλοῖ τὸ γέννημ' ὠμὸν ἐξ ὠμοῦ πατρὸς / τῆς παιδός· εἴκειν δ' οὐκ ἐπίσταται κακοῖς.

1047, 8. εἴ μοι παρείκοι: εἰ ὁ καιρὸς ἐπιτρέψειέ μοι Σ. Cf. Thuc. III 1.2 ὅπη παρείκοι 'wherever it was practicable', Thuc. IV 36.2 κατὰ τὸ αἰεὶ παρεῖκον; the impersonal παρείκει, amounting to 'it is possible', is also to be found in Plato. Probably the simplex is so used in Sappho 31.8 (where see Page). παρείκει is almost a synonym of ἐγχωρεῖ.

νῦν δ' ἑνὸς κρατῶ λόγου: 'But, as it is, I can say no more than one thing' (I have no leisure to say more). This announces, not the following lines, but 1053 (νῦν δὲ) sqq.; 1049-1053 form a parenthesis leading up to νῦν δὲ, but at the same time they contain, briefly, the justification of the conduct he professes not to have the leisure to expound circumstantially.

1049-51. οὗ γὰρ . . . ἐγώ·: Campbell is probably right to take this line in a general meaning: 'Where this or that character [1]) is needed, I am of that character' and to reject Jebb's assumption that

---

[1]) τοιούτων may be neuter.

τοιούτων is a euphemistic substitution of, for instance, δολίων. (This is the course also followed by Mazon and Webster). (γὰρ does not denote more than: 'you know' and is not causal in relation to νῦν δ' ἑνὸς κρατῶ λόγου). We are reminded of Theogn. 213-18 (see Hudson-Williams *a.l.*). What Odysseus says, is entirely in agreement with his expostulations with Neoptolemus (cf. in particular 81-85).

χὥπου: καὶ as 'aussi', first word of a sentence in French.

κρίσις: δοκιμασία, ἐξέτασις Σ.

1052, 3. νικᾶν γε: cf. 134 (and 81).

ἔφυν: with the participle, cf. *O.T.* 9 ἐπεὶ πρέπων ἔφυς πρὸ τῶνδε φωνεῖν.

πλὴν ἐς σέ: this comes as an ἀπρόσδοκητον, and introduces the 'one word' he has to say.

1054-56. ἄφετε γὰρ αὐτόν: no indention is called for: 'the γάρ clause forms a confirmation of what precedes: "For I say, release him"' (*G.P.*² p. 61).

οὐδὲ σοῦ ... / ... τά γ' ὅπλα ἔχοντες ταῦτ': 'indeed we do not need *you*, now that we have those *arms*'; there is something to be said for reading οὐδέ σου: 'indeed we do not *need* you, now that we *have* those *arms*'.

I am convinced, as I was long ago in my contestation of Tycho von Wilamawitz' interpretation of the play (*Studiën over Sophocles*, 1934, pp. 33, 4) that Odysseus' *volte-face* is a bluff made in the hope that Philoctetes will come round when he sees himself deserted and defenceless. I entirely agree with A. E. Hinds' discussion of the matter, *Prophecy of Helenus in Sophocles' Philoctetes*, Cl.Qu. 1967, pp. 177 sqq. (and see his note p. 177.4. Add to the authorities there mentioned U. von Wilamowitz, *Einleitung*, p. 27).

1056-59. Τεῦκρος ... / ἐγώ θ': these considerations are of course meant to arouse Philoctetes' ambition, but they only heighten his rage and despair.

πάρεστι ... / ... παρ' ἡμῖν: 'in our army there is Teucer at hand'.

μὲν / ... / ἐγώ θ': *G.P.*² p. 375; there is no contrast at all.

τήνδ' ἐπιστήμην: the art of archery; its specialists among the Achaeans are well-known from Homer.

οὐδὲν ... / ... μηδ': After the normal οὐ in οὐδὲν, μηδ' follows with the second infinitive. Again (see *supra* 1006) it would seem that μη is used as a stronger equivalent of οὐ; the use of μὴ with part. and inf. gradually grows more frequent in Attic. Jebb's idea viz. to take οὐδὲν with κάκιον and μηδ' with ἐπιθύνειν is not valid, because κάκιον belongs to the second clause as well (thus rightly Webster). The case is the more noticeable because there was nothing to prevent the poet from writing οὐδ'—if not a desire for emphasis. Dawe's remedy κρατύνων τῆδ' (*Studies* III, p. 133) is clever.

1060-62. τί δῆτα σοῦ δεῖ: a case of 'ring-composition' in a text not at all 'archaic' in character.

χαῖρε τὴν Λῆμνον πατῶν: up to a point *Trach.* 819 ἀλλ' ἑρπέτω χαίρουσα is comparable. The sarcasm is an instance of the utmost cruelty; in τὴν may befelt a contemptuous 'your'.

καὶ ... / ... ἔχειν: Unmistakably, it seems to me, Odysseus is attempting to allure Philoctetes by appealing to his φιλοτιμία.

1063, 4. τί δράσω δύσμορος: 'The thought of Odysseus in proud possession of the bow is almost more than he can bear' (Linforth, *o.l.* p. 136). One moment it seems that Odysseus' ruse may succeed.

σὺ ... / ... κοσμηθεὶς ... φανῇ: cf. *supra* 944.

1065. μή μ' ἀντιφώνει μηδέν: construed on the analogy of e.g. προσέφη, ἀνταμείβομαι.

ὡς στείχοντα δή: Philoctetes is to feel that Odysseus is in earnest. Hence his warning to Neoptolemus; his ruse will fail either if the latter returns the bow (which will actually happen in the next act), or if he casts doubt on the seriousness of Odysseus' declared purpose. He reckons on Philoctetes' coming round when reduced to despair.

1066, 7. ὦ σπέρμ' 'Αχιλλέως: the address in itself implies an appeal to Neoptolemus' better feelings.

οὐδὲ σοῦ φωνῆς ... / ... προσφθεγκτός: the genitive as with the adjective compounds with α *privans*; cf. *O.C.* 1722 δυσάλωτος κακῶν, *O.T.* 1437 μηδενὸς προσήγορος (K.-G. I 402 Anm. 7).

1068, 9. During the preceding scene Neoptolemus had stood silent, a bewildered and shame-faced witness of the painful goings-on; his loyalty to Odysseus has not yet completely broken down although he has not handed over the bow to him. Apparently he wants to aid Odysseus' ruse to succeed (1078); so he does not address Philoctetes.

ἡμῶν ... τὴν τύχην: 'our good fortune' (We have to assume that Odysseus is convinced of the success of his ruse).

γενναῖός περ ὤν: 'noble though you are', better to be taken with πρόσλευσσε (Jebb, Webster, Kirkwood *o.l.* pp. 145, 243) than within the final clause (von Wilamowitz-Radermacher-, Dain-Mazon).

Third scene, 1070-1080, Philoctetes, Neoptolemus, Chorus.

1070-80. Philoctetes appeals to the Chorus not to leave him alone; the Chorus relegates the request to Neoptolemus' authority. Neoptolemus decides in its favour (not addressing Philoctetes, but the Chorus): The Chorus is allowed to remain until the ship is ready to sail. He hopes that Philoctetes 'will come to a better mind' (1078, 9).

On the fictional plane of the action and the interplay of the characters and their evolution this is all very plausible, and on the real plane of stage action and structure, the poet, in this way, subtly manages to get the stage free for Philoctetes to confront the Chorus on his own, and to compose on a large scale the lyrical scene in which the hero's own sense of his situation, plunged deep in misery and full of inexorable wrath, is elaborated.

1070, 1. πρὸς ὑμῶν: with λειφθήσομαι, and cf. *Ant.* 919 ἐρῆμος πρὸς φίλων.

δή: for δή in indignant questions cf. *G.P.*² p. 236. The transmitted text has ἤδη, but elision of -αι is so rare in Tragedy (K.-B. I 238) that Wakefield's correction is generally accepted.

1072, 3. ναυκράτωρ: here: 'master of the ship'. In Hdt. and Thuc. the word means 'master of the sea' (= ναυκρατής).

1074-77. ἀκούσομαι: cf. 607.

τοῦδ': Odysseus.

τούτῳ: Philoctetes. εἰ comes near to 'since', *siquidem*.

τά τ' ἐκ νεὼς: instead of τά τ' ἐν νηΐ, since Greek has the tendency to denote adjuncts of place relating to things beyond the reach of the speaker by ἐκ rather than by ἐν. Thus some commentators. I am not convinced of the correctness of the interpretation in this case. Rather would it seem that something like 'the things that are fixed to the ship' (cf. K.-G. I 544 C) is expressed by the phrase; at any rate the rigging is meant [1]. Tournier's τά τῆς νεὼς, accepted by Pearson, is an easy way out (the second hasta of H could, with the C, have been misread as K and ⊦ then altered into E, ϵ); τ(ε) is certainly not indispensable.

1078-80. φρόνησιν ... / λῷω: 'a better way of thinking' (Long, *o.l.* p. 83); cf. *infra* 1098.

ὁρμώμεθον: on this very rare dual of the first person see Schw. I 672.4. (νώ: Odysseus and Neoptolemus). I do not see why it should

---

[1] στέλλω 'make ready', 'fit out', 'rig' is a normal meaning of the verb.

be taken as subjunctive (Jebb, Webster); the exhortation does not fit in with Neoptolemus' position at the moment of speaking. So I agree with v. Wilamowitz and Mazon in regarding it as an indicative ('Damit brechen wir auf', 'Pour nous deux, nous partons').

ὁρμᾶσθαι: probably inf. pro imper., ταχεῖς predicative. Σ λείπει γίνεσθε is hardly worthy of belief (cases of ellipse of an imperative of the copula are very rare, cf. K.-G. I 41.2, Anm 2 e). (In itself an infinitive dependent on ταχεῖς would be perfectly possible).

Kommos 1081-1217

Two antistrophic pairs: 1081-1100 = 1101-1122; 1123-1145 = 1146-1168. Epode 1169-1195, 1196-1217. Whereas the strophic pairs,—wherein both strophes and antistrophes are divided between Philoctetes and the Chorus in the same way (longer song of Philoctetes concluded by a much shorter answer by the Chorus, a sort of ephymnion),—have a formally 'regular' character, the long epodic part shows a much more diversified pattern of exchange of longer or shorter utterings and answers between the two.

1081, 2. γύαλον: properly 'hollow' (cf. Chantraine *Dict. Ét. s.v.* γύη); thus the phrase κοίλας πέτρας γύαλον is a natural denotation of the cave in the rocks, the ἄντρον.

θερμὸν καὶ παγετῶδες: cf. and contrast with 17 sqq.. παγετώδης <παγετός 'frost'; only here in Tragedy; cf. Hippocr. π. ἀέρων etc. 7. ὡς: exclamative.

1083-5. οὐκ ἔμελλον ἄρ': ἄρα with ἔμελλον 'denoting that the predestination of an event is realised *ex post facto*' (*G.P.*² p. 36). Cf. *Ai.* 926.

θνῄσκοντι συνείσῃ: 'will be witness of my death'. συνείσῃ is Reiske's conjecture, accepted by most editors, though not by Campbell, who in his commentary and again in *Paral. Soph.* tries to defend συνοίσῃ (mss), quoting for συμφέρεσθαι 'to consort with' Hdt. IV 114.4 οὐκ ἂν ὧν δυναίμεθα ἐκείνῃσι συμφέρεσθαι. But a schol. ἢ οὕτω: σὺν ἐμοὶ ἔσῃ καὶ ὄψει με ἀποθανόντα, and the parallel use of σύνοιδα at *El.* 92.3 afford strong arguments in favour of Reiske's conjecture.

1087-90. αὔλιον: cf. 19, 954, 1149.

πληρέστατον . . . / λύπας τᾶς ἀπ' ἐμοῦ τάλαν: the personification of the cave as his daily companion is continued; it is as it were infected with the λύπη exhaled from him, echoing his cries of pain. *Ai.* 307 πλῆρες ἄτης στέγος is only up to a point comparable. The personification culminates in τάλαν, echoing ὦ τάλας 1083 referring to Philoctetes himself.

τί ποτ' αὖ μοι τὸ κατ' ἆμαρ: if we retain the mss reading, the colon is an ionic dimeter; then we should read in 1110 (with Campbell and Radermacher) κραταιαῖσ<ιν> μετὰ χερσίν. If, on the other hand, we suppose that the aeolic rhythm is continued (ἔσται; / ἴσχων· whether or not belonging to the colon). the correction τίπτ' αὖ μοι (κραταιαῖς 1110) is to be recommended: with ἔσται we shall then have a hipponacteus, without it, a glyconeus followed by glyconeus. But there is much to be said for assuming period-close after ἔσται / ἴσχων. In that case the next colon is either dodrans –∪∪–∪– or dochmiac, again with period-close (ἄσκοπα 1111) [1]), unless we accept W. Theiler's conjecture οἰτονόμου (Mus. Helv. 12 (1955) p. 187) for σιτονόμου 1091; but since οἶτος means 'unhappy fate' almost everywhere I do not think that this conjecture is a happy one.

τί ποτ' or τίπτ': τὸ κατ' ἆμαρ 'my daily portion' is subject, τί predicate.

1090, 91. τοῦ: = τίνος, attribute of ἐλπίδος.

σιτονόμου . . . ἐλπίδος: 'a food-providing hope' is a bold substitute for (prosaically) 'a hope of obtaining food', 'a hope of something that will provide me with food'. ἐλπίς is sometimes 'object of hope', cf. Aesch. Choëph. 776.

τοῦ . . . πόθεν: for the two interrogatives within one sentence, cf. Ai. 1185, Ant. 401, Trach. 421. K.-G. II 521.5.

1092-94. The mss text (εἴθ' αἰθέρος ἄνω / πτωκάδες ὀξυτόνου διὰ πνεύματος / ἕλωσί μ' οὐ γὰρ ἔτ' ἰσχύω) is corrupt: (1) εἴθ' is impossible with a subjunctive; (2) αἰθέρος ἄνω is suspect; (3) the metre of the third colon, dubious in itself, does not correspond with 1115, a line unimpeachable in metre and meaning. Among the manifold attempts at correction Jackson's (Marg. Scaen., pp. 114-16) is, I think, outstanding: ἴθ' αἱ πρόσθ' ἄνω (or αἱ πάρος ἄνω)

πτωκάδες ὀξυτόνου διὰ πνεύματος·

ἅλωσιν οὐκέτ' ἴσχω.

'Come, you who once cowered aloft; come through the shrilling breeze; I can no longer bring you low'. The idea, then, is repeated in 1146-1151. ἅρπυιαι, it is true, is in the text of Q, but this seems no more than an intrusive gloss, for ἅρπυιαι is in schol. 1093 the

---

[1]) But, at a pinch, also without assuming period close, the last syllable of ἄσκοπα can be regarded as long before κρυπτά.

explication of πτωκάδες, and Webster is right in objecting that Harpies cannot be 'cowering', πτωκάδες. For ἅλωσις *capiendi via* cf. supra 61, and mark that the word is used of catching birds and fish Arist. *H.A.* 593 a 20, 600 a 3. πτωκάς occurs in the phrase πτωκάσιν αἰθυίῃσι ('Hom'. *Epigr.* 8.2[1]) and derives from πτώξ 'cowering animal' = 'hare'; πτώσσω is said of birds νέφεα πτώσσουσαι *Od.* XXII 304 (but the passage has difficulties of its own) and cf. Archil. 224 West πτώσσουσαν ὥστε πέρδικα.

1095-97. In this part there is either corruption in 1097 or in 1119 (or 1118, 1119). Those who want to retain the four dactyls as transmitted in 1119 have to alter 1097 accordingly; so Pearson and others, following Dindorf (1860[5]): ἄλλοθεν ἁ τύχα ἅδ' ἀπὸ μείζονος instead of ἄλλοθεν ἔχη τύχα τᾷδ' ἀπὸ μείζονος. This is fairly violent (somewhat less so B. Kneisel, Progr. Naumburg 1886 ἄλλοθεν ἔσχε τύχα σ' ἀπὸ μείζονος) and not very convincing. Von Wilamowitz' verdict was: '1095-1100 sind heil' (Translation, p. 113) and his metrical analysis runs as follows:

σύ τοι σύ τοι κατηξίωσας, ὦ βαρύποτμ', οὐκ ἄλλοθεν ‖ 4 iamb.
ἔχη τύχα τᾷδ' ἀπὸ μείζονος ‖ iamb. + dochm. Antistrophe:
πότμος <πότμος> σε δαιμόνων τάδ' οὐδὲ δόλος ἐμᾶς σέ γε ‖
ἔσχεν ὑπὸ χειρός· στυγεράν ἔχε ‖.

One might demur at the period close at στυγεράν ἔχε. The same objection can be made against ἔσχεν ὑπὸ χειρὸς ἁμᾶς (ἀμᾶς) Bergk, with 1117 unaltered τάδ', οὐδὲ σέ γε δόλος dochm. ∪ – ∪∪ ∪◡◡ = 1096 -σας, ὦ βαρύποτμ'· οὐκ (Then 1097 = 1119 is to be scanned –◡◡ ◡– ◡– –◡◡ –◡× iamb. + glyc. Synaphy between 1095, 96, 97 and 1116, 17, 18, 9).

1095, 6. σύ ... ὦ βαρύποτμ': 'C'est toi, c'est toi, infortuné, qui l'as voulu' (Mazon).

1097. ἔχη τύχα τᾷδ': cf. *O.C.* 1025 γνῶθι δ' ὡς ἔχων ἔχη / καί σ' εἷλε θηρῶνθ' ἡ τύχη. ἔχη amounts to ἐνέχη, συνέχη (Σ).

ἀπὸ μείζονος: explains ἄλλοθεν: 'from a stronger hand' (Jebb). After μείζονος a comma is better than a semi-colon.

1098-1100. εὖτέ γε: *quandoquidem.*

φρονῆσαι: cf. 1078.

τοῦ λῴονος δαίμονος: In my opinion to τοῦ λῴονος ––∪–, καὶ γὰρ ἐμοὶ –∪∪– (1121) can correspond. The genitive of comparison with αἱρεῖσθαι (= προαιρεῖσθαι) is also to be found at Aesch. *Ag.* 350, where see Ed. Fraenkel's comment and references. (Though A. M.

---

[1]) D. B. Monro, Oxford 1896.

Dale's idea ¹) proposed in order to obtain exact responsion viz. to read [τοῦ] λωτονος is possible—cp. Seyffert's reading of *Ai.* 1416—, it would seem a pity to omit τοῦ, cf. Theocr. XXIV 74).

δαίμων: = fate.

αἰνεῖν: G. Hermann's conjecture for ἑλεῖν is almost universally accepted and is intrinsically probable.

1101, 2. (μόχθῳ) λωβατός: maltreated, *affectus malo et contumelia* (E.). Cf. *Trach.* 1069 (κείνης) λωβητὸν εἶδος, *Ai.* 1388 λωβητὸν αὐτὸν ἐκβαλεῖν, and note ad *Ant.* 1074, 5.

1102-5. ἤδη . . . ὕστερον . . . εἰσοπίσω: 'henceforth . . . later . . . in time to come'. The gloomy prospect of his life to come is emphasized by the tautological wording; metrically the three words effectuate a climactic pattern: ‒‒, ‒◡‒ (there is period close at 1103), ‒◡◡‒. Between these words the emphatic μετ' οὐδενὸς . . . ἀνδρῶν enhances the effect.

1107-11. προσφέρων: to the cave.

οὐ: meaningfully repeats the negation, insisting on his utter helplessness.

ἴσχων: subordinate to προσφέρων: 'while holding them <as was formerly the case > . . .'; ὅπλα is to be thought as its object.

1111, 2. ἄσκοπα: ἀπροσδόκητα, . . ., ἃ οὐκ ἔστι προσκέψασθαι. This meaning seems to be suitable here, though hardly at *Ai.* 21 and *El.* 864 and 1315.

μοι: if this is correct we have mentally to supply φρένας (ἐμὰς) or the like with ὑπέδυ, for the dative with ὑποδύομαι in the sense of 'beguile' would be exceptional ²). Now, if ἀλλά μοι ἄσκοπα has to be regarded as dactylic, nothing can be said against the shortening of μοι; but if the colon has to be interpreted as aeolic, the shortening would be uncommon (to say the least). So there is something to be said in favour of Blaydes' ἀλλά μ' ἀπρόσκοπα (*A.C.S.* 1899, p. 238). ἀπρόσκοπος, it is true, occurs only once—Aesch. *Eum.* 105 ἐν ἡμέρᾳ δὲ μοῖρ' ἀπρόσκοπος βροτῶν: the verse is discarded by a number of edd. and μοῖρ' ἀπρόσκοπος is a correction (Turnebus) of μοῖρα πρόσκοπος,—but there is nothing improbable in the word nor in its, in this case, passive meaning.

1113-15. Again he passionately expresses his desire for revenge; cf. 791-95, 1043, 44. Cf. *Ant.* 927, 8, Hippon. (?) 115.14 sqq. (West).

---

¹) In Webster's commentary; the idea is much older (Froehlich, Blaydes, alii).

²) *Od.* X 398 πᾶσιν δ' ἱμερόεις ὑπέδυ γόος is not at all comparable.

1116-1119. The addition of πότμος (Erfurdt, cf. in the strophe σύ τοι σύ τοι) is accepted by most editors. Still, there is a difficulty, viz. the inconsistency¹) with 1095-97, where the whole responsibility for Philoctetes' condition is laid at his own door. We may, of course, argue that his deplorable stubbornness (deplorabe in the Chorus' opinion) is at the same time his πότμος δαιμόνων, or—simpler—that the Chorus is supposed to think of Χρύση (cf. 192-194 and 1326 sqq.). It would also be possible to interpret οὐδὲ as a case of ἀπὸ κοινοῦ negation in the second member of a sentence (K.-G. II p. 291 l., *G.P.*² 194 III (a) and cf. *ib.* 511 V), or we may reject Erfurdt's conjecture and read: <οὐ> πότμος <οὐ>. But perhaps 'the apparent inconsistency' can be understood as a symptom of the Chorus' sense of discomfort ('Unbehagen', Jens-Uwe Schmidt *o.l.* p. 191) at their own rôle (but Schmidt is not correct in stating: 'halten ihm die Matrosen mit Nachdruck entgegen, dass dazu (Philoctetes' outburst) gar kein Anlass sei, da er an allem ganz allein die Schuld trage (1095 ff.; 1116 -!-)'. *ib.* p. 190).

πότμος ... χειρός: I follow v. Wilamowitz' text (see ad 1095-97), but I prefer γε σὲ to σέ γε. τάδ', these your sufferings, this situation of yours, is probably the subject of ἔσχεν, with πότμος δαιμόνων and δόλος ἐμᾶς ὑπὸ χειρὸς as predicative adjuncts. See Webster's correct translation: 'this that caught you is fate sent by the gods, not a trick performed by my hand'.

ἐμᾶς: Bergk's conjecture ἁμᾶς is not necessary, for ◡–◡– can respond to ––◡–, nor does it yield a better sense than ἐμᾶς; ἐμᾶς is unobjectionable: the Chorus may be assumed to identify themselves with their master.

γε: γε after ἐμᾶς, it seems to me, makes more sense than after σε; but the text is the result of conjecture and σέ γε would be perfectly possible (*G.P.*², p. 122).

1119, 20. στυγερὰν ... ἄλλοις: the preceding words are sheer nonsense if not understood as meaning either that all this is Philoctetes' own fault, or that everything, the δόλος included, is the will of the gods. The present sentence, illogical in so far as there are no ἄλλοι in either case, is to be understood as a violent rejection by the Chorus of responsibility on the part of the Achaeans, themselves included.

---

¹) Campbell has felt the difficulty: (the Chorus) 'with apparent but not real inconsistency, declare that the theft of the bow was a divinely appointed act'. Σ ad 116 has: θεὸς γὰρ τῆς δυστυχίας ταύτης παραίτιος.

ἔχε: 'direct'.

1121, 2. καὶ γὰρ: 'for in fact'. καὶ does not belong to ἐμοί.

τοῦτο: announces μὴ (= ὅπως μὴ) φιλότητ' ἀπώσῃ. The words imply that they are acting for his good.

1123-27. καί που: 'and haply', 'and, so I think'. A local interpretation is not impossible, but surely less apt. Cf. *Ai.* 382 ἦ που πολὺν γέλωθ' ὑφ' ἡδονῆς ἄγεις.

Just as at 1101 Philoctetes continues as if the Chorus had said nothing whatsoever. So the subject of the words is not mentioned; the obsessive image of his worst enemy is never absent from Philoctetes' mind.

πολιᾶς: with θινὸς, although normal with forms of ἅλς. The usual explication ('because πόντου θινός is a single notion') is not quite satisfactory; why should we deny that the colour designation, hovering between 'grey', 'white', 'clear' could be used of a beach?

(θινὸς) ἐφήμενος: 'sitting upon'. The genitive as with ἐφέζομαι Pind. *Nem.* IV 67, Ap. Rh. III 1001. 'Fortasse ἐφ' ἥμενος' Cavallin.

1125. γελᾷ μου: the genit. as with καταγελῶ, καταφρονῶ (cf. K.-G. I 365). Cf. perhaps Pl. *Theaet.* 175 b. The words mean 'has the laugh on me' rather than 'is laughing at me', expressing Odysseus' unconcern with Philoctetes' fate.

1126. τροφάν: cf. 931.

1127. ἐβάστασεν: cf. 657.

1128, 9. φίλων / χειρῶν: 'loving hands' (Jebb); 'ma main' (Mazon) misses the pathos.

1130-33. The personification of the bow reaches its highest point.

ἦ που: cf. 1123.

ἐλεινὸν: pityingly, for Philoctetes and for the bow itself.

τὸν Ἡράκλειον: the comrade and heir of Heracles.

ἄθλιον ὧδε: predicative adjunct to <ἐμὲ> τὸν Ἡράκλειον. I do not share the objections against this phrase and reject ἄρθμιον (Erfurdt, Jebb, many others) and Ἡρακλείῳ ἀεθλίῳ (A. Platt, Cl. Qu. 5 (1911), 27) (better R. Y. Tyrrell, Hermath. 9 (1896), 362-368 τὸν Ἡρακλείῳ / ἄθλῳ τῷδέ σοι / οὔποτε) and τὸν Ἡράκλειον ἄθλον ἔμ' ὧδέ σοι Campbell, repeated in *Paral. Soph.*. The last vindication of the text transmitted in LA is to be found in T. C. W. Stinton, J.H.S. 97 (1977), 136.

1134, 5. ἄλλου δ' ἐν μεταλλαγῇ: G. Hermann's supplement of the defective ἀλλ' ἐν μεταλλαγῇ. The genitive is the person taken in

exchange for Philoctetes. The responsion with 1157 is not perfect
(⏤⏤⏑⏑⏑⏑⏑⏑ ∼ ⏑⏑⏑⏑⏑⏑⏑). Hartung's (1850) χεροῖν δ' ἐν μεταλλαγῇ
deserves mention and so does Stinton's ἀλλ' ἐν μεταλλαγᾷ <χε-
ροῖν> with <ἐν δαιτὶ> σαρκὸς αἰόλας in 1157 (J.H.S. 97 (1977),
136, 7). Webster proposes ὃ νῦν ἐν μεταλλαγᾷ.

ἐρέσσῃ: 'you are handled'. For various metaphorical uses of
ἐρέσσω cf. L.-Sc. s.v. II 2.

1136-39. ὁρῶν: neuter nominative.

στυγνόν . . . οὗτος: except for the Ὀδυσσεύς at the end (for which
Campbell's οὗτος is an outstanding correction; Ὀδυσσεύς has to be
regarded as an intrusive gloss), the mss text of these lines seems to
me sound. ὁρῶν has two objects, correlated by μὲν . . . τε: αἰσχρὰς
ἀπάτας and στυγνόν τε φῶτ' ἐχθοδοπὸν (no comma) . . . ἀνατέλλονθ'.
ἀνατέλλω can perfectly well be used transitively 'bring forth', cf.
L.-Sc. s.v. I 1, 2 (and Ellendt s.v.).

ἀπ' αἰσχρῶν: 'from evil thoughts', 'designs'.

ὅσ': no need of altering into ὃς (Bothe, Jebb). I think that the
alternatives for οὗτος (ὦ Ζεῦ, Dindorf, Jebb, οὐδεὶς Arndt, Radermacher, Dain-Mazon) are much more arbitrary than οὗτος. (If we
want ἀνατέλλονθ' to be intransitive, Gernhard's μυρία τ' αἰσχρῶν—
separative with ἀνατέλλονθ'—is the easiest way out).

1140-43. τὸ μὲν εὖ δίκαιον εἰπεῖν: I agree with Jebb's statement
that the only acceptable interpretation of the transmitted text is
G. Hermann's (evidently also v. Wilamowitz'), viz. 'It is the part
of a man to say that what is expedient is just'. I do not share the
objections to τὸ εὖ (cf. Eur. I.T. 580, Her. 694, Ar. Acharn. 661, 2
τὸ γὰρ εὖ μετ' ἐμοῦ καὶ τὸ δίκαιον ἔσται). But I think that the Chorus
are applying the maxim to themselves, not to Philoctetes, and that
the next words express their wish not to hurt his feelings (cf.
Masqueray's note a.l., repeated by Dain and mentioned by Webster).

εἰπόντος: the construction ἀνδρός <ἐστιν> is continued; εἰπόντος
δὲ lit. 'and it behoves a man, after having said that, not to . . .'.

φθονερὰν: 'malignant', invidiosus.

ἐξῶσαι γλώσσας ὀδύναν: Metaphor from the bee-sting, 'a common
image for forceful or spiteful speech' (Collard ad Eur. Suppl. 242
κέντρ' ἀφιᾶσιν κακά), γλώσσης πικροῖς κέντροις Eur. Her. 1288. I
think that ἐξωθέω seems a good forceful synonym of ἀφίημι;
γλώσσας ὀδύναν amounting to aculeum is the object (better than to
take γλώσσας with ἐξῶσαι). I do not share J. H. Kells' objection to
ἐξωθέω (Cl. Rev. 1963, p. 9: he proposes ἐξᾶξαι).

If we believe that the Chorus refer not to themselves in 1140-42, but to Philoctetes, Kells' (see above) substitution of ὃν for εὖ is very attractive: 'Certainly it is the part of a (true) man to assert his own case (τὸ ὃν δίκαιον, for τὸ δίκαιον 'claim', 'case' he refers to Eur. *I.A.*810 sq.), but once he has asserted it, it is no longer his part to go on to use his tongue in a malicious and painful way on another'. (Kells, *ib.* p. 8) [1].

1143-45. κεῖνος: Odysseus? It seems very difficult to think of Neoptolemus, but if Odysseus is meant τοῦδ' ἐφημοσύνᾳ cannot stand. We should read τοῦτ' or τῶνδε. With either conjecture there is redundancy. Campbell followed G. Hermann in choosing the *v.l.* ὑφημοσύνᾳ (Marc. 616), lending to this word (not to be found elsewhere) with τοῦδε the meaning: 'using as his minister Neoptolemus' (it would be better to say: 'by suborning this man—our master—'). (For ὑφίημι 'suborn' cf. *O.T.* 387). If this is rejected I should prefer to read τῶνδε, without much conviction (if κεῖνος refers to Odysseus). But perhaps a case can be made for κεῖνος referring to Neoptolemus. Odysseus is the one on whom Philoctetes' bitterness has centred. But for the sailors it is their master whose conduct has to be defended. εἷς ἀπὸ πολλῶν ταχθείς is more natural said of Neoptolemus than of Odysseus. Then τοῦδ' has to be retained ('at the behest of this one' [2]), 'the man you are speaking about'); there is often an apparent arbitrariness in the use of demonstrative pronouns.

κοινὰν ... ἀρωγάν: the profit for all concerned is emphasized. If κεῖνος refers to Neoptolemus, the intention of the Chorus' words can be rendered as follows: 'I feel it my duty to call what is useful just, but not to add spiteful and rancorous rebuke. My master, as one out of many appointed, fulfilled, at the command of Odysseus, a helpful mission for the common good'. This implies that the deceit was for the common weal, that Neoptolemus acted as a subordinate, and that the whole enterprise has to be regarded as just.

1146. Again there is no reply.

1146-48. ὦ πταναὶ θῆραι: 'O ye, my winged chase' (Campbell). χαροπῶν: 'bright-eyed' seems the most plausible meaning.

---

[1]) It is very difficult to defend the idea I once fostered, *viz.* that 1140 refers to the Chorus, 1141, 2 to Philoctetes: εἰπόντος would then be genitive absolute and the construction harshly zeugmatic.

[2]) Thus Σ, Brunck.

οὐρεσιβώτας: either acc. pl., predicative with οὓς (<βόσκομαι) or nom. sing. (<βόσκω).

1149-50. φυγᾷ ... / πελᾶτ᾽: the only reasonable interpretation of the transmitted words is G. Hermann's 'non amplius fuga vestra me ab antro meo ad vos adducetis' [1]). Σ seems to admit a harsh sylleps: ἀντὶ οὐκέτι φεύξεσθέ με, οὐκέτι μετὰ φυγῆς καὶ φόβου προσπελάσετέ μοι. Exactly the same interpretation is given by Campbell (borrowed from Bernhardy): 'No longer flying me from my cell, ye shall approach me there', *i.e.* οὐκέτι με φεύγοντες ἀπ᾽ αὐλίων, πελᾶτέ μοι εἰς αὔλια.

Neither the transmitted text nor the many conjectural attempts are convincing. I confess to some sympathy for Erfurdt's and Heimsoeth's ἐλᾶτ᾽ [2]) (the latter with the alteration φυγαῖς instead of φυγᾷ μ᾽: then ἐλᾶτ᾽ would be intransitive and φυγαῖς ἐλᾶτε = φεύξεσθε; with φυγᾷ μ᾽ left unaltered the words would mean: 'No longer, by your flight, will you cause me to leave my cave'). Note that Jebb's metrical objections to the transmitted reading are not valid.

1150-52. τὰν πρόσθεν βελέων ἀλκάν: my former strength consisting in bow and arrows.

1153-57. ἀλλ᾽ ... ἕρπετε: the words between ἀλλ᾽ ... ἕρπετε form a parenthesis with the same function as a preceding γάρ-clause. Cf. Platnauer ad Eur. *I.T.* 65.

ἀνέδην ... ἐρύκεται: an oxymoron: 'is remissly guarded' [3]) (ἀνέδην = ἀνειμένως; note that ἀνίημι means also 'to open'). ὅδε χῶρος is the subject of a passive sentence representing a separative genitive in the active form, or the construction is the passive form of an active form ἐρύκω <σοι> τὸν χῶρον instead of ἐρύκω<σε>τοῦ χώρου. Cf. *Trach.* 344 σοὶ ταῖσδέ τ᾽ οὐδὲν εἴργεται; Aesch. *Sept.* 416 εἴργειν μητρὶ πολέμιον δόρυ instead of εἴργειν μητέρα πολεμίου δορός.

ἀντίφονον: with στόμα: 'taking blood for blood' (Webster prefers to take it with χάριν; I think this needlessly difficult).

πρὸς χάριν: 'to your heart's desire' (at *Ant.* 30 the use is probably somewhat different unless we take βορᾶς with θησαυρόν).

---

[1]) Thus also von Wilamowitz (?), conjecturing ἀπαυλίῳ.

[2]) Already proposed by Canter, but as imperative combined with Auratus' μηκέτ᾽ instead of μ᾽ οὐκέτ᾽.

[3]) 'vos ab eo arcemini adeo negligenter, ut non metuendum amplius quidquam sit' (E.).

αἰόλας: ποικίλης διὰ τὰ τραύματα Σ.

1158, 9. γὰρ ... / ... γὰρ: for γὰρ 'not infrequently' introducing 'successive clauses in successive lines' (in Sophocles) cf. *G.P.*² p. 58.

1160-62. ἐν αὔραις: virtually = αὔραις, ἐξ ἀνέμων Σ. Cp. 'Leven van de wind'.

κρατύνων: = κρατῶν, as very often in Sophocles.

βιόδωρος: possibly this adjective, found in Aesch. *fr.* 355.17 M. = 168 N.², Pind. *Pae.* 3.26, and here, derives from the idea that epic ζείδωρος meant βιόδωρος (as it certainly did Emp. 151). Cf. Frisk *s.v.* ζειαί.

1163, 4. πρὸς θεῶν ... / ... πελάταν: one thing is certain in these much vexed words, viz. that πέλασσον, if taken intransitively ('approach!'), cannot be construed with the accusative of a person. So, in that case, ξένον has to be construed with σέβῃ and πελάταν, although πέλασσον intervenes, is in apposition with it. This, I feel is very improbable. So I prefer to regard πέλασσον as transitive-causative with ξένον as its object: 'allow a ξένος to approach <you>'. ξένον may be also the object of σέβῃ, but εἴ τι σέβῃ can also mean: 'if there is anything you revere' (they mean: 'friendship').

πελάταν: in its literal sense: 'one who approaches', *i.e.* in the context 'one who wants to come near to you'. Cf. Eur. *Hyps.* I. IV 12, 2 (Bond) τίνος ἐμπορίᾳ τοῦσδ' ἐγγὺς ὁρῶ / πελάτας ξείνους ... / ... πρὸς τούσδε δόμους / στείχοντας. See note ad 1190.

1165, 6. ἀλλὰ γνῶθ', εὖ γνῶθ': a maximum of urgency is expressed.

ὅτι σοί: Campbell retains this, explaining σοί here and at *O.C.* 721 by: σὸν ἔργον ἐστίν[1]). This is hardly believable. So either ἐπὶ σοί (Seyffert, Jebb, Pearson) or, ὅτι σὸν (Dindorf, D.-M.) should be read: 'it is in your power', 'it is up to you'.

κῆρα: of the νόσος also 42.

1168, 9. βόσκειν: sc. with your own flesh.

ἀδαὴς ... ξυνοικεῖ: I find it difficult to accept that in the second clause the κήρ is to be identified with the patient (see Jebb), and also to believe that ἀδαὴς here means 'incapable of teaching' (Webster). Rather should I prefer to assume change of subject and construe as follows: <οὗτος> δ' ᾧ κὴρ ξυνοικεῖ ἀδαὴς <ἐστιν>

---

[1]) Σ has λείπει τὸ πάρεστιν.

('is incapable of learning') ἔχειν ('to bear') μυρίον ἄχθος. This, of course, is only possible with the reading of A: ῷ.

1169-1217. In contradistinction to the preceding parts of the kommos there is intercourse and even interaction between Chorus and protagonist in this long epode, a piece of astrophic lyric poetry, where the swift changes of diverse metre, the many changes of speaker (also within metrical units) are suggestive of the shifting moods, the vain attempts at persuasion and, in general, of vehement emotion. The Chorus' last exhortation, in dactyls, is followed by Philoctetes' desperate assertion of his refusal to move, in dactyls (1196, 1197-1202), and, still in the same metre, his asking for a sword in order to do away with himself (1203-1207). Then there is a return to iambic and aeolo-choriambic lines.

1169-72. παλαιὸν ἄλγημ᾽: this refers to the notion, implied in the Chorus' words 1165, 6, that he could free himself of his sufferings by going to Troy.

ὑπέμνασας: 'you made mention in a suggestive way'. (It is perhaps not irrelevant to note that ὑπομιμνήσκω is used by medical authors with the meaning of provoking a dormant process, see L.-Sc. s.v. I 2 b and ὑπομνηστέον 3).

ὦ λῷστε τῶν πρὶν ἐντόπων: referring to 307 sqq. For the genitive with the superlative cf. K.-G. I 23, note ad *Ant.* 100-102 (logically ὦ λῷστε stands for ὦ λῷστε, λωίων).

ὤλεσας . . . εἴργασαι: the aorist referring to the near past, where we should use a form of the present: 'why do you . . .', the perfect expressing the result, implying 'I feel done for by your words'. The same relation between εἰργάσω, ἠπάτηκας 928, 9.

1173-75. τί τοῦτ᾽ ἔλεξας: τοῦτ᾽ refers in particular to Philoctetes' last line. His answer presupposes as apodosis ὤλεσάς με, <ἐξ>εἴρ γασαί με and makes clear to the Chorus (and the hearer) the meaning of παλαιὸν ἄλγημ᾽ ὑπέμνασας. The idea that he should go to Troy is expressed in the highly emotional ionics of 1175. Ionic metres continue as far as 1179; 1179 and 1180 form a transition to choriambs.

1176. γάρ: <ἤλπισα> for . . . 'Yes, indeed, I . . .'.

κράτιστον: sc. ὄν.

1177. ἤδη: 'forthwith'.

λείπετ᾽: the 'pressing present imperative', because at this moment the situation, to Philoctetes' emotional state of mind, requires the Chorus' immediate departure; cf. ἔκπλει 577. (Cf. W. F.

Bakker, *The Greek Imperative*, thesis Utrecht 1966, p. 55, and in general pp. 49-66; he does not discuss this passage).

1178, 9. μοι: with φίλα and with παρήγγειλας.

πράσσειν: with παρήγγειλας and with ἑκόντι.

τε: see *G.P.*² p. 497 n. 2 and my notes ad *Ant.* 383 and 653.

1179, 80. ναὸς ἵν' ἡμῖν τέτακται: <ἐκεῖσ'> ἵνα ναὸς (partitive genitive) ἡμῖν τέτακται (we are posted). 'To our station on board ship' (Campbell). Dawe ¹) wants to read λαός.

(The Chorus show signs of departure).

1181-85. πρὸς ἀραίου Διὸς: on ἀραῖος Σ notes: ὥσπερ δὲ ἱκεσίου λέγουσι τοῦ τοὺς ἱκέτας ἐποπτεύοντος οὕτως ἀραίου τοῦ τοὺς ἀρωμένους ἐπισκοποῦντος. The common meanings of ἀραῖος are 'accursed' ('under a curse') and 'cursing', 'bringing under a curse'. Webster's paraphrase brings out most clearly what is implied: 'Zeus who can carry out the curses of a suppliant who is rejected'.

μετρίαζ': 'keep measure'. First occurrence of the verb and ἅπαξ in Tragedy (though μέτριος 'moderate' is common since Hesiod). I think that 'keep measure' is better than 'be calm' (Jebb, see also Mazon) because the Weidmann commentary is right in pointing out that it refers to the invocation of Ζεὺς ἀραῖος; thus also von Wilamowitz.

τί θροεῖς: why do you cry: 'μείνατε'. The meaning becomes clear from 1191, 2.

1186, 7. δαίμων, δαίμων: exclamation rather than invocation; 'fate', 'doom' rather than 'divine power'.

1188, 9. ὦ πούς πούς: personified as at 786.

τί σ' . . . τεύξω: used and construed as ποιεῖν, δρᾶν τί τινα. 'What shall I make of you'. ἔτι *olim aliquando*, cf. Eur. *Hel.* 57, *Or.* 906.

ἐν βίῳ . . . τῷ μετόπιν: μετόπιν = μετόπισθε(ν), only here in Greek of the classical period, but κατόπιν = κατόπισθε(ν) is common (though not in the language of Tragedy).

1190. ἔλθετ' ἐπήλυδες αὖθις: 'come back again to me'. ἔπηλυς is here used in its etymological sense of: 'one who is coming to' (its common meaning is 'incomer', 'foreigner' Hdt., Aesch., Thuc., also adjectival). On ἐπήλυσις 'approach' see my note ad Archil. P. Colon. 7511, l. 33, Mnemos. 1976, p. 125. ἔπηλυς is a curious ἅπαξ in Tragedy.—What Philoctetes wants, seems to confirm my interpretation of 1163, 4; ἔπηλυς comes very near in sense to πελάτας.

---

¹) Proc. Cambr. Philol. Soc. 14, 1968, p. 17 and *Studies on the Text of Sophocles* III (1978), p. 133.

1191, 2. τί ῥέξοντες: sc. ἔλθωμεν, to be supplied from ἔλθετ'.

ἀλλοκότῳ ... προὔφαινες: the adjective ἀλλόκοτος, derivation from κότος—with weakened sense [1]), see Chantraine *Dict. Ét. s.v.* κότος, Frisk B. III p. 136—means 'of unusual nature', 'entirely different (from)'; cf. νεόκοτος 'new and strange', 'unheard of' Aesch. *Pers.* 257, *Sept.* 803. It does not occur elsewhere in Tragedy; twice in Ar. *Vesp.* 47, 71 ('strange'), and in prose (Thuc., Pl.). The dative ἀλλοκότῳ γνώμᾳ is best understood if we regard τί ῥέξοντες <ἔλθωμεν> as said instead of τί ῥέξοντας ἐλθεῖν ἐκέλευσας; at any rate it is Philoctetes' 'entirely different' γνώμη that is meant, whether we take the dative as sociative ('with') or causal; γνώμη means 'purpose' [2]).

The genitive τῶν πάρος is dependent on ἀλλο- as sometimes with ἄλλος, ἀλλοῖος, ἀλλότριος, ἕτερος; ὧν by attraction instead of ἅ.

προὔφαινες: this reading (GRQ) seems probable and metrically inoffensive: 1192, then, has to be regarded as a hipponactean with dragged close.

1193-95. νεμεσητόν: 'worthy of indignation'. This verbal adjective, fairly frequent in Homer (mostly in the form νεμεσσητόν) only here in Tragedy.

ἀλύοντα: cf. *El.* 135, *supra* 174, *O.T.* 695.

χειμερίῳ: 'raging'. Compare the metaphorical uses of χειμάζω.

καὶ παρὰ νοῦν θροεῖν: 'entfährt uns ein Wort auch gegen den eigenen Sinn' (v. Wilamowitz). This refers to 1177 and causes the Chorus to foster the illusion that Philoctetes will give in.

1197-99. ἴσθι τόδ' ἔμπεδον: ἔμπεδον is predicative adjective with τόδε. τόδ' refers to οὐδέποτε <βήσομαι εἰς "Ιλιον> (but the conciseness of the wording gives it its force).

οὐδ' εἰ ... φλογίζων: no resignation here, but a Promethean stubbornness: cf. Aesch. *Prom.* 1043 sqq..

βροντᾶς αὐγαῖς: reading from Σ. Mss have βρονταῖς αὐταῖς. The mistake would be the same as at Aesch. *Ag.* 254 (the reverse perhaps in the vexed text of Alc. 308.2 L.-P.). But it is not certain that there *is* a mistake; for βρονταῖς αὐταῖς (or better αὐταῖς βρονταῖς, the normal order in this idiom), to be taken with εἶσι (cf. *Il.* XXIII 8

---

[1]) To be compared to the 'neutral' meaning of ὀργή, cf. Phryn. *Praep. Soph.* 23 κότος = ὀργή 'temper'.

[2]) Page (Proc. Cambr. Phil. Soc. N.S. 6, 1960, p. 53) proposes τί ῥέξοντες; ἀλλόκοτος γνῶμα τῶν πάρος ἂν προφαίνεις., T. C. W. Stinton (J.H.S. 97, 1977, p. 137) ἀλλοκότῳ γνώμᾳ τῶν πάρος ὧν <σὺ> προὔφαινες.

ἀλλ' αὐτοῖς ἵπποισι καὶ ἅρμασιν ἄσσον ἰόντες, Xen. *Cyr.* III 3.40
ἥκειν εἰς τὰς τάξεις αὐτοῖς στεφάνοις), could very well mean 'with
thunder(claps) and all'. (Campbell considered this possibility).

φλογίζων: lit. 'in the act of setting me on fire'. But since εἶσι is
probably future, the notion of intention can be regarded as implied
in the main verb instead of in the participle. φλογίζω active only
here, passive *Trach.* 95, not elsewhere in Tragedy; it is a substitute
for φλέγω, common in poetry.

1200-02. ἐρρέτω: 'away with', an epic usage.

τόδ' . . . ἐμοῦ ποδὸς / ἄρθρον ἀπῶσαι: 'to reject this foot of mine'.
This, of course, is much more pathetic (and in harmony with the
personification of the foot 1188) than if he were to say: 'me, suffering from my foot'. ποδός is a genitive 'of definition'.

1202-03. If ἀλλ' is taken as forming with the last syllable of
ἀπῶσαι one longa, an uncommon and hardly acceptable synaloephe
has to be assumed. So it seems better to regard ἄρθρον ἀπῶσαι as a
dactylic dimeter in the form of an adonius at the end of a period,
and to regard ἀλλ' . . . ὀρέξατε as a colon of 'dactylo-anapaestic'
rhythm (A. M. Dale, *The Lyric Metres of Greek Drama*¹, p. 41 n. 2).
To do away with ἀλλ' altogether (Hartung, v. Blumenthal, Hermes
1934 p. 456) seems an all too easy remedy; Dawe's proposal to
write ἄ ἄ ἄ ἄ (or αἰαῖ), cf. Philp on 782, is not so very helpful
(*Studies on the Text of Sophocles* III - 1978 - p. 133): here there is
no attack of pain.

1203-05. ἀλλ': 'a break-off in the thought'. It is better not to
think of a combination of ἀλλά and γε, but to regard γε as exclusively
emphasizing ἕν.

εὖχος: 'object of prayer'; not elsewhere in Tragedy. The combination with ὀρέγνυμι is Homeric (*Il.* XII 328 ἠέ τῳ εὖχος ὀρέξομεν ἠέ τις
ἡμῖν). ὀρέξατε 'reach' is natural because what he wants is a concrete
object; Campbell feels it as 'a suppliant expression', comparing
Od. XV 312 πλάγξομαι, αἴ κέν τις κοτύλην καὶ πύρνον ὀρέξῃ.

ἐρεῖς: on the desiderative element in future forms cf. note ad
438, 9.

εἴ ποθεν: εἴ ποθεν <δύνασθε>.

προπέμψατε: I do not think that 'send forth'—from the ship—is
meant. Rather, if not simply = παράσχετε, 'pass forward' (Jebb)
would meet what is wanted here (the difference with ὀρέξατε is
slight).

βελέων τι: *aliquid telorum, quidquid id est* (Schn.-N.-R.).

1206-09. ὡς . . . ποτέ: A. M. Dale *l.c.* in note ad 1202, 3 argues for leaving out the all but generally accepted <δή> (G. Hermann) and assumes a colon – ∪∪ – – ∪∪ –∪∪, comparing 1215.

Between ποτέ (no period-close) and ὡς there is hiatus, excused by the change of speaker.

παλάμαν: not necessarily 'deed of violence' (Jebb, L.-Sc., Mazon), rather 'device'.

ἀπὸ . . . τέμω: the construction of 1206 is continued.

κρᾶτ' ἀπὸ πάντα καὶ ἄρθρα τέμω: There is no advantage in changing the transmitted word order (Bergk, Pearson). πάντα καὶ is a simple instance of hyperbaton. The form κρᾶτα has to be regarded as neuter, cf. 1457 where it is nominative. ἄρθρα refers to the 'joints of the neck'. The words are a hyperbolic expression of despair; Hermann's χρῶτ' instead of κρᾶτ', adopted by Jebb, is uncalled for.

φονᾷ φονᾷ: comparable expressive iterations are listed in Schw.-Debr. II 700. The verb is a desiderative, comparable to θανατάω, τοκάω.

1210-12. τί ποτε: the natural interpretation seems to me: 'Why <φονᾷ>'? (v. Wilamowitz, Mazon), not sc. ἔστιν (Jebb).

ποῖ γᾶς: because ματεύων implies 'going to seek'.

οὐ . . . ἔτι: Philoctetes' ideas about his father's life or death vary according to the desperateness of his situation as felt by him.

1213-17. ὦ πόλις ὦ πόλις πατρία: this is metrically very difficult [1]). Some read with Dindorf ὦ πόλις ὦ πατρία (but πατρία is not a noun, and πατριά would not be suitable). Webster adopts ὦ πόλις πόλις πατρία (Gleditsch) and this is better. But it would also be possible not to accept, as many edd. have done, G. Hermann's οὐ γὰρ ἐν φάει γ' ἔτι but to read with the mss οὐ γὰρ ἔστ' ἐν φάει γ' ἔτι and to regard this with the first ὦ πόλις as a troch. trim. sync. and catal., thus (with Radermacher):

οὐ γὰρ ἔστ' ἐν φάει γ' ἔτ'. ὦ πόλις ||
ὦ πόλις πατρία, / πῶς ἂν εἰσίδοιμί σ' ἄθλιος γ' ἀνήρ, dodr. troch. trim. catal.

πῶς ἂν εἰσίδοιμί σ': urgent wish.

ἄθλιός γ' ἀνήρ: on γ' see *G.P.*[2] p. 139.

λιβάδ': 'stream'; the Spercheüs is meant, cf. 491, 2.

ἔτ' οὐδέν εἰμι: cf. *Trach.* 161 ὡς ἔτ' οὐκ ὤν . . . . The passionate rebelliousness of 1197-1202 has sunk into the abyss of utter despair. He retires into the cave.

---

[1]) Unless we think of dochm. + cretic., as is done by Kraus, *Strophengestaltung*, p. 169.

Fourth Epeisodion 1218-1408

First scene 1218-62(o)

4 introductory trimeters by the Coryphaeus; Odysseus and Neoptolemus; stichomythia from 1224 to 1246 and again from 1250 to 1253; 1247-49 and 1254-56 stichomythia with ἀντιλαβαί; 1257-60 Odysseus and Neoptolemus each 2 trimeters.

1218-21. νεὼς ὁμοῦ / στείχων ... ἐμῆς: for ὁμοῦ with genitive Men. *fr.* 760 a and b Koerte ὁμοῦ δὲ τοῦ τίκτειν παρεγένεθ' ἡ κόρη and ἤδη γὰρ <ἡ κόρη> 'στι τοῦ τίκτειν ὁμοῦ is a parallel (schol. Ap. Rhod. II 127 and Harpocr. 137.26 note that ὁμοῦ = ἐγγύς is Attic; the genitive on the analogy of the genitive with ἐγγύς). στείχων ἂν ἦ is periphrasis of ἂν ἔστειχον, ὁμοῦ may be taken with ἦ in particular, or with the phrase στείχων ἦ. (It is not recommendable to read νεὼς πέλας / ... εἰ μή γ' ὁμοῦ—Schütz, *Stud. Soph.* 1890—for γ' would be blatantly otiose).

στείχοντα: one instance out of many (in Sophocles) of repetition of the same word within a brief compass, at which we are inclined to take offence but a Vth century poet apparently not.

σοι: ethic dative ('almost "for all you could have done about it"'', Webster).

πρὸς ἡμᾶς δεῦρ': more or less redundant.

Technically this entrance of two characters together involved in a heated dispute is unexampled in Sophocles' plays [1]; in Euripides there is the entrance of Menelaus with the Presbytes *I.A.* 304 sqq. [2]). As to its contents and its place in the structure of the play Karin Alt (*Schicksal und* φύσις *im Philoktet des Sophokles*, Hermes 1961, p. 166) makes the following pertinent comment: 'Die ganze Szene ist eine Umkehrung zu der stichomythischen Partie des Prologs (100 ff.); endete diese mit einer Einigkeit, die freilich nicht dauern konnte, so kommt es hier zur endgültigen Entscheidung'. Cf. also Jens-Uwe Schmidt, *Sophokles-Philoktet*, p. 193. We have to imagine Neoptolemus purposefully making for the cave, the bow in his hand, with Odysseus close on his heels.

1222, 3. οὐκ ἂν φράσειας: somewhat more courteous than οὐ φράσεις.

ἥντιν' ... / κέλευθον: inquires as to the purpose of his journey, as

---

[1]) There is some resemblance to *Trach.* 971 sqq. (noted by Jebb), but the difference is great.

[2]) And a few other instances listed by Stevens *Andromache*, p. 115.

to his errand. ἥντιν' . . . παλίντροπος / κέλευθον ἕρπεις belong closely together; Webster well catches the meaning in translating: 'What is this return journey that you make with such energetic haste'.

ὧδε: not local, but adverb of manner belonging to σὺν σπουδῇ ταχύς.

1224. λύσων ὅσ' ἐξήμαρτον: cf. Sappho 5.5 L.-P. ὅσσα δὲ πρ]όσθ' ἄμβροτε πάντα λῦσα[ι. λύειν combines the notions 'undo' and 'make up for'. Cf. Ar. *Ran.* 691 λῦσαι τὰς πρότερον ἁμαρτίας.

1225. δεινόν γε φωνεῖς: 'that sounds alarmingly indeed' (Campbell).

1225-28. Instance of syntactically closely knit stichomythia. Again 1230-1233. ἁμαρτία picks up ἐξήμαρτον, ἥν picks up ἁμαρτία and is internal accusative with πιθόμενος, here the omitted main verb in the first person is replaced by the second person in Odysseus' line 1227 with its object ἔργον ποῖον, and in Neoptolemus' 1228 ἑλών is predicative adjunct with either <ἐξήμαρτον> or (better) <ἔπραξα ἔργον ὧν οὔ μοι πρέπον>.

ὧν . . . πρέπον: τούτων τῶν ἔργων ἃ οὔ σοι πρᾶξαι πρέπον ἦν.

ἑλών: cf. 14, 608, 945, 948.

1229. νέον: cf. 784. Eur. *Med.* 37 δέδοικα δ'αὐτὴν μή τι βουλεύσῃ νέον. Here and at 1230 Jebb renders by 'rash', v. Wilamowitz by 'Unerhörtes'. Campbell (ad 1230) refers to 966, perhaps rightly.

1230-34. τῷ δὲ Ποίαντος τόκῳ: the dative is dependent on the notion δοῦναι (βουλεύομαι) supplied by Odysseus' δοῦναι νοεῖς 1233; τί χρῆμα δράσεις 1231 has nothing to do with it grammatically speaking.

ὥς: better to be taken as exclamative than as = ἐπεί.

παρ' οὗπερ ἔλαβον: Neoptolemus continues still as if he will supply the main verb himself. τάδε τὰ τόξα, object of ἔλαβον, is also object of <δοῦναι>; perhaps we had better leave out the comma before αὖθις πάλιν.

τί λέξεις: 'que veux-tu dire', cf. 1204 and note *a.l.*.

αἰσχρῶς γὰρ . . . ἔχω: γὰρ implies: 'yes, that is what I want to do, for'.

λαβὼν ἔχω: v. Wilamowitz' translation well renders the force of the periphrasis: 'Betrug gewann ihn. Mir gehört er nicht'.

1235, 6. πότερα: on πότερον (-α) without following second member cf. K.-G. II 532 Anm. 10. δή: 'only in AUY' (Dawe); it is excellent.

κερτομῶν: κέρτομος and its congeners, of uncertain etymology, have the meaning 'mock' (in general, tending to 'taunt', 'sneer' sometimes approaching 'jest', 'joke') and in particular (cf. L.-Sc. *Suppl.* p. 83) 'mock by false statement'. Cf. *Od.* XIII 326 σὲ δὲ κερτομέουσαν ὁτω / ταῦτ' ἀγορεύεμεναι, Theocr. I 62 οὔ τί τυ κερτομέω. The words are rather frequent in Homer, rare in prose (but Hdt. uses ἐπικερτομέω and κατακερτομέω); Pindar once has κερτομέω *fr.* 215 a 4, and so Aesch.: *Prom.* 986 ἐκερτόμησας ... ὡς παῖδ' ὄντα με; Soph. has κερτόμησις in the next line and κερτόμιος *Ant.* 956, 962; Eur. seven times κερτομέω, twice κέρτομος.

Throughout this stichomythia Neoptolemus shows himself absolutely sure of the cause he is fighting for, because he has justice on his side. He has refound his true nature and speaks accordingly. So the poet makes him speak the sublime verse 1236, one of the most impressive lines he has written, quietly.

1237, 8. Ἀχιλλέως παῖ: always when the hearer is reminded of Neoptolemus' father, the address is meaningful.

δὶς ... ἔπη: alludes to the same proverb as Socrates Pl. *Gorg.* 498 e 11: δὶς καὶ τρὶς τὸ καλόν <ἀναπολεῖν δεῖ—or the like— >, cf. *Phileb.* 59 e 10. Pind. *Nem* VII 104 also implies a contradiction of the proverb: ταὐτὰ δὲ τρὶς τετράκι τ' ἀμπολεῖν ἀπορία τελέθει, see Dodds ad *Gorg. l.c..* ἀναπολεῖν: lit. 'turn up the ground again'. The instances found are, all of them, figurative.

1239, 40. ἀρχήν ... οὐδ': for ἀρχήν with negation cf. *Ant.* 92, *El.* 439-41. (very common in Hdt.).

οὐδ' ἅπαξ: note that in Apostol. cent. VI 26 (*Paroem. Gr.* II p. 369) the wording of the proverb runs: Δὶς καὶ τρὶς τὸ καλόν, τὸ δὲ κακόν οὐδ' ἅπαξ.

εὖ ... λόγον: *i.e.* I have nothing to add nor to explain. A has ἀκήκοας, possible (but α and ω are easily confused).

1241, 2. ἔστιν τις ἔστιν: there seems to be an element of fake in Odysseus' threats. At any rate he is made to appear as unconvincing and unavailing as Neoptolemus shows himself staunch and unyielding.—For the repetition cf. *El.* 459. τις refers to himself, notwithstanding his reply 1243.

κωλύσει τὸ δρᾶν: cf. K.-G. II 44.

ἔσται ... οὑπικωλύσων: cf. *O.T.* 297 ἀλλ' οὑξελέγξων ... ἔστιν, *Ant.* 261 οὐδ' ὁ κωλύσων παρῆν.

1243, 4. ἐν δὲ τοῖς: decidedly better than τοῖσδ'; compare the fairly common instances of ἐκ τῶν.

σοφὸς ... σοφόν: he taunts him with his famous σοφία. We might say that, among other things, the course of this play demonstrates the truth of the paradox τὸ σοφὸν δ' οὐ σοφία.

1245. δρασείεις σοφά: this desiderative also at *Ai.* 326, 585; not in Aesch.; twice in Eur.: *Med.* 93, *Phoen.* 1208, twice in Ar.. σοφά, Brunck, has to be accepted.

1246-49. ἀλλ' . . . τάδε: again a 'mot sublime'. τάδε: my 'unwise' words and acts.

δίκαιον: as with σοφός, the essential fact is that δίκαιος signifies to Odysseus' mind a notion entirely different from that held by Neoptolemus. Neoptolemus has dismissed what he alleged as his excuse at 925, ὁ τῶν γὰρ ἐν τέλει κλύειν / τό τ' ἔνδικον με καὶ τὸ συμφέρον ποεῖ. And *this* ἔνδικον is to Odysseus' mind exactly τὸ δίκαιον, obedience to the army, advantage of the army.

ἅ γ' ἔλαβες βουλαῖς ἐμαῖς: implying that Neoptolemus is in fact doing an injustice to Odysseus. His βουλαί were the tricks he had taught the young man. γ' amounts to: 'mark well', 'nota bene'. Characteristically Odysseus does not use πάλιν δοῦναι, but πάλιν μεθεῖναι, stressing the idea of 'letting go out of possession'.

ἀναλαβεῖν: about the same as λῦσαι, 'make good', 'retrieve', cf. 1224 sqq..

1250, 1. στρατὸν: Odysseus reverts to the intimidating mention of the Greek army.

ξὺν: 'with . . . on my side'.

τὸν σὸν . . . φόβον: 'the (reason for fear) you are speaking of'. J. Jackson, *Marg. Scaen.*, p. 242 D, argues for reading στρατόν instead of φόβον, and to regard φόβον as the last word of the next, lost, line (idea suggested by G. Hermann and Dobree). This is perfectly plausible.

1251a, 2. There can be hardly any doubt as to the assumption of a lost line, spoken by Odysseus [1]). The attribution of 1252 to Odysseus and of 1253 to Neoptolemus in the majority of mss is impossible.

οὐδέ (τοι) σῇ χειρί, 1252, points to a threatening with force on Odysseus' part in the preceding lost verse.

οὐδέ . . . σῇ χειρὶ πείθομαι: 'neither do I allow myself to be persuaded by your threat of force', 'neither do I obey, yield to your threat of force' (which amounts to the same). πείσομαι (πεισθήσομαι Σ) Bothe, Blaydes deserves mention.

τὸ δρᾶν: = ὥστε δρᾶν. Cf. *Ant.* 1105.

---

[1]) Cf. Denniston ad Eur. *El.* 651, 2.

1253. Again this verse, eminently appropriate to the occasion in Odysseus' mouth, cannot possibly be attributed to Neoptolemus. The correct division of the following ἀντιλαβαί is a logical consequence.

1254-56. ἔστω τὸ μέλλον: Wecklein's ἴτω is still to be found in Schn.-N.-R.. But, to quote Jebb, 'the calmer word ἔστω is more dignified and more effective here'.—Almost a scene of 'épées tirées' seems to follow—something Euripidean rather than Sophoclean,—but Odysseus immediately desists. This is more or less repeated when Neoptolemus has handed over the bow and Odysseus has to retreat in a far from dignified way. The stage action vividly expresses the collapse and the discomfiture of Odysseus' persona and his designs.

ἀλλὰ κἀμέ: It is, of course, idle to wonder how Neoptolemus, while holding the bow, could be about to draw his sword [1]). It is perhaps less irrelevant to note that he is not represented as being prepared to ward Odysseus off by means of the bow. Not, surely, because 'that he knows to be beyond his strength' (Campbell) but (1) because the bow is a sacred object belonging to Philoctetes, (2) because the remnants of his loyalty to Odysseus would have prevented that (cf. 1300).

The bickering character of the close of this stichomythia reminds one of the dispute between Teucer and Menelaus, as do Odysseus' final rather lame lines.

1257, 8. καίτοι: adversative, cf. Denniston, *G.P.*[2] p. 558 (V): 'καίτοι, though it belongs properly to continuous discourse, is occasionally used at the opening of a speech, where its place is normally taken by καὶ μήν'. <Here> 'Odysseus' change of intention ignores Neoptolemus' words . . .'. 'However' (Jebb) is the best translation.

Exit Odysseus, but we must suppose that he hides somewhere nearby within hearing. I do not believe that he 'stays below the cave' (Webster), nor do I believe that the dialogue between Philoctetes and Neoptolemus takes place on the platform before the cave-door. Philoctetes will have to descend the steps leading to the stage (cf. v. Wilamowitz, p. 99).

1259, 60. These lines address Odysseus, but in the way of a 'Nachruf', cf. for instance *Ant.* 98, 9.

ἐσωφρόνησας: Jebb's 'Thou hast come to thy senses' is decidedly

---

[1]) Did the bow hang over his left shoulder?

better than Webster's 'you are sensible'. This aorist is not on a par with the aorists listed in K.-G. I pp. 163-165 (Goodwin § 60). From Odysseus' καίτοι σ᾽ ἐάσω, and his departure, Neoptolemus infers that his prudence has returned; the ingressive meaning of the aorist is unmistakable. Of course, other translations may be as correct as Jebb's, for instance Mazon's 'te voilà raisonnable': for here the fact that he has become 'raisonnable', having been 'déraisonnable' is implied, whereas this is not the case in Webster's rendering.

ἐκτὸς κλαυμάτων ἔχοις πόδα: for comparable phrases cf. L.-Sc. s.v. πούς 6 e, Eur. *Heracl.* 109; add Alc. 130.31 L.-P. κάκων ἔκτος ἔχων πόδας.

1261, 2. He addresses Philoctetes in a formal, solemn way: he contemplates a new stage in their relation. The fairly stilted wording is continued in τάσδε πετρήρεις στέγας.

ἀμείψας: 'change' > 'give and take in exchange' > 'pass', 'cross' > 'pass out and into' (a house). So here 'leave'.

Second scene 1263-1307, Phil., Neopt., Chor. (silent), Odysseus (1293-±1300).

1263, 4. θόρυβος βοῆς: 'disturbing shouting'. Cf. for the wording in a similar situation Eur. *I.A.* 317.

τί . . . ξένοι: he addresses the Chorus or Neoptolemus and the Chorus. It is not clear when exactly he becomes aware of the former's presence.

τοῦ κεχρημένοι: (lit.) 'being in want of which'. The epic use of κέχρημαι (esp. frequent in the participle) 'desire', 'be in want of' is not at all rare in Tragedy.

1265, 6. In 1265 μέγα is the mss reading; in 1266 L has κακά, AGRQ κακόν. It seems preferable to read μέγα . . . / . . . κακόν, and not νέα . . . / . . . κακά (Bergk, a number of editors).

κακὸν τὸ χρῆμα: In my opinion the meaning of χρῆμα must be determined by the preceding κεχρημένοι [1]): 'the thing you want, you require of me' (or, if ὦμοι κακὸν τὸ χρῆμα is regarded as a parenthesis not directed to Neoptolemus and the Chorus: 'they require of me': 'what they require <is certainly> a bad thing'). Page, Proc. Cambr. Philol. Soc. 1960, p. 53 proposes reading ὦμοι κακῶν· τί χρῆμα; (with μέγα 1265 and κακόν 1266). If we follow him, the same holds good for χρῆμα.

---

[1]) This was maintained by G. Hermann: 'mala res, qua opus sit vobis' and scornfully rejected by Ellendt.

πέμποντες: perhaps simply 'bringing'. Jebb argues in favour of 'heralding', comparing *Ant.* 1286 ὦ κακάγγελτά μοι / προπέμψας ἄχη. Among the many conjectures (πέσσοντες, ῥάπτοντες, τεύχοντες) none is convincing.

The μέγα κακόν he fears is being abducted by force to Troy.

1268, 9. δέδοικ': answering Neoptolemus' θάρσει.

ἐκ λόγων / καλῶν: taking up Neoptolemus' λόγους and in strong contrast with κακῶς ἔπραξα: the harsh *facts* of what happened with me were the result of specious *words*, I *fared* badly through your specious *words*. This is reinforced by the bitter and reproachful σοῖς πεισθεὶς λόγοις.

1270. μεταγνῶναι: 'change one's mind' > 'repent'. Cf. μετάγνοια *El.* 581 with the note. Cf. *supra* 961, 2 εἰ καὶ πάλιν γνώμην μετοίσεις.

1271, 2. τοῖς λόγοισι: cf. 1267, 8, 9; dative of respect; τοιοῦτος τοῖς λόγοισι is explained by πιστός (sc. τοῖς λόγοισι) 'trustworthy', followed by the harsh adversative asyndeton: ἀτηρὸς λάθρᾳ '<but> baneful underneath' (Webster).

1273-75. ἀλλ' οὔ τι μὴν: cf. *El.* 817.

μένοντι καρτερεῖν: on καρτερέω with participle see K.-G. II 55.5.

Again, as in the previous scene, the ἀντιλαβαί are symptoms of emotionality.

1275, 6. παῦε: 'leave off'. Only here in Soph. (reading of T), common in Comedy.

ἂν εἴπῃς γε: 'anything you *do* say' (*G.P.*² p. 124).

1277. καὶ πέρα γ' ἴσθ' ἢ λέγω: either καὶ πέρα γε <δεδογμένον> ἴσθι ἢ λέγω, or καὶ πέρα γε <δέδοκται>, ἴσθ', ἢ λέγω. There is some similarity in the lively passage Men. *Sam.* 116-18, where see Austin.

1278-80. ἤθελον ... ἄν: cf. Goodwin *G.M.T.* §§ 246, 426. 'I could have wished'.

εἰ ... / κυρῶ: 'if my words are of no avail'.

πέπαυμαι: 'I have done'. The perfect as final as the future perfect *Ant.* 91.

1280-84. γάρ: '<you are right to stop> for' (*G.P.*² p. 76).

οὐ γάρ ... φρένα: amounting to: οὐ γάρ ποτε τὴν τῆς ἐμῆς φρενὸς εὔνοιαν κτήσῃ.

ὅστις γ': *quippe qui.*

ἐμοῦ ... λαβὼν / ἀπεστέρηκας: cf. 931; genitive and accusative ἀπὸ κοινοῦ with λαβὼν and ἀπεστέρηκας, though the construction ἀποστερέω τί τινος is uncommon (but ἀποστερέω τι in itself is of frequent occurrence. Cf. 931 *supra*, also for τὸν βίον) [1]).

κᾶτα νουθετεῖς ἐμὲ / ἐλθών: 'and then you come and preach to me'.

ἀρίστου πατρὸς ἔχθιστος γεγώς: with characteristic condensation: for γεγώς has a double function and combines the notions 'born of' and 'having shown himself'. Or we could say that ἀρίστου πατρὸς alone expresses: 'son of an excellent father' and ἔχθιστος γεγώς 'who turned out to be most hateful'. Pierson's αἴσχιστος, an easy conjecture, accepted by many, lacks compelling force.

1285-87. Here he includes Neoptolemus in his imprecation; at 961 he said ὄλοιο μήπω. — Now Neoptolemus intervenes and puts into effect his resolve. This act, springing from the young man's conscience and his true nature, effectuates a real peripeteia in the action of the play.

'πεύξῃ: ἐπεύχομαι 'imprecate upon', L.-Sc. *s.v.* III.

καὶ σύ: καὶ σύ . . . is not to be excluded, in view of πέρα [2]).

δέχου . . . τάδε: the wording is impressive by its very simplicity.

1288-92. Neoptolemus' oath and the deed itself are needed to overcome Philoctetes' doubt and suspicion. Clear gradation between 1288, 90, 95 (τέκνον).

ἆρα: οὐκ ἆρα (ἄρα) mss is impossible, ἆρ' οὐ unsuitable; οὐκ is probably an intrusive gloss. ἆρα well renders the question as one uttered between hope and fear.

ἀπώμοσ': 'I swear "no"'; the meaning of the aorist, expressive of emotional urgency, may be paraphrased by: 'I want to have denied on oath'. Cf. K.-G. I 165, Schw. Debr. II 282. Cf. *infra* 1434.

ἁγνοῦ . . . ὕψιστον: Wakefield's interchange of the attributes, adopted by many edd., seems unnecessary.

τοὔργον: contrasting with the promise.

παρέσται: παρ- as in Dutch 'de daad *bij* het woord'.

φανερόν: 'beyond the possibility of doubt' (Campbell). Cf. *Trach.* 223, 4 τάδ' ἀντίπρωρα δή σοι / βλέπειν πάρεστ' ἐναργῆ.

He hands over the bow to Philoctetes and Odysseus shouts from his hiding place in vain and appears one moment too late.

κράτει: be (and remain) master of your arms.

1293, 4. ὡς θεοὶ ξυνίστορες: the ellipse of the copula is somewhat remarkable in the ὡς clause, but does not warrant Reiske's ὦ.

---

[1]) E. Mehler, Mnemosyne 1889, p. 100 and A. von Blumenthal, Hermes 1934, pp. 454-57, want to read βιὸν here.

[2]) Nauck (1867) wanted to divide καί—NE. σὺ μή.

ὑπέρ: comes near to 'in the name of'.

1295, 6. τέκνον: see note 1288-92.

ἐπῃσθόμην: again the aorist is emotional; but, in this case, even in a modern language, a past tense would be as natural as the present. Possibly: τίνος φώνημα; μῶν 'Οδυσσέως / ἐπῃσθόμην; (thus Campbell, Jebb).

1296-98. σάφ' ἴσθι: cf. 977.

καὶ πέλας γ' ὁρᾷς, / ὅς . . . ἀποστελῶ βίᾳ: καὶ πέλας γ' ὁρᾷς <ἐμὲ> ὅς . . . ἀποστελῶ. The threats of 981-83 are repeated with a vengeance. For 1298 cf. 981, 2.

1299. ἀλλ' οὔ τι χαίρων: repeatedly occurring in threats with a future tense expressed or implied (here we can mentally supply ἀποστελεῖς με, or τοῦτο τολμήσεις or the like). Cf. *O.T.* 363.

ὀρθωθῇ: most commentators understand this to mean: 'will be carried to its aim' ('= ὀρθῶς ἐνεχθῇ' Campbell). Better v. Wilamowitz (p. 114) ἣν . . . βέλος 'meint nicht, dass das Geschoss zum rechten Ziele gelangt ist, sondern wenn er den Pfeil gerichtet hat'. He has taken an arrow and is about to put it on the bow. Ironically, Odysseus' fear (75, 103-106) seems to be coming true. But Neoptolemus grasps Philoctetes' arm and prevents him from adjusting the arrow. In the meantime Odysseus makes an inglorious exit.

1300, 1. ἆ: lending an emotional tone to a prohibition also *O.T.* 1147; cf. Kannicht ad Eur. *Hel.* 445.

μεθῇς: 'let loose', meaning 'shoot'. Nauck would read ἀφῇς.

μέθες: 'let go', meaning 'release your grip'.

με . . . χεῖρα: κάθ' ὅλον καὶ κατὰ μέρος.

1302, 3. ἀφεῖλου: construed with μὴ and infinitive as the verba impediendi (instances listed by L.-Sc. *s.v.* II 3). ἄνδρα πολέμιον ἐχθρόν τ' is object of κτανεῖν. The infinitive with μὴ has to be supplied Eur. *Andr.* 913.

πολέμιον ἐχθρόν τε: 'hostile' (*i.e.* to be treated as an enemy) 'and hated'.

1304. καλόν: 'honourable', *honestum*.

1305-07. ἀλλ' οὖν . . . γ': 'well, at least', introducing a more moderate suggestion, made as a *pis aller* (*G.P.*² p. 443). Cf. *Ant.* 84 ἀλλ' οὖν προμηνύσῃς γε τοῦτο μηδενὶ / τοὔργον, *El.* 1035 ἀλλ' οὖν ἐπίστω γ' οἷ μ' ἀτιμίας ἄγεις.

τοὺς πρώτους στρατοῦ, / τοὺς τῶν 'Αχαιῶν ψευδοκήρυκας: generic plural referring to Odysseus, in particular to his boasts which have not come true and to the frauds he has attempted in vain. Jebb is right in pointing to the examples in Tragedy where a κῆρυξ is convicted of 'unsuccessful bluster'. The whole sentence conveys a devastating comment on the Odysseus of this play and, because it is couched in general terms, on those men he is supposed to represent.

κακούς / . . . πρὸς αἰχμήν: 'cowards when it comes to a fight'.

Third scene 1308-1408, Neopt., Philoct., Chor. (silent).

1308, 9. εἶέν: this Attic particle, used 'in passing to the next point', occurs in Tragedy (four times in Aesch., five in Soph., frequently in Eur), in Ar., Pl. and Orr. 'Quite so', 'good', are possible renderings. 'Soit' (Mazon) is misleading, for it has nothing to do with εἰμί. See Barrett ad Eur. *Hipp.* 297. Cf. Eur. *Hel.* 761 εἶέν· τὰ μὲν δὴ δεῦρ' ἀεὶ καλῶς ἔχει.

τὰ μὲν: he has in mind what he is going to say at 1315.

κοὐκ ἔσθ' ὅτου: Turnebus' ὅτου (causal genitive) seems preferable to ὅπου; *Ai.* 1103, 4, quoted by Campbell, offers no good parallel.

ἔχοις . . . μέμψιν: see A. A. Long, *Language and Thought in Sophocles*, p. 84 n. 70 for periphrases with -σις nouns as alternatives to the finite verb.

μέμψιν εἰς ἐμέ: cf. *Rhes.* 50, 1 ὡς / μή ποτέ τιν' ἐς ἐμὲ μέμψιν εἴπῃς.

1310-13. τὴν φύσιν . . . / ἐξ ἧς: because the φύσις is Achilles' as well as Neoptolemus' τὴν φύσιν . . . ἐξ ἧς can be said instead of τὴν τοῦ πατρὸς φύσιν ἐξ οὗ; it seems, plausible moreover, that we have to borrow from ἐξ ἧς ἔβλαστες <βλαστὼν> closely to be connected with ἔδειξας; Σισύφου πατρός and ἐξ Ἀχιλλέως are dependent on this notion βλαστών. Or we can say that Σισύφου πατρός and ἐξ Ἀχιλλέως are genitives of origin dependent on an omitted ὤν, again closely to be connected with ἔδειξας. At any rate there is some measure of contamination in the construction. — Cf. Eur. *Heracl.* 539, 40.

μετὰ ζώντων θ' . . . / . . . νῦν δὲ: if we read θ' in 1312 (θ' is the reading of AUᵖᶜY, Dawe, *Studies on the Text of Sophocles* III, p. 9), this is no reason for altering δὲ into τε (Turnebus and others): cf. *G.P.*² p. 513. But, as Denniston notes *ib.* pp. 516, 7, θ' in 1312 'is the only place in Sophocles . . . where τε is postponed after a preposition'. θ' is certainly not indispensable; the Budé editors leave it out, retaining of course δὲ in the next line.

τῶν τεθνηκότων: sc. ἄριστ' ἀκούει.

1314-16. ἥσθην: cf. note ad 1289.

πατέρα . . . εὐλογοῦντά σε: We have to choose between πατέρα τὸν ἁμὸν (T) and πατέρα τε τὸν ἐμὸν (add. AUY, Dawe l.c.); the latter stands perhaps a somewhat better chance of authenticity.

τυχεῖν: here with genitive *rei* and *personae*.

After the remarkable link by which Neoptolemus' rhesis is attached to the preceding dialogue [1]) there follows by way of introduction a bi-membered reflection, mainly general, but in the second member explicitly applied to Philoctetes. This is explained by a description of Philoctetes' attitude. Then Neoptolemus proceeds to expound the real causes of Philoctetes' plight, and why he should comply with the divine decree as to the fall of Troy. Friis Johansen, pp. 116 sq., has a good discussion of this somewhat laborious and not very regular discourse, in which the 'general' and the 'particular' are indissolubly intertwined [2]).

1316-20. This long sentence, antithetical in form, does not contain a real antithesis (here I disagree with Friis Johansen). The general truth of 1316, 17 does not form a contrast with 1318-20; what is conveyed by these lines is rather an *a fortiori* inference from the former. The application of ἀνθρώποισι . . . φέρειν to Philoctetes' plight is made at 1326 sqq.; the contents of 1318-1320 are immediately applied to his attitude. I do not think that the poet wants us to believe that what he makes Neoptolemus say here to Philoctetes is his, the poet's, own verdict on the latter's attitude. Rather would it seem that the clumsiness of Neoptolemus' argumentation is expressive of the fact that the young man still does not even now, understand the inmost motives of Philoctetes' conduct.

ἑκουσίοισιν: sometimes of two endings.

ἔγκεινται: 'are involved in'.

1321-23. ἠγρίωσαι: cf. 226. But there referring to his bodily appearance, here rather to his mental inaccessibility as a result of isolation, his intractability.

νουθετῇ: cf. 1283. εὐνοίᾳ is Triclinius' reading.

πολέμιον δυσμενῆ θ᾽: cf. 1302, 3.

1324, 5. ὅμως: notwithstanding the risk of being regarded as an enemy.

Ζῆνα . . . καλῶ: cf. 1289. What he is going to say will be nothing but the truth.

---

[1]) See H. Friis Johansen, *General Reflection in Tragic Rhesis*, 1959, p. 116, n. 47.

[2]) See also E. Wolf, *Sentenz und Reflexion bei Sophokles*, 1910, p. 10 and p. 107.

γράφου φρενῶν ἔσω: cf. Aesch. *Choeph.* 450 τοιαῦτ' ἀκούων . . . ἐν φρεσὶν γράφου, *Prom.* 789 ἣν ἐγγράφου σὺ μνήμοσιν δέλτοις φρενῶν (with Groeneboom's very full comment).

1326-28. γὰρ: introduces the argument proper. What Neoptolemus keeps before Philoctetes' eyes is essentially the same as his explanation to the Chorus 192 sqq., combined with the Helenus oracle told by the 'ἔμπορος' 605 sqq.[1]). What is new is the promise about his healing by the Asclepiadae (though perhaps alluded to in 919), belonging to Helenus' prophecy.

ἐκ θείας τύχης: there is no question of any guilt on Philoctetes' part.

πελασθείς: with the genitive; cf. K.-G. I 353.

ὅς . . . / . . . ὄφις: the complex apposition κρύφιος οἰκουρῶν ὄφις is drawn into the relative clause; this is normal, but the placing of the apposition at the close of sentence and verse lends it a remarkable, somewhat sinister effect.

τὸν ἀκαλυφῆ σηκὸν: the roofless precinct. For illustrations of Chryse's statue and altar on contemporaneous vases Webster refers to E. M. Hooker, J.H.S. 70, (1950), p. 35. The snake as watchman is compared by many commentators with the οἰκουρὸς ὄφις in the Erechtheüm, cf. Hdt. VIII 41.2 (ὄφιν μέγαν φύλακα τῆς ἀκροπόλιος), Ar. *Lys.* 759 (τὸν ὄφιν . . . τὸν οἰκουρόν).

1329-31. ἐντυχεῖν: mss; this, with παῦλαν as subject, can very well mean 'turn up', 'present itself', Germ. 'eintreffen', as was argued by H. Jurenka, *Pindaros neugefundener Paean für Abdera*, Philol. 71, 1912, pp. 173-210, followed by S. L. Radt, *Pindars Zweiter und Sechster Paian*, 1958, p. 72, ad *Pae.* 2.75, ὁ ἐν δὲ μηνὸς πρῶτον τύχεν ἆμαρ [2]). It is not necessary at all to adopt Porson's ἂν τυχεῖν; on the contrary, the potential ἂν τυχεῖν is uncalled for (μήποτ' lends to the statement the character of an oath) and the aor. inf. can perfectly well refer to the future (cf. Schw.-Debr. II 296 β). It can not be regarded as a valid objection that at 1333 ἐντυγχάνω occurs with a different meaning.

ἕως: where ὡς is transmitted and the meaning must be 'until' or 'while' ('so long as') this (or another) correction has to be made. We have to choose between ἕως (with synizesis) and ἔστ' (cf. *El.* 105; some older edd.).

---

[1]) On this 'full and authoritative' knowledge of Neoptolemus see Kirkwood's pertinent remarks, *Sophoclean Drama*, p. 81 with n. 44.
[2]) But see Slater *s.v.* ἐν B.

ἕως ... / ... πάλιν: cf. Hdt. VIII 143.2. ἔστ' ἂν ὁ ἥλιος τὴν αὐτὴν ὁδὸν ἴῃ τῇπερ καὶ νῦν ἔρχεται. Comparable Theogn. I 252.

αὐτός: αὐτὸς mss. We have to write either αὐτὸς or οὗτος.

αἴρῃ: intr.; no other instances are known in the sense of *orior*. (Cf. Dale ad Eur. *Alc.* 450).

1332-35. ἑκὼν αὐτός: the pleonasm emphasizes the *conditio sine qua non* on which Odysseus had encroached.

τοῖν 'Ασκληπίδαιν: the dual is not in the mss; but it is a practical way out of the difficult genitive with ἐντυχών. If τῶν 'Ασκληπιδῶν (Machaon and Podalirius, the patronymic is irregularly formed *metri causa*) is retained, we have to assume, with Jebb and others, that ἐντυγχάνω here combines the notions 'encounter' and 'obtain the aid from'.

νόσου μαλαχθῆς τῆσδε: the genitive as with κουφίζω 'relieve', παύομαι and the like.

ξὺν τοῖσδε τόξοις: this ξὺν reinforces the instrumental dative. Cf. Theogn. I 237.

If we take the whole sentence 1229-1336 absolutely literally, it would seem that the νόσος must end only after the capture of Troy, and the latter occur after a previous alleviation of the νόσος by the intervention of the Asclepiadae. This can hardly have been intended: the healing and the capture are regarded as intertwined to such a degree that they are put on a par by the grammar of the wording.

1337-42. Cf. 604 sqq..

ἀνὴρ ... ἔστιν ἐκ Τροίας ἁλούς: better ἔστιν than ἐστιν as is well observed by Jebb.

ἁλούς: cf. εἷλε 608. Odysseus' rôle is left out.

ἀριστόμαντις: comparable on the one hand with ψευδόμαντις, ἀληθόμαντις, on the other with ἀριστοπολίτης, 'best citizen' (*I.G.* 5(1) 335), ἀριστοχειρουργός 'best of surgeons' (*Pap. Oxyr.* 437): 'best of prophets'.

πρὸς τοῖσδ' ἔτι: what follows was not in the story told by the emporos.

τοῦ παρεστῶτος θέρους: 'this present summer'; for the genitive denoting the time within which cf. K.-G. I 386.

ἢ δίδωσ' ἑκὼν / κτείνειν ἑαυτόν: ἢ 'else', expanded by the ἢν clause.

1343. συγχώρει θέλων: only now does the imperative occur corresponding with ὧν δέ σου τυχεῖν ἐφίεμαι 1315.

1344-47. καλὴ γὰρ ἡ 'πίκτησις: ἡ ἐπίκτησις τῆς δόξης (Σ). So the main element in the elaboration of this statement is expressed by the participial clause Ἑλλήνων ἕνα κριθέντ' ἄριστον, resumed more fully by the second member of the accusative with infinitive. It is very common in Greek that a participle clause contains the main burden of what is said.

In simple prose the intention of the utterance can be rendered thus: your gain is to be healed, but your additional gain is the glory of being reputed the best of the Greeks by the capture of Troy. Again, as in 1329-1335, the healing and the capture are represented as indissolubly belonging together.

ἕνα / . . . ἄριστον: common intensification of the superlative.

τοῦτο μὲν . . . / . . . εἶτα: 'first' . . . 'then' (also). Commentators compare *Ant.* 61-63: τοῦτο μὲν . . . ἔπειτα δ'.

1348, 9. Philoctetes feels himself in a quandary, caused by conflicting sentiments. His trust in Neoptolemus has been restored, but his abhorrence of the Atreidae and Odysseus remains overwhelming, and his pathetic speech ends in a passionate refusal.

αἰών: personified; personification of life itself under the aspect of time has its roots in the idea that time grows old with the individual man. So αἰών can be said to be left by man, and inversely, to leave man. In στυγνός the weariness of his long sufferings is pathetically expressed.

τί με, τί δῆτ': for δῆτα when a speaker 'echoes or endorses his own words' see *G.P.*² p. 277; cf. *supra* 760, *El.* 1164. This is more forceful than τί μ' ἔτι δῆτ' (Toup, many edd.).

ἔχεις: 'are you holding me'.

βλέποντα: amounting to ζῶντα, a common usage.

Cf. for the outcry as a whole, *supra* 797, 8.

1350, 1. ἀπιστήσω: 'not comply with' (not: 'distrust').

εὔνους ὢν: cf. 1322 εὐνοίᾳ λέγων.

1352, 3. εἰκάθω: aor. subj.; 'yield'. Sophoclean heroes do not yield, unless to a god, and even then not always.

ἐς φῶς . . . εἶμι: 'shall I come into men's sight' (Jebb), 'into public' (L.-Sc.). This use of φῶς recurs in later authors.

τῷ προσήγορος: προσήγορος can mean: 'addressing' and 'addressed', in both cases the genitive is the normal construction. But it can also be used to express a mutual relation. This is the case in Pl. *Theaet.* 146 a φίλους τε καὶ προσηγόρους ἀλλήλοις. But it is not correct to use this passage in order to defend the dative with προσήγορος by regarding it as passive. Rather would it seem that we have to interpret: 'with whom shall I be conversant'. Philoctetes is not afraid lest nobody will speak to him; what he shrinks from is addressing anybody in the Greek army. τάδ' in τάδ' ἔρξας refers to a supposed yielding, a shame in his own, not in other men's eyes.

1354-57. κύκλοι; κύκλοι repeatedly used for 'eyes' by Sophocles; cf. *O.T.* 1270, *Ant.* 974. (The interpretation of Σ ἐνιαυτοί, τοῦ αἰῶνος χρόνοι is surely mistaken). Like his foot, and his hands, his eyes, too, are personified. 'The lonely man's eyes have a life of their own, like his hands (1004) and his bow (1128—and elsewhere—)' (Webster). This is a striking symptom of the poet's power to imagine the inner life of his creatures.

τὰ πάντα . . . ἀμφ' ἐμοί: compressed for ἰδόντες ἀμφ' ἐμοὶ πάντα τὰ ἀμφ' ἐμοὶ and amounting to πάντα τὰ περὶ ἐμὲ πάθη (Σ).

ταῦτ': announces what is said in the participial clause (ἀνέχομαι with accus. personae and participle is a normal construction). But it would also be possible to interpret: ταῦτ' sc. τὰ ἀμφ' ἐμοὶ <ὁρῶντες> <ὁρῶντες> ἐμὲ ξύνοντα τοῖσιν 'Ατρέως παισίν; the difference, however, would be slight at the cost of assuming a strained construction. The π-alliteration, π̱ῶς τὰ π̱αντ', παισίν, ἀπωλεσαν, π̱ῶς, πανώλει π̱αιδὶ by means of identical or semantically connected words is very expressive. The hearer directly perceives the increase of his passion.

1358-60. τῶν παρελθόντων: referring to τὰ πάντ' . . . ἀμφ' ἐμοί.

δάκνει: cf. 378. All the instances of δάκνω in Sophocles are figurative. οὐ γάρ: 'sc. τοσοῦτον' (Campbell).

οἷα χρὴ παθεῖν με πρὸς τούτων: referring to what is, at any rate, implied in ταῦτ' ἐξανασχήσεσθε κτλ. 1355-57.

προλεύσσειν: 'foresee', a hapax instead of the intractable προορᾶν.

1360, 1. οἷς . . . κακῶν / μήτηρ γένηται, τἄλλα παιδεύει κακά: if this text (mss) is retained, Campbell's interpretation seems to be indicated: 'For men's thoughts, when they have once brought forth an evil progeny, rear nothing but mischief afterwards'. 'Thought or Mind, is imagined as the mother of results for which man is responsible. The mind that had once had bad children will go on, and will bring up an evil brood. The figure is lost if κακούς is read for κακά'. Similarly Mazon: 'Quand la pensée a une fois donné le jour à quelque crime, de tout ce qui s'ensuit elle fait d'autres crimes'. It goes without saying that, in this interpretation, the supposed antecedent of οἷς should be τούτοις. For figurative use of μήτηρ cf. *Ai.* 174 ὦ μεγάλα φάτις, ὦ μᾶτερ αἰσχύνας ἐμᾶς, Aesch. *Sept.* 224, 5

Πειθαρχία γάρ ἐστι τῆς Εὐπραξίας μήτηρ, *Prom.* 460, 1 γραμμάτων τε συνθέσεις, / μνήμην ἁπάντων, μουσομήτορ' ἐργάνην. παιδεύω, it is true, means as a rule, 'train', 'teach', 'educate', but sometimes 'bring up', 'rear': Soph. *fr.* 648 P. λευκὸν αὐτὴν ἐπαίδευσεν γάλα, Eur. *Ion* 953 "Αιδου δ' ἐν δόμοις παιδεύεται; παίδευμα can mean 'nursling': Eur. *Andr.* 1100 μῆλα, φυλλάδος Παρνασίας παιδεύματ', Eur. *fr.* 939 N.² ὦ παγκάκιστα χθόνια γῆς παιδεύματα. Von Wilamowitz has another interpretation of the transmitted text (Translation, p. 114): 'Wenn die γνώμη κακά geboren hat, so erzieht sie auch alles übrige, also auch alles was von aussen an sie herankommt, zu κακά. Die Atreiden werden alles was Pyrrhos bewirken will, zu Schanden machen'. 'Geistreich', but too subtle.

Dawe (*Studies on the Text of Sophocles* III, 1978, pp. 133, 4) rejects the lines 1360, 1 (as transmitted and if 'corrected': κακούς —Dobree, Jebb, alii—,πάντα (Reiske) κακούς—Pearson,—τἄργα ... κακά—Erfurdt) because they are inapposite; he suspects the two preceding vss. too.

1362-64. καὶ δ': only example of this combination in Sophocles. Denniston would regard δέ as the connective and καί as adverb: 'And in thee also' (*G.P.*² p. 200 and cf. p. 199 n. 1; Jebb is of the opposite opinion).

σοῦ ... θαυμάσας ἔχω τόδε: 'I wonder at this in you'. This construction, very common in prose, is rare in poetry. The genitive is possibly possessive rather than partitive.

θαυμάσας ἔχω: emphatic periphrasis of the perfect, fairly common in Sophocles.

χρῆν ... μολεῖν: must refer to Neoptolemus' present intention, not to the past. The text would be easier if it ran μηκέτ' αὐτὸν ἐς; but μή(τ) ... ποτ' may be a substitute for 'not at all', 'on no account' (cf. *numquam* and 'never').

1364-65. The words οἱ τὸν ἄθλιον / ... / ... ἔκριναν are bracketed as spurious since Brunck and rightly so: the wording is clumsy, and Philoctetes is supposed to speak of what he cannot possibly know —it is really foolish to suppose that this information is implied in 412, 3.—See the further objections in Jebb's *Appendix a.l.*.

Dawe [1]) is right in considering the possibility that either after συλῶντες—Pearson's idea—or, better, after ἀπείργειν some genuine part of the text has been lost, displaced by the interpolation. He

---

[1]) *Studies on the Text of Sophocles* III, p. 135.

notes that not a single ms has οἵ γε (Heath's conjecture instead of τε) and impugns the customary interpretation of οἵ γε *quippe qui* as picking up an antecedent inherent in Τροίαν. Perhaps Pearson's idea is sufficient and we might read: οἵ τε σοῦ καθύβρισαν / πατρὸς γέρας συλῶντες ὕστερόν τε σὲ / 'Οδυσσέως ἔκριναν,— εἶτα τοῖσδε σὺ κτλ. But the whole passage shows too much signs of corruption and interpolation to allow of even moderately attractive correction.

Philoctetes remains unaware of the fact that Neoptolemus' story about the arms belonged to the fraud, nor is this error rectified by his interlocutor. Again (see comment ad 363-66) this seems true psychology and wise dramatic economy.

1366, 7. εἰ ξυμμαχήσων: εἰ is best regarded as present tense; the construction with future participle as in Homer, *e.g. Il.* III 383 'Ελένην καλέουσ' ἴε.

κἄμ' ἀναγκάζεις τόδε: τόδε instead of the infinitive construction ἰέναι ξυμμαχήσοντα. τόδε LGRQ (το δὲ Λ) is decidedly better than τάδε (A and *v.l.* in G).

μὴ δῆτα: cf. *G.P.*² p. 276 (2).

1367-69. ἀλλ' ἅ μοι ξυνώμοσας: 'what you agreed with me under oath', 'promised me by oath'. There is some pregnancy in the use of ξυνώμοσας = ξυνήνεσας ὀμόσας, but this is certainly no reason for conjecturing ξυνήνεσας. Since μὴ δῆτα is elliptical for μὴ δῆτα <τόδε με ἀναγκάσῃς>, the object of πέμψον can easily be supplied (from κἄμ' and from μοι). One could consider the desirability of reading ὃ, but it seems hardly necessary; cf. 1398. <ταῦτα> ἃ ξυνώμοσας (or if you prefer <τοῦτο> ὃ ξυνώμοσας) is apposition to πέμψον πρὸς οἴκους. Should we venture to rewrite the passionate words in lifeless prose, the result would be: μὴ δῆτα τοῦτο δράσῃς, τέκνον, ἀλλὰ δρᾶ ταῦτα ἅ μοι ξυνώμοσας· πέμψον με πρὸς οἴκους.

ἔα κακῶς ... κακούς: in this verse without caesura (for the 'caesura media' is not 'excused' by perispomenon of the preceding syllable, nor otherwise) various conjectures have been made (though it must be said that verses of the same metrical structure are not absent in Sophocles: cf. *supra* 101, *Ant.* 1021, *O.T.* 738 (quoted by Webster ad 101): *e.g.* Cobet proposed ἔα κακῶς τούσδ' ἐξαπόλλυσθαι κακούς (Mncm. N.S. 5 (1877) 225), Nauck ἔα κακῶς νιν ἐξαπόλλυσθαι κακούς, F. Polle ἔα κακῶς σὺ τούσδ' ἀπόλλυσθαι κακῶς (Philol. 51 (1892) 247 sqq.), Dawe (*Studies*, III p. 136) ἔα κακῶς αὐτοῦ (at Troy) 'ξαπόλλυσθαι κακούς. One of these proposals may be right, but the transmitted text itself is not downright objectionable.

1370-72. διπλῆν μὲν ἐξ ἐμοῦ κτήσῃ χάριν, / διπλῆν δὲ πατρός: if the text were to run *e.g.* διπλῆν μὲν ἐξ ἐμοῦ κτήσῃ χάριν / πατρός τε the interpretation would surely have to be: 'you will win gratitude from me as well as from my father'; διπλῆ χάρις would surely mean thankfulness on the part of two persons. Cf. *Trach.* 618, 9 ἔπειθ' ὅπως ἂν ἡ χάρις κείνου τέ σοι / κἀμοῦ ξυνελθοῦσ' ἐξ ἁπλῆς διπλῆ φανῇ. Dain-Mazon take our text to mean just that, regarding διπλῆν δὲ as purely stylistic figure, an anaphora which does not add anything to the meaning of the sentence. (Campbell leaves this open as an alternative course). The current interpretation is that Philoctetes and his father will be grateful for two reasons: for Philoctetes' return home and for Neoptolemus' desertion of the Atreidae. It is an interesting fact that von Wilamowitz regards πατρός as referring not to Poeas ('Das wird N. wenig imponieren') but to Achilles, deeming this interpretation to be corroborated by the next words: 'wenn er anders handelte, würde man sagen, er wäre so schlecht πεφυκώς wie Odysseus, der Sohn des Sisyphos'. This interpretation is certainly worth mentioning and perhaps to be preferred.

1373-75. εἰκότ': 'reasonable' ('plausible') things; cf. Eur. *I.A.* 1134 σὺ δ', ἤν γ' ἐρωτᾷς εἰκότ', εἰκότ' ἂν κλύοις.

πιστεύσαντα: 'putting faith in' (rather than 'obeying'). Cf. 1350.

θεοῖς: refers to the Helenus prophecy.

φίλου . . . τοῦδε: with great emphasis.

1376, 7. Of course Philoctetes is supposed to have understood the somewhat ambiguous phrase τῆσδ' ἐκπλεῖν χθονός.

I cannot believe that τῷδε δυστήνῳ ποδί is dependent on ἔχθιστον, as Webster will have it. It is sociative dative (Jebb and others).

1378, 9. μὲν οὖν: *immo vero*, 'say rather'. Cf. *Ai.* 1363 (ἡμᾶς σὺ δειλοὺς τῇδε θημέρα φανεῖς). Οδ. ἄνδρας μὲν οὖν Ἕλλησι πᾶσιν ἐνδίκους.

ἔμπυον: only here in poetry, common in medical writers. 'Suppurating' (from πύον = τὸ πύος; cf. Chantraine, *Dict. Ét. s.v.* πύθομαι).

βάσις: concrete use of a -σις word. But in using βάσις instead of πούς, his miserable gait is implied.

σε . . . τήνδε τ' ἔμπυον βάσιν: for this coupling cf. *Ant.* 95 ἔα με καὶ τὴν ἐξ ἐμοῦ δυσβουλίαν, *Ai.* 1147 σὲ καὶ τὸ σὸν λάβρον στόμα, *O.C.* 750 σὲ καὶ τὸ σὸν κάρα. See Bruhn, *Anhang* § 237, Long, *Language and Thought in Sophocles*, p. 108 with note 155.

κἀποσώσοντας: Heath's simple emendation seems necessary.

1380. ὦ δεινὸν αἶνον αἰνέσας: Webster and Verdenius (Mnem.

1962, p. 389) want to stick to the proper meaning of αἶνος 'tale'
('allusive tale' Verdenius; 'teller of cruel fiction' Webster). This is
impugned by Knock, (*The Heroic Temper*, p. 12 and note 27 at
p. 167), who opts for Jebb's interpretation: 'You who give me this
terrible advice', rightly in my opinion. We have to take αἰνέσας in
the not uncommon sense of 'recommending', and to assume that the
meaning of αἶνος is adapted to that of the participle. We have to
bear in mind that αἰνέω can be substituted for both ἐπαινέω and
παραινέω, and that αἶνος as used in Hes. *Erg.* 202 implies a warning
advice, as in fact is the function of the αἶνοι in *Ai.* 1142-1156.
Moreover, we should not forget Philoctetes' words after Neoptolemus' first attempt at persuasion in this scene:, 1350, 1: πῶς ἀπιστήσω λόγοις / τοῖς τοῦδ', ὃς εὔνους ὢν ἐμοὶ παρήνεσεν;

1381. ἃ ... τελούμενα: καλῶς ὁρῶ LGRQ, κάλ' ὁρῶ AUY. The
favoured correction is Dindorf's λῷσθ' ὁρῶ (we might suppose that
a scribe repeated κα, omitted to delete κα, or inadvertently wrote
καλῶς, which seemingly made sense; κάλ' ὁρῶ in the A class was
intended as a metrical correction). καλά γ' ὁρῶ would be another
possibility (emphatic γε after καλά). Broadhead (B.I.C.S. 8 -1961 -
p. 57) suggested κλέος 'to our glory', not convincingly. We have to
construe ἃ λῷσθ' ὁρῶ<ὄντα> τελούμενα 'when being accomplished'.
(τελούμενα is probably present participle).

1382. λέξας ... θεούς: the participle to be closely connected
with the finite verb. The accus. with καταισχύνεσθαι as at *O.T.* 1424,
5. Philoctetes does not give any credence to the Helenus oracle; we
should not forget that he first heard of it from the 'emporos'.

1383, 4. 'So befindet sich Philoktetes am Ende in einer Situation,
die der des Neoptolemos zu Beginn durchaus vergleichbar ist; und
wieder stehen Vorteil und Erfolg unter der Bedingung des unehren-
haften Handelns' (J.-U. Schmidt, *Sophokles-Philoktet*, p. 237).

ὠφελούμενος: this must be passive and the words as they stand
can only imply: neither I nor you need be ashamed when we
receive benefits (which is what my words have in view), I by the
capture of Troy, you by your healing in addition to this capture. It
must be said that the conjecture of Buttmann ὠφελῶν φίλους,
adopted by Jebb, praised by Campbell in *Paral. Soph.* p. 229, and
by Radermacher, and accepted by von Wilamowitz (translation),
makes things much easier and fits better with Philoctetes' retort.
(Though even with the transmitted reading this makes sense, thus:
<you speak of ὠφελεῖσθαι>, do you mean ὄφελος for the Atreidae etc.).

ἐπ' ἐμοί: 'with reference to me'.

τόδε: reading of GQ (Dawe, *Studies* III, p. 61). τάδε in itself is perfectly defensible: 'do you mean a benefit for the Atreidae, or do you say these words with reference to me'. But τόδε is perhaps easier in connection with the next verse.

1385. σοί που φίλος γ' ὤν: sc. τόδε ὄφελος λέγω. The verse is well rendered by Mazon: 'Pour toi, me semble-t-il. Je suis ton ami, je parle comme tel'.

1386. πῶς: <can you be my friend>.

1387. ὦ τᾶν: cf. note ad *O.T.* 1145.

διδάσκου μὴ θρασύνεσθαι κακοῖς: μάνθανε, φησί, μὴ ἐν τοῖς κακοῖς ἐπαίρεσθαι. κακοῖς· λείπει ἡ ἐπί (Σ) and so many commentators; the dative is then possibly a dative of circumstance [1]). Tournier *Exercices critiques* (1875) p. 121 proposed μὴ 'νθρασύνεσθαι or 'ν κακοῖς. Others interpret: 'to be hardened by misfortune' (Campbell), 'driven to excess by misery' (Webster).

The commentary of Tournier-Desrousseaux connects κακοῖς with διδάσκου (instrumental dative) 'Que tes malheurs t'apprennent à montrer moins de confidence' and thus Mazon: 'apprends de tes malheurs à ne pas trop faire le fier', and this is an attractive solution.

1388. ὀλεῖς ... λόγοις: ὀλεῖς με, γιγνώσκω σε: more vivid than γιγνώσκω σε ὅτι ὀλεῖς με. τοῖσδε τοῖς λόγοις has to be connected with ὀλεῖς (thus correctly Campbell and Jebb). What Philoctetes means by these words is that he will be morally ruined if he allows himself to be persuaded by Neoptolemus' arguments; morally ruined, because in that case he will have yielded and will be the sport of the Atreidae.

1389. οὔκουν ἔγωγε: ὀλῶ σε.

οὐ σε μανθάνειν: that you do not <want to> learn <the meaning of my words>, more generally 'that you are "unbelehrbar"'.

1390. ἐγὼ οὐκ ... οἶδά με: Philoctetes picks up οὐ μανθάνειν and asks with indignation: 'do I not know that the Atreidae threw me out', implying that from them he can expect anything in the future and that it would be a shame to yield to them. For ἐκβάλλω cf. 257, 600, 1034.

1391. ἀλλ' ... ὅρα: 'The force of this is not "see if they will save you", but rather "if they save you, consider what that means"' (Webster). Compare Mazon's translation: 'Et si ceux qui t' ont

---

[1]) Cf. *O.C.* 592 ὦ μῶρε, θυμὸς δ' ἐν κακοῖς οὐ ξύμφορον.

rejeté te sauvaient la vie cette fois'. πάλιν: a clear case of πάλιν used 'ad significandam actionem eam, qua ... tollitur ante facta res' (Ellendt).

1392. οὐδέποθ', ... ἰδεῖν: Jebb is right in putting a comma after οὐδέποθ'. οὐδέποθ' is used as at 999; we may mentally supply 'ὄψομαι' ('I'll never consider it' Webster) or something like 'shall I allow them to "save" me'.

ὥστε: 'on the condition that'. This use of ὥστε, common in prose, is rare in poetry (see K.-G. II 504, 5, Jebb quotes O.C. 602 and cf. Collard ad Eur. Suppl. 876).

ἑκόντα γ': a common case of Sophoclean hyperbaton, lending emphasis to ἑκόντα.

ἰδεῖν: A and Lˢ; surely the correct reading; ἰδεῖν amounts to 'visit'.

1393, 4. Neoptolemus' means of persuasion are exhausted.

ἐν λόγοις: by means of words.

πείσειν: on the future infinitive after verbs signifying 'to be able', 'to wish' etc. see Goodwin § 113, Hudson-Williams ad Theogn. 184, 5.

1395, 6. ὡς: since τί δῆτ' ἂν ἡμεῖς δρῷμεν amounts to 'we are not able to do anything', ὡς 'for', (Dutch) 'immers' connects these lines in a logical way with the preceding words.

ῥᾷστα: cf. 524 αἰσχρά. It is the easiest way for Neoptolemus to cease his attempts at persuasion, and to let Philoctetes live on as he does, in misery (Mazon's translation: 'et pour toi de vivre ...' is incorrect).

ἐμοὶ μὲν τῶν λόγων λῆξαι: i.e. ἐμοὶ <αὐτὸν> μὲν τῶν λόγων λῆξαι (thus rightly Jebb). <σοὶ> is not to be supplied in the δέ clause.

1397. πάσχειν ... παθεῖν: the present infinitive is used in exactly the same way as ζῆν 1396. παθεῖν implies that after his death people will say, summing up his fate: ταῦτ' ἔπαθεν ὁ Φιλοκτήτης.

1398-1401. ἃ δ' ᾔνεσας ... θιγών: ᾔνεσας = συνῄνεσας, cf. Eur. Alc. 12, and see note ad 1367. For δεξιᾶς ἐμῆς θιγών cf. 803. Philoctetes regards the promise made under the false pretences of the fraud as a promise to be fulfilled, and so does Neoptolemus after his 'last lingering look at the cherished object of his ambition' (Campbell ad 1395, 6).

μηδ' ἐπιμνησθῇς ἔτι / Τροίας: 'do not mention Troy any more'.

τεθρήνηται: a perfect comparable with κεκαρτέρηται τἀμά Eur. Hipp. 1457, 'my enduring is done' (Barrett) and perhaps Men.

Dysc. 692 τεθάρρητ' (or τεθάρρηκ', but see Gomme-Sandbach *a.l.*).

γόοις: seems definitely better than λόγοις, and τεθρήνηται is better when taken as impersonal than with Troy as subject (*pace* Σ, who paraphrases (after 'γράφε γόοις') πολλὰ διὰ Τροίαν πέπονθα, φησίν). This would seem plausible (ἄλις γάρ . . . γόοις referring above all to μὴ βράδυνε rather than to μηδ' . . . / Τροίας) if we could be sure that τεθρήνηται is the correct reading. But there exists a *v.l.* τεθρύλληται, corrected by G. Hermann into τεθρύληται and Zf^m (Par. gr. 2884) has τεθρήληται (Dawe, *Studies* III 61). Hermann and Ellendt preferred to read ἄλις γάρ μοι τεθρύληται λόγοις (Τροία subject). Now Dawe has discovered the reading τοι (instead of σοι) in Zg (Laur. 32.2) and Zo (Vat. Palat. gr. 287), and K (Laur. 31.10) AUY have λόγος, not λόγοις (the rest of the mss, γόοις *v.l.* in LGUYT). So Dawe proposes to read ἄλις γάρ τοι τεθρύληται λόγος ('Philoctetes underlines his exasperation by using the particle which is designed to bring home the point to the hearer'). θρυλέω 'repeat over and over' does not occur in Aesch., nor elsewhere in Soph., but it does in Eur. *El.* 910 and *fr.* 285.1. Philoctetes' final words amount to 'your argument, you know, has been repeated *ad nauseam*'. With Dawe's text Neoptolemus is supposed to yield to a final scornful dismissal of his argumentation by Philoctetes; with the text as found in Jebb, Pearson and others, he is supposed to yield to a last pathetic appeal. I still should prefer the latter, despite my admiration for the critical acumen and exhaustive learning displayed by Dawe.

1402, 3. εἰ δοκεῖ . . . ἔπος: It is a well-known stumbling-block that in this tetrameter the diaeresis after the second metron is not observed. But is this really so insurmountable a difficulty as to warrant conjecture or excision? The tetrameters in Sophocles' transmitted plays are very few in number, and how can we set a boundary to the freedom he permitted himself in handling them [1]), especially in a case like this where the verse introduces a turning-point in the action, and is divided between the two speakers in such a way that the brief word of resignation on Neoptolemus' part is as it were overflowed by the other's effusive exclamation.

ἀντέρειδε τὴν βάσιν: 'Lean now thy steps on mine' (Campbell). ἀντέρειδε is a compression of ἀντέχου (sc. ἐμοῦ, cf. 893) ἐρείδων τὴν βάσιν. εἰς ὅσον γ' ἐγὼ σθένω refers to the concept ἐρείδων τὴν βάσιν in the preceding pregnant phrase. The reader will understand why

---

[1]) Cf. Ed. Fraenkel in *Due Seminari Romani* (1977), p. 76: 'evidentemente i poeti avevano più libertà dei nostri manuali di metrica'.

I impugn the whole-sale rejection of these lines by Dawe (*Studies* III, 136, 7).

1404, 5. αἰτίαν ... φεύξομαι: In my view it is a convincing μίμησις of human conduct to make Neoptolemus utter this scruple after having taken his fundamental decision.

τί γάρ: on γάρ see *G.P.*² pp. 81, 2.

1406. προσωφέλησιν ἔρξεις: προσωφέλησις is 'hapax', probably coined by the poet (cf. Long, *Language and Thought*, p. 32); on the periphrasis of προσωφελεῖν see id. *ib.* p. 67.

Ἡρακλέοις: Wackernagel's correction of the mss Ἡρακλείοις (*Kleine Schriften* II, 1358). Edd. have Brunck's Ἡρακλέους.

1407, 8. Between πελάζειν and στεῖχε there is serious corruption in the mss. The easiest way out is to omit σῆς πάτρας — αὐδᾶς (Dindorf, Jebb and many others). In my opinion the best restoration of the verses is Housman's (partly following, or inspired by, Porson's): Νε. πῶς λέγεις; Φι. εἴρξω πελάζειν σῆς πάτρας. Νε. ἀλλ' εἰ <θέλεις> | δρᾶν <σὺ> ταῦθ' ὅπωσπερ αὐδᾶς, στεῖχε προσκύσας χθόνα. (Cl. Rev. 39 (1925) p. 78. Pearson's text is a good second). I think, that in this case tentative restoration is to be preferred to excision because Φι. εἴρξω πελάζειν. Νε. στεῖχε προσκύσας χθόνα is much too abrupt.

It is surely noteworthy that the reminder of the Heraclean origin of Philoctetes' bow and arrows comes just before Heracles' appearance.

προσκύσας: cf. 533.

Exodos proper, 1409-1471

As a rule edd. let the Exodos begin at 1218, and it is true that at the end of 1218-1408 we could speak of a pseudo-exodos, a *faux départ*. Nevertheless, this part has the character more of an 'act' than of an exodos, be it not that of an epeisodion in the traditional (Aristotelean) sense of the word.

Heracles appears, probably on the roof of the skene.

1409-12. Heracles, of course, is probably recognizable for the audience by his array (see further note ad 1420); moreover, his close relation with Philoctetes has been repeatedly mentioned in the course of the play. We have to imagine that at the start of his anapaests Philoctetes and Neoptolemus turn, and at any rate at 1411, where he names himself.

Up to a point he is a *deus ex machina*, but one so closely connected with Philoctetes' life and fate that he is the sole figure whose pronouncements we may regard as acceptable—psychologically speaking—to Philoctetes, so that this man who has been pictured as indifferent (or nearly so) to any mortal's exhortations, even the most friendly and reasonable, now yields without protest.

μήπω γε: 'No! not yet'.

ἡμετέρων, if anywhere, this is pluralis maiestatis.

ἄιης: possibly aorist, but not necessarily so.

φάσκειν: as at *El.* 9.

ἀκοῇ τε: for the irregular place of τε cf. *G.P.*² pp. 519, 20.

1413-17. κατερητύσων: only here in Tragedy; an epic verb, just as its simplex.

σύ . . . ἐπάκουσον: cf. 1410. A simple instance of 'Ringkomposition', an old-established stylistic device, but surely not restricted to 'archaic' poetry.

Here follows Heracles' speech consisting of four parts, closely connected.

(1) A reference to Heracles' own ἀθάνατος ἀρετή as a guarantee to Philoctetes that he is to win εὐκλεᾶ βίον ἐκ τῶν πόνων τῶνδε.

(2) He will go to Troy, with Neoptolemus, will be healed, kill Paris by means of Heracles' bow, destroy Troy, send the prize of his ἀρετή, the assigned spoils, home to his father.

(3) Neoptolemus' lot is to be the faithful companion of Philoctetes in the capture of Troy; they have to be guardians of each other (Heracles will send Asclepius as healer of the wound; for it is fated that Troy shall fall a second time by means of Heracles' bow).

(4) A reminder that, when Troy is destroyed, they should act piously towards the gods.

1418-20. πρῶτα μέν: μέν *solitarium*, not in correlation with δὲ 1423; I do not agree with Jebb and others that it 'would properly have been answered by ἔπειτα δὲ in 1421'. πρῶτα μέν refers to 1418-1422, containing a sort of preliminary parallel between Heracles' and Philoctetes' destiny.

λέξω: the future conveys a desire, as often.

ἀθάνατον ἀρετήν: surely not 'immortal glory', but 'glory of immortality' (see Webster's pertinent remarks).

ὡς πάρεσθ' ὁρᾶν: in itself the 'epiphany' of Heracles is sufficient for an understanding of these words. Webster observes that, as an immortal, he may have been represented as 'young and beautiful'. (He compares a picture on a late fifth-century vase).

1421, 2. καὶ σοί: 'Eh bien! toi aussi . . .' (Mazon).

τοῦτ': either playing on the ambiguity of ἀθάνατον ἀρετήν, or = τοιοῦτο, or simply announcing the next verse (thus Jebb, comparing 1440, and this seems the best solution).

ὀφείλεται: 'is owing to you'. On the passive of ὀφείλειν with inf. see L.-Sc. s.v. II 1.

ἐκ τῶν πόνων τῶνδ': 'after these (your) sufferings', not 'through', as is well observed by I. M. Linforth, *Philoctetes, The Play and the Man*, Univ. of Calif. Publ. in Cl. Philology 15.3. (1956) p. 154 n. 32: 'in itself it is not an idea of moral or religious import'.

εὐκλεᾶ θέσθαι βίον: 'to make your life glorious'.

πόνων: picks up πονήσας, πόνους 1419, εὐκλεᾶ θέσθαι βίον answers (in a sense) ἀθάνατον ἀρετὴν ἔσχον.

1423, 4. δὲ: connective, where γάρ could be used.

πρῶτον μὲν: Heracles returns to this 1437, 8. μὲν *solitarium* (τε in 1425 has nothing to do with it).

1425-27. ἀρετῇ . . . ἐκκριθείς: chosen as the outstanding hero in ἀρετή, probably referring to his fame as archer: for the audience is supposed to remember his μονομαχία with Paris, mentioned in Lesches' Ἰλιὰς μικρά, 213, 4 Severijns, probably in Sophocles' Φιλοκτήτης ἐν Τροίᾳ.

μέν: in correlation with τε (after πέρσεις) 1428. (Wakefield, of course, may be right in altering this into δὲ; or L's reading νοσφίσεις could point to a corruption from νοσφίσας; μέν, then, would be *solitarium*).

νοσφιεῖς βίου: 'deprive of life', 'kill', a far from common phrase.

The connection between Paris' primordial guilt and the rôle of Heracles' bow is a remarkable feature.

1428-30. πέρσεις: 'sack' seems the most satisfying rendering.

πέμψεις: either 'convey' or simply 'send', as Jebb rightly observes.

σκῦλα . . . / . . . ἀριστεῖ': σκῦλα is either object of πέμψεις alone, or of both πέμψεις and ἐκλαβών, with ἀριστεῖ' as predicative adjunct; in the former case, of course, ἀριστεῖ' is object of ἐκλαβών.

ἀριστεῖ' ἐκλαβὼν στρατεύματος: 'having received the meed of valour from the army'. (L.-Sc.). For ἀριστεῖα cf. *Ai*. 464.

πρὸς πάτρας Οἴτης πλάκα: to the plateau of Mount Oeta in your native land.

1431-33. ἃ δ' ἂν . . . σκῦλα . . . / τόξων ἐμῶν μνημεῖα . . . / κόμιζε:

In my view, it is needlessly complicated, to distinguish between σκῦλα and ἀριστεῖα as two separate parts of the booty to be assigned to Philoctetes, as is done by Schn.-N.-R. and by Dain-Mazon. (Mazon's rendering of the passage: 'Pour celle, en revanche, que tu recevras de l'armée en mémoire de mes flèches, porte-la à ma tombe' seems to be due to a misunderstanding of the words). It is much more plausible mentally to supply τούτων as the antecedent of ἃ (thus Jebb, Webster and others), to be regarded as a partitive genitive, whereas τόξων ἐμῶν μνημεῖα is the object of κόμιζε. 'Take a portion of all the booty you will have received and bring this to my pyre as a memory-offering for my bow' (but grammatically μνημεῖα is not a predicative adjunct).

τοῦδε τοῦ στρατοῦ: not Τρωϊκοῦ, but the Achaean army (ἐξ Ἀχαιικοῦ Σ) and dependent on λάβῃς, just as στρατεύματος 1429 on ἐκλαβών; 'in diesem Krieg' (von Wilamowitz) is an impossible translation—if it is meant as a translation—. ὅδε can be used referring to what precedes (K.-G. I 647, this use is frequent in Hdt.).

In these lines there seems to be adumbrated an aetiological myth (note the frequency and elaboration of aetiological myths put in the mouths of dei ex machina at the close of Euripides' plays), for the cult of Heracles' pyre on Mount Oeta had existed at least since archaic times (cf. Nilsson, Der Flammentod des Herakles auf dem Oete, Arch. f. Religionsw. XXI, 1922, pp. 310 sqq. = Opusc. I pp. 348 sqq., id. G.G.R.² I p. 131).

1433-35. ταῦτ': ταῦτ' (Heath, Pearson) is downright impossible. Perhaps the best interpretation is: 'these counsels concern you too'; 'ταῦτ' refers to the general tenor of the preceding verses' (Jebb's first alternative). The other course, mentioned by Jebb and preferred by Webster, is to regard ταῦτ' as referring to what follows: the aorist, then, would be comparable to ἀπώμοσ' 1289, where see note, and γάρ amounts to 'namely'.

οὔτε . . . σθένεις / . . . οὔθ' . . . σέθεν: cf. supra 115.

1436, 7. The comparison is reminiscent of Il. V 554 sq., X 297.

συννόμῳ: 'feeding together', implying the notion 'partnership'. As a noun it is commonly used for 'partner', 'consort', cf. Aesch. Sept. 354, Soph. El. 600, O.C. 340; in later Greek συννέμω can mean 'make one's partner'.

οὗτος . . . τόνδ': cf. El. 981, Eur. Hipp. 194 τοῦδ' . . . τοῦτο(?).

1437-40. Ἀσκληπιὸν: Heracles' promise outbids Neoptolemus' 1333.

τὸ δεύτερον γὰρ ... / τόξοις ἁλῶναι: γὰρ refers to the implied thought that Philoctetes must be healed in order to be equal to the task assigned to him by fate. This sentence, moreover, serves as a transition to the final warning.

τὸ δεύτερον: on the first capture of Troy, by Heracles, see *Il.* V 638-642, Eur. *Andr. 796, 7.* Webster makes the pertinent remark that Heracles appears as an archer on the East pediment of the temple at Aegina, where the earlier Trojan war is represented.

1440-44. ἐννοεῖσθ': 'bear in mind'. The audience will have remembered that Neoptolemus, in the event, did not heed the warning.

δεύτερ' ἡγεῖται: for the phrase cf. *O.C.* 351. 'Pour Zeus Père, tout passe après cela'.

οὐ γὰρ ηὐσέβεια: Dawes' reading, forestalled by Gataker (*Advers. misc. posth.* (1659)), accepted by many editors. The mss text, ἡ γὰρ εὐσέβεια, is hard to accept. Radermacher retains it with the following note, furnished by von Wilamowitz: 'Die εὐσέβεια stirbt mit dem Menschen — nicht in dem Sinne des Vergehens [1]), sondern so dass sie ihn ins Jenseits begleitet, und wenn sie tot sind, geht sie nicht zugrunde, so gut wie sie mit ihnen lebte. Der χῶρος εὐσεβῶν im Hades rechtfertigt den Spruch' (but in his translation v. Wilamowitz renders Dawes' text). The mss text is retained by Masqueray (in contradistinction to the later Budé edition), with some hesitation; he refers (as others have done) to Eur. (*Temenid.*) *fr.* 734 N.[2] ἀρετὴ δέ, κἂν θάνῃ τις, οὐκ ἀπόλλυται, / ζῇ δ' οὐκέτ' ὄντος σώματος· κακοῖσι δὲ / ἅπαντα φροῦδα συνθανόνθ' ὑπὸ χθονός. But Pohlenz (*Erläuterungen*[2] p. 138) seems right in contending that this passage, if anything, supports the conjectural text. Nor can Eur. *Hel.* 1013-1016 καὶ γὰρ τίσις τῶνδ' ἐστὶ τοῖς τε νερτέροις / καὶ τοῖς ἄνωθεν πᾶσιν ἀνθρώποις· ὁ νοῦς / τῶν κατθανόντων ζῇ μὲν οὔ, γνώμην δ' ἔχει / ἀθάνατον εἰς ἀθάνατον αἰθέρ' ἐμπεσών. serve as support for the transmitted text. (Its last defender is J. Trencsényi-Waldapfel, *Sophokles, Philoktet v. 1443* in *Misc. crit.* 1964, vol. I, pp. 281-294). (It goes without saying that 1443, 4 have often been deleted; so, lastly, by M. D. Reeve, Gr. Rom. Byz. Stud. 14 (1973) p. 169, and see Ed. Fraenkel, *o.l.*, p. 76, who supports the athetesis).

The passage has been most ably discussed by I. M. Linforth, *Philoctetes the Play and the Man,* p. 149 n. 30: 'When the spectator

---

[1]) Similarly C. del Grande, Τραγῳδία[2], 1962, p. 97 'La pietas segue i mortali nella tomba, e per essi, vivi o morti, non è mai perduta'.

hears the words "piety dies with men" he cannot be expected to understand just the opposite, that piety continues, in some sense, to live'. So he accepts the conjecture, but his interpretation differs from Jebb's: Jebb's explanation runs: 'the effect of εὐσέβεια does not cease with man's life on earth, but is imperishable. That is, it brings happiness to the εὐσεβής in the life beyond the grave; and it is also of good example to the men who come after'. In Linforth's view Jebb's statements miss the central thought. Starting from 1420 ἀθάνατον ἀρετὴν ἔσχον, where ἀρετή = the reputation, the glory of ἀρετή, and comparing *Ant.* 924 τὴν δυσσέβειαν εὐσεβοῦσ' ἐκτησάμην, he argues that our verses mean: 'Philoctetes and Neoptolemus can win the name and fame of piety by sparing the shrines of the gods. If a man distinguishes himself for piety, the name and fame of it survive among men after death'. In my opinion this is the correct interpretation of the conjectural text. I adopt the conjecture after long hesitation, for I fail to see the cause of the corruption and I should welcome that really convincing interpretation of the transmitted text for which I have sought in vain.

1445-47. ποθεινὸν . . . / χρόνιος: Philoctetes' emotion, his longing for Heracles, that has been so long in vain, find a moving expression in these two terms. His obedience to the divine dispensations, authenticated by Zeus' son, object of his reverence and trust, is immediate.

1448. γνώμην ταύτῃ τίθεμαι: mss have γνώμῃ (with the exception of Zn (Paris gr. 2787 = Pearson's B), which has, according to Pearson, γνώμην ταύτην with ταύτῃ *s.l.*). 'I give my voice in this sense' (Jebb). γνώμην τίθεσθαι can be explained as a condensation of γνώμῃ ψῆφον τίθεσθαι. Σ read, with the mss, γνώμῃ and glossed τίθεμαι by συγκατατίθεμαι; I do not regard this as absolutely impossible: ψῆφον has to be understood and ταύτῃ is pronoun.

1449-51. καιρὸς καὶ πλοῦς / ὅδ' ·: semi-colon after ὅδ', as in mss, seems necessary; καιρὸς καὶ πλοῦς are to be regarded as a hendiadys. Without a stop after ὅδ', ὅδ' is hardly understandable; moreover, the place of γὰρ would be unexampled in Tragedy.

ἐπείγει: the subject, οὖρος, is to be borrowed from καιρὸς καὶ πλοῦς (πλοῦς in itself can be used for the 'time or tide for sailing').

πρύμναν: πρύμνᾰ is Attic, πρύμνη Epic and Ionic; at 482 πρύμνην is used; that is no reason why we should read it here. For the phrase κατὰ πρύμναν cf. *supra* 639, 40.—Exit Heracles.

1452-68. Philoctetes' leave-taking recitative, except perhaps for the last three lines, could also serve for a play without Heracles' intervention. 1452 (στείχων!) would be perfectly fitting after 1408. The poetic quality of this finale is remarkably more impressive than Heracles' dispassionate and somewhat rambling rhesis (cf. Campbell's comment ad 1443).

1452. στείχων: we must imagine that Philoctetes during this recitative is slowly moving away from the centre of the stage.

καλέσω: aor. coniunct.

1453, 4. μέλαθρον ξύμφρουρον ἐμοί: 'the chamber that kept watch with me' (L.-Sc.). The cave is as much a 'person' as the Nymphs. Cf. his address 1081 sqq.; *Ant.* 892 ὦ κατασκαφῆς οἴκησις αἰείφρουρος.

λειμωνιάδες: 'of the meadows'. This feminine form only here and Ap. Rh. II 655. Cf. *Il.* XX 8, 9 νυμφάων, αἵ τ' ἄλσεα καλὰ νέμονται / καὶ πηγὰς ποταμῶν καὶ πίσεα ποιήεντα. On the many categories of Nymphs see Nilsson *G.G.R.* I² pp. 244 sqq. and the article *Nymphai* in *Der kleine Pauly* 19. kol. 207-215 (1970) by H. Herter.

1455-57. κτύπος ἄρσην: ἄρσην 'mighty', 'bass' (Campbell); cf. ἄρσην βοή Ar. *Thesm.* 125.

πόντου προβολῆς: G. Hermann, instead of προβλής. Dawe discovered the reading προβολῆς in Zo (*Studies* III p. 62; Zo = Vatic. Palat. gr. 287); προβλής <θ'> (Musgrave) seems inferior to προβολῆς, which has now a support in the transmission. προβολή = cape, foreland, jutting rock is only known from late authors (Quint. Sm. IX 378 has ἐπὶ προβολῆσι θαλάσσης), but is found in medical authors in the sense of 'prominence'. On the other hand we have προβλῆτες 'headlands' at 936. But προβλής <θ'> strikes one as somewhat bald after κτύπος ἄρσην πόντου; we could, however, regard κτύπος ... προβλής θ' as a bold hendiadys. Webster's rendering of κτύπος ... προβολῆς is satisfactory: 'strong beat on the seacape'.

οὗ: if we reject προβλής θ', the antecedent can still be προβολῆς, in or near which Philoctetes' cave is supposed to be.

κρᾶτ': nomin. sing.

ἐνδόμυχον: 'même au fond de cet antre' (Mazon); the adj. is found Call. *Dem.* 88 and Nonnus *Dion.* VIII 329. ἐνδομυχέω 'lurk in the recesses of a house' in schol. Ar. *Vesp.* 964. ἐνδο-compounds are rare, the only other classical instance being ἐνδομάχας 'fighting at home', Pind. *Ol.* XII 14.

πληγῆσι νότου: Philoctetes' cave is exposed to the rainy νότος.

1458-60. πολλά: adverbial, answering πολλάκι.

φωνῆς τῆς ἡμετέρας / . . . / στόνον ἀντίτυπον: 'a groaning echoing my voice'. Cf. 693, 4 στόνον ἀντίτυπον and 188-190.

χειμαζομένῳ: cf. χειμερίῳ / λυπᾳ 1194, 5. There is a striking harmony between the pictures of sea, wind, landscape and of his own distress.

Ἑρμαῖον ὄρος: mentioned in Aesch. *Ag.* 283 Ἑρμαῖον λέπας / Λήμνου.

1461-63. Λύκιόν τε ποτόν: indubitably a spring sacred to Apollo Lycius, probably known to the audience, but for us unknown from elsewhere. (γλύκιον is surely a corruption).

λείπομεν ὑμᾶς, λείπομεν ἤδη: the repetition, combined with ἤδη [1]) 'at last' is very pathetic. I do not agree with Webster's enthusiasm for G. Hermann's λείπομεν, οὐ δὴ / δόξης ποτὲ τῆσδ' ἐπιβάντες (in order to obtain a paroemiac before the last section; see Jebb's pertinent objections).

ἐπιβάντες: 'entered on', 'embarked upon'. For metaphorical uses of the verb cf. L.-Sc. *s.v.* A I 4. δόξης comes near to 'hope', but there is some ambiguity in the word. 'He refers partly to his steady refusal to go to Troy, and partly to his abnegation of all hope' (Campbell) may be right.

1464, 5. ἀμέμπτως: 'to heart's content' (Campbell).

1466-68. ἔνθ': ἐκεῖσε οἷ.

ἡ μεγάλη Μοῖρα: Fate as described by Neoptolemus 1337 sqq., and by Heracles.

γνώμη . . . φίλων: Heracles and Neoptolemus.

πανδαμάτωρ / δαίμων: probably Zeus (cf. 1415, and *Ant.* 604 sqq.).

ἐπέκρανεν: 'brought to pass'. But the meaning 'ordain', despite Ed. Fraenkel's remark ad Aesch. *Ag.* 369 ('In Pindar and Sophocles, though κραίνειν is common, it is not used with this meaning'), is surely not absent. I cannot subscribe to W. Chase Greene's interpretation: 'the all-subduing power of his personal destiny' (*Moira*, Harper Torchbook 1963, p. 164).

We are reminded of the end of Aesch. *Eum.* 1045, 6 Ζεὺς παντόπτας / οὕτω Μοῖρά τε συγκατέβα and of the famous κοὐδὲν τούτων ὅ τι μὴ Ζεύς. *Trach.* 1278.

1469-71. σωτῆρας: cf. *O.T.* 80, 1 τύχη . . . / σωτῆρι.

νόστου: both 'return' and 'journey' are possible.

---

[1]) Not: 'tout de suite' (Mazon).